Why I Left

The Nine Speeches of the Vickery Boulevard, Fort Worth, Texas, Lectureship of October 25 to 29 and November 1 to 4, 1948.

EDITORS:

GUY V. CASKEY—THOS. L. CAMPBELL

Order From
THE CASKEY-CAMPBELL PUBLISHING CO.
1036 EAST POWELL
FORT WORTH, TEXAS

Printed By
GOSPEL LIGHT PUBLISHING CO.
DELIGHT, ARKANSAS

ISBN 978-1-60135-803-5

COPYRIGHT, 1949
GUY V. CASKEY AND THOS. L. CAMPBELL

INTRODUCTION TO LECTURES

Every year many individuals leave denominational affiliations and become members of the church of Christ. The church of Christ must possess something which no other church can claim for many to forsake their former teaching and associates and cleave to a different doctrine and a new people. That "something" is the doctrine of Christ. If other religious bodies had "it," they, too, would be absorbed into the church of Christ.

We are not a great people for pomp, ceremony, affectation, or emotionalism; on the contrary we shun the very appearance of these things. Sectarian preachers can equal or surpass our brethren when preaching on morality, but in doctrine we have no equal. There is our strength! Shorn of doctrine we are as helpless as Samson in the hands of the Philistines, we become as weak as the sects and head pell-mell for the temple of Dagon.

Because denominationalism has softened its doctrinal teaching, there is a breakdown in the moral and religious fiber of the people. This is to be expected. If God's Word is not authoritative on religious issues, it is useless in the moral as well. One hole in the dike invites destruction of the whole dam.

Believing that we should keep these truths always squarely before the church, I suggested this type of lectureship program to the elders of the Vickery Boulevard congregation. They consented, and asked me to arrange the program. With the help of various preachers of the gospel in the city of Fort Worth, I eventually evolved the nine speech lectureship for October 25 to November 4, 1948.

The house was filled every night during the series, and on the last night when Brother Malone spoke on Catholicism people had to be turned away. Many who attended spoke words of commendation of the spirit and lessons delivered. Never before did we realize the fight that goes on within those who leave earthly institutions to become a part of the kingdom of heaven. May God bless this book to stir our hearts into the direction of appreciation for the Lamb's bride, the church of the Lord Jesus Christ.

THOMAS L. CAMPBELL, Minister
Vickery Blvd., Church of Christ
Fort Worth, Texas

WHY THIS BOOK?

This book proposes to present the deep, emotional conflicts and personal struggles of these men (the speakers) in leaving denominationalism for the truth of God. Those of us who have been "reared in the church", so to speak, taught the scriptures from childhood, can scarcely appreciate the problems and emotional encounters arising in the process of such changes. We have heard about these problems, but because we have not experienced them, it is exceedingly difficult, if not impossible, for us to know the tumult of feelings as well as the sacrifices involved.

In making these changes, many former impressions, stamped almost indelibly from early youth, had to be erased completely. This was not easy. Their sacrifices were varied and numerous, and this was no light matter.

But these men were not unduly disturbed; they had reasons—very sound reasons. They did not change because they were desirous of adventure, nor because they were fascinated by something that was new to them. Had it been a matter of personal preference, doubtless, not one of them would have left his former relationship. They changed, but WHY? This book proceeds to answer that question.

It was not the aim of the speakers to present and refute all the false doctrines of the denominations from which they came, but to give you the reasons why *they* left. But we believe that each speaker presented sufficient and irrefutable reasons to convince the judgment and convert the sinner.

We sincerely hope that you will read this book with pleasure and profit, and when you have done with it, pass it to some friend, who, by the careful reading of its pages, may be turned from darkness to light.

GUY V. CASKEY, Minister
South Summit Church of Christ
Fort Worth, Texas

CONTENTS

	PAGE
WHY I LEFT THE CHRISTIAN CHURCH	7
Floyd A. Decker	
WHY I LEFT THE PRESBYTERIAN CHURCH	31
Horace W. Busby	
WHY I LEFT THE BAPTIST CHURCH	53
Grover Stevens	
WHY I LEFT THE METHODIST CHURCH	93
Claude B. Holcomb	
WHY I LEFT THE NAZARENE CHURCH	117
Waymon D. Miller	
WHY I LEFT THE LUTHERAN CHURCH	141
Claude Guild	
WHY I LEFT THE WORLD	163
Luther Blackmon	
WHY I LEFT THE CATHOLIC CHURCH	181
Joe Malone	
WHY I LEFT THE ANTI-CLASS POSITION	223
L. W. Hayhurst	

BIOGRAPHIES—

Floyd A. Decker	6
Horace W. Busby	30
Grover Stevens	52
Claude B. Holcomb	92
Waymon D. Miller	116
Claude Guild	140
Luther Blackmon	162
Joe Malone	180
L. W. Hayhurst	222

FLOYD A. DECKER

(A Biographical Sketch)

Floyd A. Decker, son of Mr. and Mrs. E. A. Decker, was born December 26, 1898 at Geneva, Kentucky. In 1905 the Decker family moved to Ballard County in Western Kentucky. Later the family moved to Cairo, Illinois, where they were living at the time that Floyd A. Decker volunteered for Army duty April 15, 1918 in which service he served three years. When he was discharged from the service he returned to work as an automobile mechanic. He married Miss Elizabeth Hodges of Bandana, Kentucky, and moved to Tulsa, Oklahoma. Under the preaching of Billy Sunday he "hit the saw-dust trail." Soon after, he was invited to hear a Christian Church preacher preach in nearby Sand Springs. The sermons he heard were along the line of "What Must I Do To Be Saved," and upon hearing the second sermon he went forward and made the confession and was baptized. By January he was preaching and continued to preach for the Christian Church for about seven years. His wife, Elizabeth, died in Paris, Texas, in 1933, leaving him with two young girls to rear. From November 1929 to July 1933 he preached for the Highland Avenue Church of Christ in Montgomery, Alabama. In June of 1935 he was married to Miss Barbara Couch, of Paris, whose father is still elder in that congregation. He has two sons by the later marriage.

Brother Decker has preached in many states and loves evangelistic work. He preached for the Gladewater, Texas, church for five years, and spent about two years in Louisiana supported by the Gladewater brethren. He now lives at Haynesville, Louisiana, and is serving the church there for the second time.

Why I Left The Christian Church

By Floyd A. Decker

(Charles Herron, minister of the Arlington, Texas, church of Christ introduced Mr. Decker to the audience).

Thank you, Brother Herron, very much. I was not prepared for such an introduction; however, I appreciate it very much indeed.

I have never had an occasion to have any regrets for the change I made from the Christian Church to the church of Christ. I have learned as days and years have gone by to appreciate my present association with brethren in Christ. The more I learn of my brethren in the Lord the more I am convinced that they are sincerely endeavoring to serve the Lord Jesus from purity of purpose. I am happy, as I view the situation today, to see the progress which has been made. I am glad to be among those who are optimistic concerning the cause of our Lord. Brother Herron mentioned our association together back in Kentucky. To me those were great days—both before I learned the truth and after I took my stand for the plain New Testament position. I owe much for the discovery of the truth I hold tonight to the preacher, T. C. Wilcox, and his attitude, who followed up every lead and strengthened every tie of friendship that could be made. There are many things, purely personal, I would like to say concerning many men and brethren who are here tonight, but that is not the purpose of the meeting. I shall proceed with the lesson.

If I were going to take a text of any kind I think I should go to Ephesians 3:21, "To him be glory in the church by Christ Jesus throughout all ages, world without end." This shows us where we must glorify God—"in the church." It also shows us that it was not reserved for the first century church but—"throughout all ages." One other verse should be considered in this study or in any study of divine importance, 1 Thessalonians 5:21. This verse tells us: "Prove all things; hold fast that which is good." This is a principle essential to the study of any important matter. Let us search for truth always rather than try to protect some pre-conceived idea. Let us go to the Bible to *find* our doctrine rather than to go there to try to prove it!

BECAME A MEMBER OF THE CHRISTIAN CHURCH

I became a member of the Christian Church on February 10, 1922. I began to try to preach in July of the same year. I gave up my job in Tulsa, Oklahoma, and began full time preaching January 1, 1923, less than a year after I was baptized. My enthusiasm over what I thought I had found, my earnestness in the things I believed, caused me to go out believing others could be converted to the same truths I was taught to believe. My first "pastorate" (that is what they were called) was Kellyville, Oklahoma. You may not believe it, but they allowed me, my ignorance and all, to stay there five months. I moved to Vienna, Illinois from Kellyville and spent enough time there to borrow some money from the brethren and go to school—Cincinnati Bible Institute, of which John W. Tyndale was president. During this time I preached at Hartsville, Burnsville and Brownstown—all in Indiana.

MOVES TO PADUCAH, KENTUCKY

I think it was October of 1925 that I moved to Paducah, Kentucky, and became "pastor" of the Murrell Boulevard Christian Church. As I look back upon it now I think they must have been down to the bottom, with hope about all gone, or they never would have called me. They had an indebtedness of more than thirty thousand dollars. I did not know how much thirty thousand dollars was, so I did not know we could not pay it back. For some hitherto unknown reason things began to pick up and we began to pay off, and at the time I left them they owed about seventeen thousand dollars. We baptized a large number of people, many of whom are now in the church of Christ. I loved those people very much. I still love them. We were friends then, and we are friends now. I see no reason to lose the friendship of a man because you disagree with him. I confess to you that it was a great strain on me to have to leave those people.

On July 21st I left the Christian Church and took my stand with the church of Christ worshipping at 19th and Broadway. I went into the Christian Church because I thought I had found *the* church. I believed the Bible then as I do now. I believed as firmly then as I do tonight that Jesus is the Christ the Son of the living God. I have learned many things since, but my convictions on these things are the same. I firmly believe that when we settle the question concerning the Sonship of Jesus Christ and really believe him to be the Son of God, that, then, everything else can be settled that needs to be settled.

HONESTY SEEKING THE WAY

After I went into the Christian Church I was seven years finding out that I had not found the real, true church. I then found out by stumbling onto the real thing. Though I did not recognize my discovery at first when I began to compare the two churches with each other and both with the word of God, I saw wherein I had missed the way. It was rather like a person having a cut glass, thinking that it is a diamond. After awhile he finds a real diamond, and begins to examine his own so-called stone in the light of the real thing. He sees at once the cheapness of his own ring. To me, my religious experience was rather like that. I trust that if anything is ever said concerning me by my good friends, I hope it will prove true that I am "an honest man." A very fine statement, attributed to George Washington, made a profound impression upon me about the time of my spiritual upheaval—here it is: "I hope that I shall always possess virtue and courage enough to maintain what I consider the most enviable of all human titles, the character of an honest man." When we can get the world to look with real honesty upon the things we teach and when we teach with a clarity with which we should teach, we will see a great change coming about as never before. My attitude when I was with the Christian Church was aggressive. It was sure. It was honest. It was earnest. To be an honest man I had to accept what I saw to be truth regardless of results to myself or others.

OPPOSES INNOVATIONS

After entering the Christian Church and beginning my work as an aggressive preacher, I soon saw we had some serious divisions among us. Never being a "yes man" on any occasion, though a firm believer in the word of God, I was naturally on the conservative side. Thus I was lined up with those who supported the view of the "Christian Standard", and the brethren who wrote for that publication. Liberals nauseated me then, as they do now, and nauseate is the right word for it—for the man who takes liberties with God's word breathes out spiritual halitosis any one who loves and studies the Bible can detect. Policy men in the church, my dear friends, are not God's men—and I am not talking about those of you who are selling insurance for a living. I am talking of those who stand for certain things if it is to their own immediate interests to do so—standing for one thing in one place and quite another in another community. So again, I say, policy men are not God's men. We must stand for what we earnestly believe to be the truth regardless of the suffering and heartache resulting from such a stand.

OPPOSES MISSIONARY SOCIETIES

This being my attitude I was soon in a fight against the U. C. M. S.—that is, The United Christian Missionary Society, or, as we used to say: "The United Christening Money-Getters Society", and I think this came nearer representing that organization. The scraps we had with the "Society" taught me much about the evils of the organization of men or any organization other than the church of the Lord in the realm of religion. I learned from the beginning, somehow, that the church and the church alone with its elders, deacons, and members was the only organization in the universe God had ever authorized for the salvation of the souls of men. I believed that then, and I believe it now. If I am wrong I wish some of you brethren would set me right before I leave Fort Worth. Anyway, that taught me much about evils arising from human organizations. It taught me how men would work subtilly, carefully, and undercover, until they thought the time was ripe to close in for the kill. No, brethren, Hitler did not invent the fifth column.

Efforts by the fifth columnist to sabotage the work of faithful gospel preachers is no new thing. Those who would set aside God's will assumed an air of piety and extreme religious fervor as they do now. They assumed the role of the sweet-spirited tolerant, educated persons who were patient with those of us less forward looking than themselves—they were just waiting for the proper time to completely denominationalize the church —and did what they started out to do. But God's organization is the church of the Lord and there is no other.

TO BECOME TRIBUTARY IS SOON TO BECOME SUBSIDIARY

Brethren, to become tributary to an organization is soon to become subsidiary to the same. You may think you can have as organization auxiliary to the church, but it will not be long until you will find that the church is auxiliary to the organization. The church and the church alone, functioning after God's own order is sufficient for the advancement of the cause of Christ on the earth. I saw what happened in the Christian Church when men take liberties with the word of God. I saw how they would creep into this community and that community and like a giant octopus, with all its tentacles running in every direction, grasping the throat of this preacher and that—this "church board" and another—choking into submission by any means possible and taking control. Of course there were exceptions, for there were "fanatics" like myself who refused to be controlled.

READY TO BE TAUGHT

As I look back to that time nearly twenty years ago, I can now see that I was ready for some one to teach me. I believe there are many other preachers in the Christian Church tonight who are ready for some one to teach them. You remember the story of the man at the pool of Bethesda (John 5). When Jesus asked him if he would be made whole, he responded, "Sir I have no man, when the water is troubled, to put me into the pool . . . . . ." Well, the waters were troubled for me, everything was just right, the proper time had arrived for me and there were some men to "put me in." You may think that some certain persons can never be reached, but our job is to watch for the proper time—when the "waters are troubled" and then be there to help. Who would have thought that Saul of Tarsus could have been reached—but he was. I have already mentioned T. C. Wilcox, the local preacher at 19th and Broadway, who with patience continued to teach me and to associate with me—taking advantage of every opportunity. I do not know how much he was criticized by his brethren for even associating with me and being contaminated by me, nevertheless he did so and I shall be eternally grateful.

DEFENDS INSTRUMENTAL MUSIC

Another preacher of blessed memory to me and to whom I owe much was J. Petty Ezzell. He was my friend when I needed a friend. He made me sufficiently angry one night, when I heard him preach on the difference between the Christian Church and the church of Christ, to respond to him the next Sunday night from the pulpit at Murrell Boulevard. After I responded to his speech I followed it up later with some more preachments on instrumental music. Brother Wilcox could not be there to hear me but they sent Charles Houser Jr. to hear me. After listening courteously, Brother Houser asked me if I would repeat the same sermon at 19th and Broadway the next Thursday night. I responded, "I would be glad to." "Well," he said, "we want Brother Wilcox to answer it." I said, "I don't care who answers it; I'd be glad to make the speech." So we arranged two nights of public discussion. The discussion was held at 19th and Broadway. We discussed only the music issue as I was already solidly lined up against all unauthorized organizations. The first night of the discussion I took Brother Wilcox to the basement of the building and said, "Look here, T. C., you lay off me about this Ladies' Aid stuff. You lay off of this other stuff. We are just going to discuss instrumental music." He agreed. We had no moderators and we needed none.

The reason I stayed in the Christian church so long, after being convinced on the organizational question, may be explained by the fact that I believed instrumental music to be scriptural. The very week I was convinced that instrumental music in worship was unauthorized by the Lord's holy word, I prepared to oppose it and left the Christian Church when my pleas were denied.

SEES SERIOUS INCONSISTENCY

As far as the debate was concerned, one thing was accomplished which caused me to finally see the light. Brother Joe Morris, one of our outstanding gospel preachers now, was then an elder in the Murrell Boulevard Christian Church. Brother Morris was unable to attend the discussion and later asked me how I thought I had come out. I said: "Oh, pretty good I guess. I did fairly well I suppose, but you know Joe, there is just one thing I am afraid of. I would not enter into the discussion unless they let me have the first hour's speech to introduce the subject. I had to have an hour to introduce my arguments before I would agree to the debate and defend our practice. If you ask me about the subject of baptism I can settle it in just a few words and give direct quotations from the New Testament. But ask me about instrumental music and I'll say, 'now let me have an hour to make my first speech and I'll discuss it with you'. So that is what has me worried." I began to weaken from the day I lost confidence in my arguments. I was now looking for a real answer that would stand.

As I look upon my predicament, I was more or less like the story I heard concerning the first World War. During that war it is said there was a negro who was running down one of those trenches that they had then. I was over there too, but I wasn't that negro! Anyhow, this negro was running down a trench and ran "smack-dab" into a German as he turned a corner. The negro made a swipe at the German with his trusty razor. The German said, "Yeah, you thought you got me, didn't you?" The negro just looked back at him and said, "Yo' jes' shake yo' head—yo' jes' shake yo' head!" I was in that position, I suppose. I had my head cut off too, and did not realize it.

THE LAW OF EXCLUSION CONVINCES

It was through Brother N. B. Hardeman that I learned about the "law of exclusion." He sat down by my side and drew out the illustration on some note paper, and I was shaken up considerably and could think of no reply. I went away wondering, trying to think of some adequate answer. Brother Hardeman pointed out that Noah's ark was made of gopher wood, as God had ordered, and that God did not have to give a long list of the available woods and say: "Do not make the ark of gum, maple, cedar, oak, pine, etc." So also with the passover animal—it was to be a lamb, a male of the first year, etc. And, with regard to music—there are two kinds of music in the world, instrumental and vocal; and the fact that God ordained the vocal—singing, and did not authorize the instrument, was sufficient to show the kind of music God wanted in His church. So I continued to wonder, to examine and re-examine my old arguments. Finally I wrote out all the arguments I had ever heard in favor of instrumental music and mailed copies to several outstanding preachers in the church of Christ. I am sorry to state that some of the brethren never replied, and some who did, their replies were of no help. Brother Hardeman replied with some penciled references on the margin of my manuscript. This was of considerable value to me, and showed beyond all doubt that I had nothing now to stand upon in my defence of the musical instrument's use in the worship of God. (See addenda at the end of this speech for fuller explanation of the "law of exclusion.")

LEAVES THE CHRISTIAN CHURCH

The very week I was converted that instrumental music in the worship was wrong, I wrote to the Gospel Advocate and Firm Foundation and set forth my reasons for the change I was making. They kindly printed what I wrote which involved instrumental music in the worship and organizations of men in the work of the church. I have learned much more since that time, but have not seen fit to change a single argument since.

Here is something that may be of interest to you. The week of July 7th, 1929, I made up my mind and wrote out the article referred to before. I decided to preach on organizations in the work of the church on the following Sunday morning, and on instrumental music in the worship the same Sunday night. This was given to the daily papers with an urgent note for all to attend. Well, all went well until about Thursday night. I took violently ill of ptomaine poisoning. I do not know just how sick a horse gets, but I've seen some pretty sick and I venture I had him beat all to pieces. The doctor came to see me four or five times a day and several times each night. On the Sunday that I was scheduled to make my "big" speeches I could hardly raise my head from the pillow. Before the next Sunday came around considerable talking had been done in the congregation about what was in the papers and what others had said. Some few asked me some questions and without evading the issue I told them about what I had in mind. This of course resulting in what happened the next Sunday morning, July 21, 1929.

I went to church about fifteen minutes before time to preach, still very sick. When I got there I was called into the choir room for a conference with the elders and deacons—Joe Morris and all. Our conference resulted in my being barred from preaching from that day on. I told them that all I wanted to do was to make some corrections of a number of mistakes I had made in the past with reference to my teaching. I had to leave. I left the building and started to 19th and Broadway to place my membership and to make a statement there, but before I arrived I was overtaken by some of the men of the church who said I was permitted to return and make a short statement. I went back and made a short talk. I knew that as full as I was at the time, and as highly emotional as the situation was, I could do no teaching. I simply arose and said, "Brethren, I have come to the conclusion that I have been wrong, and that I have taught you wrong. I wanted to teach you right. I am not going to force the issue with you. I do not want you to follow me; I want you to follow the Lord. I want you to study this thing all over again, and do what the Book of God teaches you to do." That, in virtually a five minute talk, is what I had to say. Then I picked up my Bible, and went out to 19th and Broadway, and at the singing of their second invitation hymn I walked down the aisle and took my stand with the true church of the Lord Jesus Christ.

APPRECIATES THE BRETHREN IN CHRIST

I have never regretted my taking a stand with brethren in the church of Christ. I know that some of my brethren may not be sprouting wings, but there are not very many that are sprouting horns either. I appreciate my brethren highly for their firm stand for the truth. I am enthusiastic about the cause of Christ. I am happy over the progress we have made and am confident we are going to win our battle for the truth in the estimation of all who love the truth of God. Surely there are troubles and difficulties within the church; there were difficulties in the church of the first Century—at Corinth and other places, and there will ever be. If the world stands until the thirtieth Century the people will still have their problems —but we will have loyal and faithful brethren who will stand for and defend the truth of God. May God grant that they predominate in number, and I am hopeful they will. (From the audience, "Amen".) I may be wrong about it, brethren, but that is my attitude. I do not believe we can afford to have any other attitude. Let us go forward enthusiastically in the cause which cost the life of Jesus Christ and the Cause which will mean our salvation if we are truly loyal.

CHOOSING TRUTH OVER GAIN

But why did I make the change? This is the question I came here to answer, and I have not fully done it yet. Brother Herron has told you a little about the congregation I was serving. It had grown to be a popular congregation in the city. I think 19th and Broadway church of Christ and Murrell Boulevard Christian Church were about evenly matched as to popularity and number of members. At least I was getting along pretty well, thank you, in 1925-29 as far as financial affairs were concerned. In fact, financial affairs were better with me then than they were a few years later. However, I made up my mind before I ever started preaching to never permit financial affairs to control in any way my decisions concerning things of the church. So as I talked to my wife about the change, the difference in popularity, financial ability and opportunities for advancement—between the Christian Church and the church of Christ, I finally said, "If this is the truth, it is the truth, and I am willing to stand for it even if there were but a half dozen members of the church of Christ in the world and all of them were paupers! So since it is the truth we will just stand for the truth!" Brethren, I firmly believe that this kind of disposition must characterize us tonight. If it is the truth, stand for it. If it is not the truth, give it up. This is the only attitude God's people can afford to have toward the gospel of Christ.

A QUESTION OF AUTHORITY

But, why did I do it? My friends, it is a question of authority. You hear a lot about the differences between the Christian Church and the church of Christ. You have heard that there are many differences. Well, now I am not speaking disparagingly of what Brother Coleman Overby has outlined concerning some fifty-two differences. If we were to itemize certain practices as differences I suppose he would be about right. But all these fifty-two differences and others may be summed under one heading—just *one* difference. What is that difference? Instrumental music? That is it, is it not? Oh, no! Instrumental music has been represented as the only difference. This is not so. The real issue and the only difference between the Christian Church and the church of Christ exists in the attitude each group has toward the authority of God's word—the Bible.

ZWINGLI'S DIFFERENCE WITH LUTHER

The difference between Martin Luther and Zwingli—the German and Swiss reformers, serves to illustrate the difference between the Christian Church and the church of Christ. Luther was in favor of anything in the work and worship of the church which the Bible did not specifically condemn, whereas the Swiss reformer would have only that which the Bible specifically authorized. If we have the attitude of Luther we could have anything under the sun, including the modern dance in the worship of the church. If we have the attitude of Zwingli we would wait until we find a "thus saith the Lord", and thus have only that which the New Testament authorizes.

That would include the dancing and the instrumental music along with many other things. The same difference that exists between the church of Christ and the Christian Church is the same that exists between the church of Christ and any denomination in the world. This real difference which exists between us and any denomination is shown in the difference in our attitude as to what constitutes authority in religion. That is the real issue. I saw this finally, and was ready to say, "It is time to get out of this thing and follow only the truth of God as revealed in the Bible."

THE SIN OF PRESUMPTION

Unscriptural worship, organizations and plans are but items stemming from that parent sin—the sin of presumption. Presumption is presuming to speak for God or act for God where God has not authorized us to act or speak. This is the difference and the only difference!

ITEMIZING SOME UNSCRIPTURAL DIFFERENCES

As for itemizing the differences in practice let me read you this list, and lump it all together, and then maybe we can do as the song leader over in Oklahoma said, "Rest our 'vocalbules' a little bit." The local organizations are such as: the Ladies' Aid Society, Ladies' Missionary Society, Christian Endeavor Society with their national and international hook-up, organized Sunday Schools with their superintendents, assistant superintendent, secretaries, treasurers—operating as a separate order—not the church but operating for the church. Also under the heading of local organizations we would mention the choir, often facetiously called "The War Department," because so many wars and rumors of wars have started in their choir loft. Too, there are the men's clubs, boys' clubs, ladies' clubs and as we think about the many clubs we are forced to the conclusion that the church has had about all the spiritual life "clubbed" out of it. It was hard to get people together unless we would have a soup social or supper—a show or an entertainment of some sort. Paul Henry Packard, an outstanding evangelist in the Christian Church, said in a meeting at

Montgomery, Alabama, a few years ago, "The church is the most over-organized institution in the world." He was and is right on that.

JUNIOR CHURCHES

I am holding up before you an issue of the Christian Standard, dated September 17, 1932. They must have been very proud of the story as they gave it the front page prominence one would expect a highly recommended practice to have. This picture you see is a "Little Folks' New Testament Church." It is said to have its own elders, its little deacons, and a Mrs. Smith, the local preacher's wife is its pastor! You know from reading the Bible I somehow got the idea that elders of the "New Testament Church" should be old enough to shave! But this "Little Folks' New Testament Church"— a thing unknown to the Bible—met in the basement of the building at the same time the old folks met upstairs, observed the Lord's Supper and everything. They may not be doing it now as fads come and go, but they were then, in Ada, Oklahoma.

This reminds me of the story of the man and his cats. A man had a big cat and a little cat, and in order for them to go in and out of the house at will he cut a big hole in the door for the big cat. Beside the big hole he cut a little hole so the little cat could go in and out too. So, it seems with the Junior Church idea; it requires two churches—a big one for the old folks and a little one for the little folks—so that all might go to heaven. The young people will be no special problem unless we make one out of them. Teach them the soul saving gospel of Christ, and encourage them to believe it and obey it, and you will not have to have any church except that one redeemed by the blood of our Lord. The young people will be a part of it.

MISSIONARY SOCIETIES

The national organizations were: The U. C. M. S., the Restoration Association, Pension Boards, Educational Boards, Conventions or their counterparts. Every one of these are innovations in the realm of the work of the church. The worship and work of the Christian Church require both more and less than the New Testament requires. Instrumental music is an innovation in the realm of the worship of the church—God has not ordained it. Missionary Societies, and these other organizations already named, are innovations in the realm of the work of the church. Presumptuous innovators have, throughout the centuries, caused more heartaches and troubles and divisions in the church of the Lord than all other persecutions combined. There were (and still are) fifth columnists in the church from the modernist up or down—and so corruptions continued to increase. We, who are in the church of Christ, would do well to keep an eye on anything that might have a possible tendency to corrupt New Testament doctrine or practice.

OPEN MEMBERSHIP

Special days, women preachers, modernism, open-membership and human organizations were the main things which caused divisions, and they were the main issues over which we fought when I was in the Christian Church. Open membership means receiving and fellowshipping unbaptized—"sprinkled" —people and some who had received no so-called form of baptism at all—had not even been sprinkled. They practice this today more than ever in the Christian Churches and some Baptist Churches. It has not been long since the Christian Standard admitted that more than 200 of their churches were openly practicing open membership. When I went to Cincinnati in 1923, all we knew about were six congregations following such a practice. There is no doubt to my mind about there being more than 200 congregations of the Disciples of Christ or Christian Churches that now practice open membership. I will venture to say that there are many more than two hundred preachers among them that do not believe in the virgin birth of Christ or His resurrection from the grave.

The Christian Church observes special days, such as Easter, Lent, Christmas, and about all the other "special days" the Catholics and other sects observe. I remember when many Christian Church preachers would fight against special titles for preachers which would lift the preacher above the pew. But now the terms "Reverend", "Doctor", and "Pastor" are accepted fully by almost all of them. These things have no place in the hearts of simple Christians.

Let me tell you of this experience to illustrate what I have said concerning the authority of God's word. After I left the Christian Church, I went back to Brookport, Illinois, where I had preached for the Christian Church several months before. I went to see one of the good ladies of the Christian Church, president of the "Aid" I think. We were sitting on her porch talking about why I had made the change. Among other things this conversation developed:

"Sister, I noticed when I was preaching over here that you folks sing in your worship to God. Why do you sing?"

She said, "The Bible says so."

I then asked, "Sister, I noticed that you gave of your means —money, and have the Lord's Supper on the first day of the week. Why do you do these things?"

She said "The Bible says so."

I then replied, "Sister, I then noticed that you had instrumental music in the worship and the Aid Society in the work of the church. Why do you do these things?"

Her only answer was a red face and a quick catching of the breath. However, I will say to her credit, she gave as adequate and as reasonable an answer as any of her preachers could have done, or as good an answer as any of them can do tonight. I submit this in all kindness.

"NO PLACE TO STOP"

A great change has taken place in the Christian Church since that day I walked out nearly twenty years ago. I go back to Murrell Boulevard in the fall 1950 for a meeting, the Lord willing. I was there in a meeting in 1937 and assisted them in getting the church of the Lord Jesus Christ started off in that same building. At the close of about a month's meeting we took over the property in the name of the church of Christ, as the Christian Church had ceased to function there. It is a beautiful building. Alonzo Williams is preaching there now and has done a wonderful work the past several years. But, as I started to say, there have been many changes in the Christian Church since 1929; and many of you here tonight who were members, and some of you who are members of the Christian Church, will know I am telling the truth. It grieves me to have to make such a speech. There is more modernism and spiritual corruption among you now than ever. There is more worldliness among you than ever before. It is growing worse and worse and will continue to grow worse. *When you give up the authority of God's word there is no place to stop.* I plead with you to give up the things you know are without authority of God's word and take your stand upon the foundation of the Book of God.

THE DOWNWARD ROAD OF APOSTACY

My friends, departures from God's word, in church organization, resulted in the establishment of the Roman Catholic Church. Would you argue with me about that? I think not. Departures in church organization resulted in putting the Pope upon the throne and the establishment of the Roman Church. Every departure from the truth, as far as I know, had its beginning in the organization of the church and then from there spread out into other fields. I say once more, when the authority of God's word is given up there is no place to stop.

Let us have a care. History does sometime repeat itself. Let us be careful in the field of education, in the field of benevolence and in the field of evangelism. Institutions, brethren, do not reform. I hoped twenty years ago that I would be able to save that congregation I was preaching for. I was unable to make an impression on them to that end. Many of them came along as months and years came and went, but they did so individually. There is no way to go out and convert people on a wholesale basis and turn whole denominational bodies over. There is no easy way to build up the church of the Lord in the world. There is no easy way to convert the world. Victory comes most of the time as Churchill said, "Through blood, sweat, and tears." Men and women must be of earnest anxious hearts, enthusiastic souls who refuse to quit when quitting would be easier. Institutions fail sometimes and break up, but reform them, never! It cannot be done.

THE WORD OF GOD SUFFICIENT

I am told the church did pretty well in the first century. What do you think about it? Oh, if we could, with all our modern machinery, do half as well! The first century church got along pretty well without instrumental music and seemed to prosper without human organizations of any kind—just the church with its elders, deacons and members. I have strong suspicion that the Lord knew what the church needed then, and gave it all it was ever to have in order to propagate itself in the world. Yes, the word of God is sufficient—read it from II Timothy 3:16-17.

Brother Hardeman made a statement at 19th and Broadway church of Christ while in a meeting there, that made a profound impression on me. Brother Hardeman stated in the conclusion of a sermon one night:

"Here we are, and here is the Bible. You come and watch us in our worship of God and in our work for Him, and if you find us doing anything in the work or worship of the church for which we can not give a 'Thus saith the Lord' we pledge you that we will quit it. On the other hand, if there is anything which you think we ought to be doing, if you read it to us from the word of the Lord, we will begin it."

"Well", I thought, "I can say that and do that."

So the next Lord's day at Murrell Boulevard Christian Church I proceeded to say the same that I had heard Brother Hardeman say, and ended up with the assertion that if that congregation would not so do that I would do so anyway—regardless of their action. That statement means more and is bigger than I had thought. It was loaded with dynamite, but I knew that if I could not harmonize myself with that principle that I might as well give up claiming to believe the Bible.

Brethren, what is your attitude tonight? Can you brethren here in Fort Worth make the statement just referred to? Is there anything we are doing for which we can not give a "Thus saith the Lord"? Is there anything we are leaving off for which scriptural authority can be given? What is our attitude toward God's Holy Book tonight? May God help us in promoting these principles throughout the whole world.

I have never for one moment regretted my stand, taken at the cost of the loss of many dear friends. I have wanted very much to teach those of my former connections the full truth, but have at no time longed to go back and practice with them that which the Bible does not authorize. I left the Christian Church because of its unscriptural teachings and practices and plead with them even now to give it up, too, for the very same reasons. Come out of it, my friends, and call Bible things by Bible names, and do Bible things in Bible ways. May God bless this present effort to that end.

Addenda On Instrumental Music

THE LAW OF EXCLUSION

1. J. M. Pendleton, D. D., in his "Church Manual, designed for the use of Baptists Churches," in discussing infant baptism, brings out the point I have in mind concerning the "Law of Exclusion." He says: "It may be laid down as a principle of common sense, which commends itself to every candid mind, that *a commission to do a thing authorizes only the doing of the thing specified.* The doing of all other things is virtually forbidden. There is a maxim of law, that *the expression of one thing is the exclusion of another.* It must necessarily be so; for otherwise there could be no definiteness in contracts, and no precision in legislative enactments or judicial decrees. This maxim may be illustrated in a thousand ways. Numerous scriptural illustrations are at hand. For example:

"God commanded Noah to make an ark of gopher-wood. He assigns no reason why gopher wood should be used. The command, however, is positive, and it forbids the use of every other kind of wood.

"Abraham was commanded to offer his son Isaac for a burnt-offering, he was virtually forbidden to offer any other member of the family. Aye, more, he could not offer an animal till the order was revoked by Him who gave it and a second order was given, requiring the sacrifice of a ram in the place of Isaac.

"The institution of the Passover furnishes an illustration, or rather a combination of illustrations.

"A lamb was to be killed—not a heifer.

"It was to be of the first year—not of the second or third.

"It was to be male—not a female.

"Without blemish—not with a blemish.

"On the fourteenth day of the month—not some other day.

"The blood was to be applied on the door-post and lintels —not elsewhere." Pages 81, 82.

Dr. Pendleton gave other illustrations and examples from the Constitution of the United States, showing that "the expression of one thing is the exclusion of another." While his argument completely removes "infant baptism" from even a remote possibility of being acceptable to God, the same maxim as surely excludes instrumental music. Let us apply Pendleton's argument to mechanical music and note the results.

There are two kinds of music in the world. If God had not expressed Himself on one kind, no kind would have been excluded. But God did express Himself, and *SPECIFIED* the kind of music to be used in His worship. Singing (vocal music) and instrumental (mechanical) music are the only kinds of music in the world. The fact that God specified singing is enough to exclude any other kind. You ask: "Where did God say not to use mechanical music?" Well, where did God say: "Thou shalt not use hickory, ash or elm in making the ark, Noah?" Where did God say: "Do not offer a pig, cat or dog in the Passover, Moses?" When God specified gopher wood he excluded all other kinds of wood. When He designated the lamb for the Passover, He excluded all other animals. When God authorized *SINGING* for the New Testament Church, He excluded all other kinds of music. "Speaking to yourselves in psalms and hymns and spiritual songs, singing and making melody in your heart to the Lord" (Eph. 5:19). "By him therefore let us offer up the sacrifice of praise to God continually, that is, the fruit of our lips, giving thanks to his name." (Heb. 13:15; See also Col. 3:16, 17; Jas. 5:13; I Cor. 14:15; Heb. 2:12, etc.).

THE SUFFICIENCY OF THE WORD OF GOD

1. "The baptism of John, whence was it? from heaven, or men?....." (Matt. 21:25). A correct answer to this question would have gone far in settling the issues between Jesus and the Jews. John the Baptist said: "A man can receive nothing, except it be given him from heaven" (John 3:27). Where did the authority to use instruments of music in the worship of the New Testament Church come from? Heaven or men? It did not come from heaven; hence, we should not receive it.

2. In Acts 20:20, Paul the apostle said: ".....I kept back nothing that was profitable unto you.....", and in verse 27 he continues: "For I have not shunned to declare unto you all the counsel of God." In keeping back "nothing profitable" and in declaring "all the counsel"—advice of God, the apostle did not authorize—give them instrumental music for the worship of the church, hence, it is not in "the whole counsel of God" to the church is, therefore, unprofitable.

3. "Whosoever transgresseth (goeth onward—Revised Version), and abideth not in the doctrine of Christ, hath not God. He that abideth in the doctrine of Christ, he hath both the Father and the Son" (II John 9). Does the "doctrine of Christ" teach the use of instrumental music in the church worship? It does not. Then, can we use it, and not go beyond or transgress the teaching of God's word? We must *"abide in the doctrine of Christ"* to have God. But we cannot "abide in the doctrine" and practice things not taught. Instrumental music is not taught; hence, he who practices things unauthorized in the "doctrine of Christ"—HATH NOT GOD.

4. "All scripture is given by inspiration of God, and is profitable for doctrine, for reproof, for correction, for instruction in righteousness: that the man of God may be perfect, thoroughly furnished unto all good works" (II Tim. 3:16, 17). The scriptures furnish us "unto all good works," but do not furnish us the authority for instrumental music. Therefore, instrumental music is not among the "good works" furnished by scriptural authority.

THE ORIGIN OF INSTRUMENTAL MUSIC IN CHURCH WORSHIP

1. The American Cyclopedia says: "Pope Vitalian is related to have first introduced organs into some of the churches in western Europe about 670: but the earliest trustworthy account is that of the one sent as a present by the Greek emperor Constantine Copronymus to Pepin, king of the Franks, in 755." (Vol. 12, p. 688). So we can see that instrumental music did not originate with the apostles who were guided by the Holy Spirit, but by the Roman Church without the authority of God's word.

2. No argument was ever presented in favor of mechanical music until AFTER it was introduced and practiced. Hence, it could not have been put into the worship to please God, but man. It is kept there for the same reason. Gal. 1:10 says: "..... for if I yet pleased men, I should not be the servant of Christ."

QUESTIONS COMMONLY ASKED

1. *Did not the Jews of the Old Testament use instrumental music in their worship?* Yes, it is true that mechanical music was used by them, as shown in many Old Testament passages. But we are living under the New Testament, and we are concerned only with what it teaches and authorizes. I would not know how to go back to the Old Testament for instruments of music and not also observe the many other things authorized in the same book, such as: burning of incense, the males going to Jerusalem three times a year to worship, animal sacrifice, polygamy and many other things tolerated and even commanded in the Old Testament. See Gal. 3:16-25; Col. 2:11-17; Heb. 1:1-3; 7:11; 8:1-13; 10:1-10. There are many other passages but these will show definitely that we are not under the Old Testament.

2. *Will there not be instruments of music in heaven?* If there are or are to be, we should wait until we get there to play them; then we can play them by God's authority. Here upon earth we cannot, for God has nowhere authorized such for New Testament church worship. If we go to the book of Revelation—a book of symbols, for literal, material harps—

instruments of music, why not accept also incense, the beast, horses, etc., as literal and use these things in church worship?

3. *If you have instruments of music in your home why do you not have them in church worship?* In this connection read I Corinthians 11:19-34. Here you find an apostle rebuking the church at Corinth for doing, "when ye come together in the church," what he told them to do "at home". "If any man hunger, let him eat at home; that ye come not together unto condemnation." There are many things we do at home which we are not privileged to do in worship. The home is governed by moral law; the church and its worship by direct religious law. This is so obvious I shall comment no further.

4. *Does the Bible say not to use mechanical music?* Please see section on "The Law of Exclusion." The Bible does not, in just so many words, say: "Thou shalt not dance, gamble, sprinkle babies, burn incense in the worship or pray to the 'Virgin Mary'." Are we to conclude, therefore, that these things are permissible? I fear even though the Bible did say, "Thou shalt not use instruments of music," that many would disregard it and use it anyway. Such are they who say, "We want it and we are going to have it." And they do, for the word of God and its authority is not important to them. What surprises me is that such a person would claim to love God and respect His will. "Why call ye me, Lord, Lord, and do not the things which I say?" (Luke 6:46).

5. *Would not a proper translation* of Rom. 15:9; I Cor. 14:15; Eph. 5:19, and James 5:13, *furnish authority for instrumental music?* I have used in this addenda, the Authorized (King James) Version and have referred to the Revised Version. The King James Version was translated by forty-seven of the world's ripest scholars. The Revised Version was translated by one hundred and one of the greatest scholars of their day. To reject their work, one hundred and forty-eight of the world's greatest scholars—the cream of the world's scholarship, could be nothing short of a repudiation—a setting aside of our English Bible. If they did not give us a correct translation of the verses under consideration, how could we trust

them in giving us a true translation of the "Sermon on the Mount"?

ACCEPTABLE WORSHIP MUST BE BY FAITH

Acceptable worship must be of faith. "Without faith it is impossible to please Him: for he that cometh to God must believe that he is, and that He is a rewarder of them that diligently seek him" (Heb. 11:6). All we do in the work and worship of the church must be directed by faith. How do we obtain faith? "So then faith cometh by hearing, and hearing by the word of God" (Rom. 10:17). If there is any other way to get faith I have never heard of it. Since it is true that faith comes by hearing God's word, in the absence of God's word there can be no faith in things Christian. That is, if God's word does not teach it we cannot believe it. In II Cor. 5:7 we read, "For we walk by faith and not by sight." Of course we must have faith before we can "walk by faith." But since faith comes by hearing God's word, and God's word does not teach instrumental music in the worship of the church, we cannot walk by faith and use it any more than we could, by faith, burn incense, pray to the "Virgin Mary" or anything else not taught in the New Testament. Note the following with reference to these three verses:

(1) In the absence of God's word there can be no faith;
(2) In the absence of faith we cannot walk by faith;
(3) Walking without faith we cannot please God.

These things being true and the word of God giving no authority for the use of instrumental music, we cannot use it and please God.

The writer would be pleased to discuss any other question on this subject of interest to the reader in person or by mail.

HORACE W. BUSBY

(A Biographical Sketch)

Horace Wooten Busby was born in Lawrenceburg, Tennessee, the son of John S. and Frances Wooten Busby. When he was about seven years of age his father moved to Ellis County in Texas and settled near Waxahachie, where he grew to manhood. Here he taught school, married Miss May Wise, and began his work as a preacher of the gospel.

As he relates in his discourse his wife and he were baptized into Christ by Henry E. Warlick in Mangum, Oklahoma, after which time he spent four years in special preparation and study to preach the gospel.

His first and only local work with a congregation was with the Glenwood (Vickery Boulevard) congregation in F o r t Worth. After five years labor with this congregation the invitations were so numerous for meetings that he decided to give up the local work and hold meetings altogether. For the past thirty years he has been an outstanding evangelist in the church of Christ in gospel meeting work. He has never held less than twenty-five meetings annually, and during 1948 he held twenty-eight. He has held meetings in many of our larger cities, and in most of the states. Approximately 17,000 souls have obeyed the gospel under his preaching, with many more reclaimed, and a number of congregations started. He has held over one hundred meetings in his home town, Fort Worth, and his converts are numbered among the hundreds here. Many of our leading preachers and educators are among the number who have been led into Christ in the evangelistic work of Bro. Busby.

Why I Left The Presbyterian Church

By Horace W. Busby

It is with the greatest pleasure that we come together tonight, and especially on my part. We see so many people, and the house is filled with honest listeners.

My subject happens to be, "Why I Left the Presbyterian Church." It is not the big thing in my life just to leave something. Sometimes people come in among us like they go into various churches because they became angry at somebody. They did not think they were treated right; so they wanted to leave. But that is not so in my case; I did not get mad at anybody. I have just as many friends among the Presbyterians as I ever had. I know I have no enemies. They all conceded that I had a right to do as I pleased about religion, and I saw fit to obey my Lord more fully than I could and be a first-rate Presbyterian.

A SHORT HISTORY OF PRESBYTERIANISM

Presbyterianism is that form of church life where elders, the presbytery, rule. We call them elders, and they call them elders. The elders with their preachers—and the preacher might be one of the elders like it is with us—govern the local bodies. Therefore it is called Presbyterianism. There are many churches in that fellowship, as opposed to what we have in England where we have the Episcopal form of church government in which one man rules. There was a great fight in England a long time ago when Presbyterianism first made its appearance through John Knox and others. It looked like it would conquer the empire, and it almost did. They had a monarchy, and the English government had something to do with the religion of all those countries. When those monarchs began to seek for power, and all those people were members of a state religion, the Presbyterian form of religion was contrary to their wishes, because they taught the rule should be in the hands of several like we have in our government, and like we have in the English government now, but did not then. So the fight began between the Episcopalian idea where a bishop ruled a whole province, and where elders would rule locally.

John Calvin is the author, we might say, of Presbyterianism. The Geneva preacher's teaching has formed the basis of the creeds of many churches. John Knox was his disciple. He was a very eloquent man and a very great preacher. He went from Geneva over to Scotland, and from there started the Presbyterian Church in Scotland. It became the Scotch church—the Scotch Presbyterian Church. We are quite familiar, perhaps, with the history about these men. I am familiar with it for several reasons: I was raised on it, I read a lot about it. If you were Presbyterians you did, too.

NOT ASHAMED OF THE PEOPLE

Well, we notice the Presbyterian Church planted in Scotland back in the middle of the Sixteenth Century became a very great power. I am not ashamed of the crowd that I ran with when I was a Presbyterian as far as the people are concerned. Some of the greatest men of our country have been Presbyterian. We have had more presidents of the United States from Presbyterian families than any other. In Scotland that has been true, and other nations we might mention. It has been a big thing. They have contributed largely to our great government. Their form of government is not adverse to the New Testament idea, but they raised it to a political power in a measure to where the greatest political leaders we have had had that idea of religion. Woodrow Wilson was a Presbyterian as was also Grover Cleveland and William Jennings Bryan and others who were prominent in our government. They usually made great men in our political affairs. They were men who dealt with the people more. They did not try to assume too much rule like some others.

BUT CANNOT FOLLOW CHRIST AND CREEDS

So I did not leave the Presbyterian Church because I was mad at them or ashamed of the people, or anything like that, but it was purely in principle. The church of the Lord Jesus

Christ was something that Jesus founded on earth; and where Christ's teaching goes contrary to any human theory, if we want to love the Lord and be blessed by Him we have got to say good-bye to every earthly tie, and follow where we believe Jesus is leading. Jesus says, "Unless you take up your cross daily and follow me, you cannot be my disciple." (Matt. 16:24). Well, then, we cannot follow men and do that. Where men make a creed we cannot follow that creed without more or less following men. Nearly all the creeds of the great reformers carried that very strongly in them this principle: that we take the Bible as our rule of faith and practice. That is, among Protestant people. John Calvin did that; John Knox did that, as did John Wesley and Martin Luther. They all took the position that the Bible is a sufficient rule, and the people all started for the same position where we stand tonight. But as time went on and they had a great group of people, they had to form a creed to hold what they had together, they thought. That is how creeds were formed: each man wanting to hold his group together. There has got to be some leading principle before anybody knows what his faction is. There is some idea that he has, and he wants to hold his group to it. He builds him a church and magnifies that one idea that separates him from all other disciples of the Lord. That was the way creed-making started. They all started away from Rome and its corruptions back in the days of Martin Luther. He is called the "Morning-star of the Reformation." John Calvin gave it life and power. For good life and dignified living, John Calvin headed all the rest. He was very strict in moral teaching; so much so that he became a burden to some people that wanted to mix up worldliness and their religion. We call them Puritans in our country. We know what the Puritan laws were. Well, they were people from Scotland and England that had been touched with Presbyterianism, and therefore with the creed that came from Westminister by John Knox—the disciple of John Calvin. Of course that modified some of the Calvinist views quite a bit. The Presbyterian Church in the United States has divided a time or two, but still it is Presbyterianism.

DIVISIONS AMONG THE PRESBYTERIANS

In 1810 in Tennessee there was a division among the Presbyterians, and a part of them were then called Cumberland Presbyterians—but they were still Presbyterians. They were governed by elders in the local group. My father happened to be a member of the Cumberland Presbyterian Church. I remember seeing him appointed an elder in one of the local Cumberland Presbyterian churches. My great-grandfather, Samuel McClean, was at the organization of the Cumberland Presbyterian Church, and was an elder in it the day it was organized. I have a walking-cane over at home that he cut there that day between sessions of that presbytery. It has been in the family since 1810. He walked with it until he died, and willed it to my father, and he willed it to Horace Jr., and it is in our home. My wife's mother was crippled a good while you know, and she used that stick to walk with around home until she passed on; but the stick is still there—a memorial of the organization of the Cumberland Presbyterian Church.

THE CUMBERLAND PRESBYTERIAN CHURCH

The Cumberland Presbyterian Church modified the views of the old Calvinistic teaching much more than the regular branch of the Presbyterian Church in this country, especially concerning foreordination and predestination, and infants dying in infancy going to hell. They eliminated those things, but otherwise held to the Westminister Confession of Faith or to Calvinistic views. The Primitive Baptists took off from the Calvinistic views too, and through them the Philadelphia Confession of Faith was formed. So the Cumberland Presbyterian Church finally reached the point where they thought some of their claims were unnecessary. It started because of a great religious revival in Kentucky and Tennessee, and people were converted so fast that they did not have enough preachers to take care of the great number of converts. The old Presbyterians thought that a man had to pass a certain degree in their seminaries before he could be ordained to preach, hold communion, or baptize and marry people. The Presbytery of the Cumberland raised the question:

THE PRESBYTERIAN CHURCH 35

"We need to ordain any faithful man that is capable of preaching. He can go out and convert people and administer to them, and where he knows enough to do that, and can do it in a dignified way, we ought to authorize him to do it."

The fight became rather bitter. So the Cumberland presbytery—a presbytery in the Presbyterian Church—in February, 1810 withdrew from the general Presbyterian Church and started the Cumberland Presbyterian Church. Well, that continued until about 1903 when they decided they could take care of the situation by following the old school idea. They had a general election, and I voted in that election for the two bodies to go back together. The vote carried almost unanimously. After the election was over, a lot of the "lay members" began to raise a question over some points which they differed with the regular Presbyterians. They said, "We didn't vote for this; we believe we had rather be Cumberland Presbyterians." So the Cumberland Presbyterian Church really continued, but according to the election they lost their property. It was just a church without any property or deed to it. They finally took it to the Supreme Court to settle whether the property should continue Cumberland Presbyterian property, or whether it was now the property of the Presbyterian Church of the United States of America. But I voted for that union when I was yet a Presbyterian. I was in it, and that is my lesson tonight, "Why I Left It." I am not ashamed of why I left, nor why I am what I am, or anything else. I want to tell it. It might be helpful to somebody, and hurtful to nobody.

STUDIES THE BIBLE

Well, then, we have in this lesson tonight, "Why I Left The Presbyterian Church". Now, here is the reason:

I began to read my Bible early in life. My mother taught me the scriptures before I could read. I could quote many passages from memory. In fact, many of the passages of scripture that I can quote easily today I learned before I could read. My mother taught me. She knew a great deal about the Bible. That was not foreign to Presbyterianism either. They were great Bible students. Most of the works in your library as Christian men and gospel preachers—their authors were Presbyterian scholars. They were scholarly men, and are yet. When it comes to the life of Christ and the Old Testament, you cannot find any better commentaries on that part of the Bible than by Presbyterian authors. The only question that I could bring up is, that they do not know how to rightly divide the scriptures—that they do not give the proper division of the Old Testament from the New. That is where I became dissatisfied with my part of it.

BECOME DISSATISFIED WITH THE NAME

I began to read and study my Bible. After I was grown I continued to study it, and to study it hard. I studied to midnight. My father who was then an elder in the Presbyterian Church would often come to my room and want me to go to bed. He said, "You will go crazy reading the Bible so much. You don't need to read it so much." When he would go back to sleep, I would still want to finish a thought. In that way I became dissatisfied with a good many things. One was the name. "Why do I have to tell people that I am a Presbyterian, when I read my Bible, and became a follower of Christ? Why do that?" Well, that was the question, and I could not answer it by the Bible.

COULD NOT FIND INFANT BAPTISM

Another question that bothered me was: We believed and taught infant baptism. I began to read and search the Bible for it, but could not find anything about it. I wanted to be able to answer everybody that asked me why we did so and so. But I could not find it in the Bible, and I tried hard. I went to Dallas and called on the pastor of the largest Presbyterian Church in the state. When I asked him, he just referred me to the library to read some books. He did not answer my question. That threw me into greater dissatisfaction. One of the greatest men among them referred me to some books of men instead of to the Bible—the book that I was anxious about. So I went back home and studied some more.

SPRINKLE OR IMMERSE FOR BAPTISM?

I began to wonder about the mode of baptism—that was a great question then. I had been sprinkled when I was a child. I was old enough to remember what they did. The preacher said, "Horace, arise and be baptized." And so I stood up, and he dipped his finger in a glass of water, and placed it on my face. He said the same ceremony that I have said hundreds of times in baptizing people now. That was the way it was done. I could not find any proof for that, and it made me very greatly dissatisfied that I had to tell people that I had been sprinkled or water poured on my face for baptism.

However, they did not force sprinkling or pouring on us. The first immersion I ever saw was performed by a Presbyterian preacher. Over at Ovella when I was about like little John, my grandson, over here on my left, I went down to Red Oak Creek one Sunday afternoon, and the preacher named Bunch, the pastor of the church where my father was an elder, had a group of people who wanted to join his church, but they had heard a part of the gospel, or read it like I had, and they said, "We will not come into the Presbyterian Church unless we can be immersed."

They only made a confession of faith in Christ, too; they did not say, "We believe that God for Christ's sake has pardoned our sins," like some denominational people do. They just made a simple confession, and Bunch baptized all that bunch sure enough, in Red Oak Creek. That was the first immersion I ever saw. Everybody commented on how well he did it—how nice and dignified the baptizing was conducted—they did not think it could be done by immersion. Some had made fun of it, and said that it was indecent to immerse people. But when the man I have just referred to did that baptizing they could see that it was done in a very fine way.

They were not dogmatic about sprinkling and pouring, but that was their doctrine. They believed that baptism could be done by pouring water on the individual instead of immersing the whole body. And so, I began to study the question, and perhaps it bothered me more than any other one thing.

WORRIES ABOUT THE PURPOSE OF BAPTISM

Another question came into that particular study and that was, "What was I baptized for?" The answer that they wanted me to give was: to get into the visible church on earth. When you believed on the Lord you entered the spiritual or invisible church, but now baptism is to put you into the visible church. And so when I read in my New Testament that we are baptized into Christ (Rom. 6:3; Gal. 3:27), I could not fix that thing, and my conscience was not at ease. I would talk to my Presbyterian friends and my own family about it often. There was no quarreling over it, but just discussing it so that we might understand it. That question could not be answered by staying where I was, and letting the Presbyterians answer for me.

BAPTISM IS FOR THE REMISSION OF SINS

In studying the question of what baptism is for, I noticed it was the remission of sins (Acts 2:38). The Bible said that. Ananias said, "Arise, and be baptized and wash away thy sins....." (Acts 22:16). Well, the preacher told me to arise and be baptized, but he did not say to me what Ananias said to Paul. When I began to compare mine with Saul's, it disturbed me. Then I read Paul's explanation of his baptism when he said, "As many of us (including himself) as were baptized into Christ, have put on Christ" (Gal. 3:27). His baptism was into Christ—mine was not. Paul also said, "We are buried with him by baptism into death, and raised to walk a new life" (Rom. 6:4). I thought I had the new life before I went into it, and as a child of God I was obeying a simple command that placed me into the visible church here on earth. Of course I was dissatisfied. Reading my Bible made me so. I was not dissatisfied with the group I was running with. They were my kin people. They were the ones I went to school with, had dates with, and loved very dearly. It was really a hard fight to have to leave that group religiously over nothing but doctrinal differences, but I did.

THE PRESBYTERIAN CHURCH 39

EVENTS IN OKLAHOMA

Well, we kept on reading, and finally I married. My wife is present to check on the rest of it. She was not a member of the church of Christ either. We went to Oklahoma, and while I was there I heard Henry Warlick preach a sermon. It was very much along the line that I had been studying. I was disturbed. It was out in a community where there was no church. They did not have the Lord's Supper there that day. Somebody had invited him there to make a talk about like I am. Well, I listened to it, and I saw that he had something that I had been craving. And so I went home and gave up a job I had as a bookkeeper in a wholesale grocery store in Mangum. I went out to an uncle's home whose wife was a very fine Bible student.

I said, "Aunt Lizzie, I want to study the Bible—just study it. My mind craves to know more of the Book, and you are an able teacher."

She said, "Horace, I'll let the girls take care of the house, and we will just study."

And so sure enough the girls did it, and from breakfast at six o'clock, until midnight every night for ten days we just sat there and studied the Bible on these questions that were hard for me to grasp. She did not say a word about my religion, nor the people with whom I associated, nor the church I was a member of, but showed me in the Book what the New Testament Church was. That was all I cared about. I knew about the other. There was no need for her to waste time, and to say those other things were wrong.

IS BAPTIZED INTO CHRIST

My uncle was not much of a Bible scholar, but a Christian who was doing the best that he could. It was something like Priscilla and Aquila; they taught Apollos the way of the Lord more perfectly. Priscilla is mentioned first which shows that she did the teaching while Aquila sat there like uncle did and listened. That straightened Apollos out (Acts 18:26), and that straightened me out.

My uncle said, "Horace, if you ever decide that you would

like to be baptized and become a New Testament Christian, I'll go get a preacher to do the baptizing."

I said, "I am ready now, Uncle Tom."

So he got up early the next morning and hitched two great big grey horses to an old-fashioned Spaulding hack, and drove twenty-two miles to Marie, and called for Brother Henry E. Warlick.

He said, "I have a nephew over home that is not satisfied with his religious work, and he has decided to be baptized into Christ for the remission of sins. We could do it, but I just thought you were accessible, and I'd come and tell you about it."

"All right, Tom, I'll be over in the morning. Just announce that on tomorrow, Sunday, I'll preach in Mangum."

Well, my uncle came back and stopped at every farm house and had them telephone to everybody that the telephone would reach, that he had a nephew that was a Presbyterian, and was going to be baptized in Mangum Sunday morning. The house was as full as this, and Henry preached. But my mind was made up before I heard his sermon, and so before the invitation song started, I started down the aisle to make my confession. I told them that I wanted to be baptized into Christ for the remission of sins. I did not want to be anything but just a Christian. I did not want any church affiliation except the New Testament church, which is called the church of Christ, the church of God, or the church of the Lord (Rom. 16:16; I Tim. 3:15; Acts 20:28). Brother Warlick said that he would do that. My wife went with me, and my uncle's daughter-in-law went with us—three of us. We were baptized that afternoon in Brother Wetston's tank. A good many of the good old sisters came around—God bless them—and slapped me on the back and said, "Horace, the next time we hear from you, we want to hear of your being a gospel preacher."

BEGINS PREACHING THE GOSPEL

We left there in about a week and came to Ellis County, Texas. There I began to study hard the scriptures, and finally hired a man to work in my place that my father-in-law had arranged for me. For four years I studied the Bible—not

THE PRESBYTERIAN CHURCH

doctrine. I had studied doctrine nearly all of my life. But I studied the Bible that I might know how to preach it acceptably. At the end of that four years I was preaching. I had been teaching the Bible every Sunday, for the elders had put me right to work at that. I was teaching the church house packed full of people every Sunday, chapter by chapter. They had a preacher out of me before I knew it. At the end of those four years I was called to come to a church near Midlothian and hold a meeting. We baptized more than twenty, and it went out broadcast that I had become a preacher. Then I went to Lockney Bible College for a meeting. There I baptized my father. My mother came into the church there, and my brothers and sisters heard me, and my sisters were baptized, and one of them is here tonight.

The next time, I got a call to go back to Mangum, and those good old sisters were still living. They came around and beat me on the back, and one of them even hugged and kissed me! The old lady said, "Horace, I knew it was in you—God bless you!"

I cannot forget it. It was the same place where I was baptized just a few years before.

HEART'S DESIRE TO SAVE THOSE IN ERROR

So that is the story of a man who changed by just following his conscience. I am not mad at anybody. I love all those people. Paul was that way. He came up among the Jews, was a Jew, a Pharisee, and he preached to the Jews. He tried his best to convert them. Some of them mistreated him, and some did not. Yet I hear Paul speaking just like I would like to speak. He said, "My heart's desire and prayer to God for Israel is, that they might be saved. For I bear them record that they have a zeal for God, but not according to knowledge. For they being ignorant of God's righteousness, and going about to establish their own righteousness, they have not submitted themselves to the righteousness of God." (Rom. 10:1-3).

Now, friends, you can see the likeness, and you can see what I have in my heart when I pray that same prayer tonight. Presbyterians are good, honest people, and they have a great zeal. Sometimes they make me ashamed of our zeal even yet, and certainly as we read their history. Many people were put to death because they preached so earnestly what they believed was right. But when I began to read my Bible, and I could not read of infant baptism, I said, "There is where man has changed God's message." They are preaching that, and are ignorant of God's righteousness, and going about to establish their own. They would get up and talk about foreordination and predestination, and some people being ordained to eternal life. Of course I had a little modified view of that teaching, but yet that was in our background. They were good people, and they loved me and still do. They want me to preach when I come around where they are. They nearly always endorse it some way or other if I am just preaching the plain Bible. They say, "That is it, and we cannot deny it."

THE GREAT LARIMORE MEETING IN LAWRENCEBURG

Well, I will tell you another little thing which may be of interest. Over in Tennessee the descendants of that great-grand-father that was made an elder in the first Cumberland Presbyterian Church in Dickson County, Tennessee, in February 1810, were McCleans. There was a large family of them. I have almost a hundred McClean cousins in Lawrenceburg or vicinity. Brother T. B. Larimore of former days came there to hold the first gospel meeting in that town which now has one of the largest churches of Tennessee. Well, the doctrine was strange, and they would talk on the streets about that new religion that was coming to town. They talked about it in such terms the boys and girls thought it was some dangerous thing. Brother Larimore held the meeting in an old academy that had stood during a battle skirmish during the Civil War. A cannon had been placed out yonder somewhere, and a ball was shot across, cracking down through the roof. The ceiling was still standing.

Well, one of those McClean boys was called Doc, a great, big, old awkward boy—my cousin—decided he would beat them to it. He would go down there and hide, and hear that fellow and just see what went on. So he went down before night, climbed up in the loft, and he got to where that cannon-ball hole just served his purpose to see where the preacher would stand. He hid himself. He was afraid they would hear him breathe, so he was very quiet.

Directly the crowd began to gather, and they began to sing, "On Jordan's Stormy Banks We Stand," "Amazing Grace, How Sweet the Sound," and "Rock of Ages, Cleft for Me."

"Well," he thought, "there's nothing bad about that. That is the best singing I ever heard."

After awhile somebody led a prayer, and he thought, "Well, there's nothing wrong about that. It seems like they were talking to God."

Then Brother Larimore came up; he was a young man then, but with as big feet as he ever had. He walked to the edge of the pulpit, and two-thirds of his feet stuck over. I heard him preach when he was eighty-five, and he still had that same habit. Well, Doc saw him come out and stand just that way, and he never did move. He preached a wonderful sermon, as he was capable of doing. He had a great flow of intelligent words and oratory; in fact it was so great in those days that the railroads out of Nashville would give Dollar Excursions to the Larimore meetings even as far down as Alabama. When they would start, the train would be loaded between the cars, on top of the cars, and out of the windows, and everywhere, going to the Larimore revival—a dollar a round trip. So the railroads made lots of money selling tickets to the Larimore Meetings.

Well, anyway, this was one of them, and Doc was up there looking through that cannon-ball hole at the preacher. When he saw there was nothing dangerous about it, the next night he went down and took a seat at the back. It was so great that the following night he went up closer to the front, and on the fourth night he obeyed the gospel. That was Doc. He was the first of the McCleans to obey the gospel. The last time I was in Lawrenceburg, all those cousins of the McCleans and their descendants were members of the church of Christ. Two or three of them are elders and deacons in that congregation. It all started with Doc listening through a cannon-ball hole to Brother Larimore away back in about 1876!

My grandfather and grandmother were baptized in that meeting, and all my uncles except one. All except that uncle and my father obeyed the gospel; they did not. That shows how the work can radiate out through the influence of one or two members of a family— and that is still going on. We have preachers of the gospel among those descendants that nobody in the world would be ashamed of, as they used to say about Jesse Sewell—the grandfather of our Jesse—that he was a man of one Book. He had only read the Bible, but he knew it. His speeches would grace the halls of Congress. We have some of them over there whose speeches would "grace the halls of Congress" as they defend the old-fashioned way—the gospel of Jesus Christ, the blood-stained message that began in Jerusalem about 1915 years ago this past June, and has been rolling over hills and through the valleys, and touching the hearts of honest men and women, boys and girls through all the centuries and all nations, and today it is spreading anew.

THE KINGDOM IS SPREADING

This is something that is almost marvelous. Since the War started we have had boys in the army who were Christians, and they dropped the seed of the kingdom in Manila. We now have a preacher preaching in Manila, and baptizing people as fast as we are in Fort Worth. This has occurred in just the past two or three years. We have people in Germany preaching to as many people on Sunday night as we have here tonight. Brother Gatewood told me that he thought there would be a hundred or two baptized in a very short time, because they were studying hard, and he was taking time that they might not do something too early before they understood it. That is the work that happened as a result of that terrible calamity on human society—the World War II. Over in England we have had boys to go over there and have had very successful meetings. Brother McGaughey has just closed a series of meetings in Scotland where he baptized as many people as he would have if he had stayed in Texas. He was right back where John Knox taught in the middle of the Sixteenth Century, teaching Presbyterianism and turning the whole world upside down. Ellis McGaughey was back over that same ground, preaching the same gospel that I have found so precious to my soul.

John Allen Hudson was sent over to England to hold some meetings and was successful. He has written some interesting material about how those English people are a little more pious than we are as a rule. They have their religion at heart perhaps a little more, because they might be persecuted, looked down on a little more from the crown. The king is the head of the English church; the Episcopal church is the English church.

CAMPBELL LEFT THE PRESBYTERIAN CHURCH

Now we come back to 1948 and back to Glenwood (Vickery Boulevard) where most of you heard me start preaching at Fort Worth. Some of the gray-headed people here obeyed the gospel back in those days. I am enjoying my visit here tonight. You know that in our Restoration Movement Alexander Campbell was a leading light. He was not the one who started this movement, but he was a scholarly man. He wrote lots, and edited the Christian Baptist. People read his works when they would not read anything else. He was a Scotch Presbyterian when he came to this country. He later affiliated himself with the Baptist people because they would immerse him. He was a Bible student, and he came to the point where he wanted to be simply a New Testament saint or Christian, or a member of the church of Christ, and to drop any other name or doctrine that he could not read about in the New Testament. There were a great number of men with him such as Barton W. Stone, his father, Thomas Campbell, and Walter Scott—all who came from the Presbyterians. They came to this country and learned the truth. They were implicated in leading many souls to Christ when the great cry went up, "We must go back to the Bible, and speak where the Bible speaks, and be silent where it is silent." On this slogan we take our stand tonight.

CANNOT AFFORD TO COMPROMISE

No, we are not mad at anybody. We want everybody to go to heaven. We are not trying to send anybody to hell. We are not tickled when somebody is wrong, but we want everybody to be right. We want to treat them like our brothers if we can, and pray for them like Paul did for the Jews (Rom. 10:1-3). But we cannot afford to compromise the truth even with father or mother or ourselves, because it will not do us any good.

I cannot afford to compromise one thing. If I wanted to compromise any truth at all, I would have remained with the Presbyterians, because that is as fine a body of Protestant people as can be found. But I cannot do that. I want to go to heaven, and I cannot go to heaven weakening on the truth of God Almighty, and preaching it some other way than is found in the New Testament.

I have sat down with preachers of that group, and we have talked about those things. I said, "Now, here, I'm not mad at you. I am not a denominationalist. I am nothing of the kind. I believe this Book, do you?"

"Well," he said, "Yes, I do believe this book."

I said, "Well, now, this is what this Book says."

He said, "I admit that. I think you are all right, and I think you will go to heaven, but I believe I can go to heaven too."

That is about as far as some of them would ever go. Just close the Book, their mouth, and their head, and everything else to the truth, when I was doing the greatest thing I could possibly do for their soul. They have always treated me very fine, but they would not pay any attention when I tried to teach them God's ways. I did not get offended, of course; it is their business.

THE TESTIMONY FROM HEAVEN

You can be what you want to be. You are. If you do not want to be a good, faithful Christian, you are a backslider, and it is of your own making. Nobody wants you to be. God does not want you to be. The church does not want you to be. I am sure you have a perfect right to be what you want to be, but we have a convincing argument from heaven—and that is what the Bible is. When Peter spoke on Pentecost's glorious morning—the day the Holy Spirit came to bring the mind of Christ to the mind of men, the record says he spake "as the Spirit gave them utterance," and therefore, the apostolic utterances are the Holy Ghost's utterances. It was brought right from heaven that day, and Peter speaking about it thirty years later in I Peter 1:2 said, "the gospel was preached by the Holy Ghost sent down from heaven." That is the way the gospel came—not through a conference of men—not through a presbytery made up of elders and preachers, and a few presbyteries making a synod that could vote and make a law equal to the pope and his cardinals. I saw this thing standing out clearly in my Bible which you can read easily. The little boys can read it. It is not hard to read God's word.

THE LAW OF THE LORD IS PERFECT

David says in Psalm 19, "The law of the Lord is perfect, converting the soul." What men makes is not the Lord's law. Jesus said in Matthew 15:9, "In vain you worship me teaching for doctrine, the commandments of men." Then the worship based on what men say about it, Jesus says is vain. You see that. Then we read again in that New Testament that we are following, that the apostles preached the law of the Lord, and it convicted the people on that Pentecost morning. In their conviction they cried out and said, "Men and brethren, what shall we do?" Peter did not preach a lot of theology, but simply spake from heaven as the Spirit spake, "Repent and be baptized everyone of you in the name of Jesus Christ for the remission of sins." "They that gladly received the word" did obey that day for it was a message from heaven. That is genuine Holy Ghost religion. That is the old-time religion that makes men happy, because it associates with the angels and the redeemed of the ages around our Father's throne through Jesus Christ our Lord.

We come a little further and quote James on this, too. James says, "Lay aside all filthiness and superfluity of naughtiness, and receive with meekness the engrafted word which is able to save your souls" (James 1:21). You can see that the word of God is sufficient, friends. Again Peter speaks in I Peter 1:22, "Seeing you have purified your souls in obeying the truth....." Jesus says, "Thy word is truth" (John 17:17). When the truth of God Almighty is preached, the Holy

Spirit's message is preached, and when that convicts men of error, it is the Holy Spirit that does the convicting through these words. When men open their hearts and believe and obey the word, they become followers of the Holy Spirit. Paul says, "As many of you as are led by the Spirit of God, these are the sons of God" (Rom. 8:14). "If we are sons, then heirs, and joint-heirs with Jesus." We know we are children of God tonight, if we are following the Spirit's message. Not the Holy Spirit in some mystical way that we cannot explain, but his plain message of divine truth which will sink deep into your heart and show them exactly how to walk and please God.

THE CHURCH BUILT ON CHRIST

The apostle speaks of men who had heard, believed, and had been baptized into Christ, and thus become members of the church at Ephesus, "You are builded upon the foundation of the apostles and prophets, Jesus Christ himself being the chief cornerstone." (Eph. 2:20). The chief cornerstone is Jesus Christ. In I Cor. 3:11, Paul said, "There is no other foundation that any man can lay but that which is laid, which is Christ Jesus." Brother John Cash over here is one of our fine builders. We know we must first lay a foundation, and then build a house on that foundation. When we build a house on that foundation we have got to lay another foundation to build another house. The church of the apostolic age built theirs on Jesus Christ as the chief foundation, and Paul says, "There is none other." Then if there is any church built by men alongside the church of the New Testament, it would have to have another foundation, for Christ is the foundation of the church that he built. He says, "Upon this rock I will build my church, and the gates of hell shall not prevail against it." (Matt. 16:18). He says that it is his. Paul called it, "the church of the Lord, which he purchased with his own blood." (Acts 20:28). Then that church that was built by Christ was built by the power of God, and if we build another, we would have to build another foundation. That would be another Christ, and Paul says, "There is one Lord, one faith, one baptism" and one body (Eph. 4:4-6). He also says, "We were all baptized into one body..... whether Jew or Greek, bond or free" (I Cor. 12:13).

HEAVEN'S CONDEMNATION OF DIVISION

Jesus prayed that his disciples be not divided, that the unbelieving world might believe (John 17:20-23). Paul condemns the Corinthian church because they allowed divisions to creep in among them (I Cor. 1:10-13). Here some were saying, I am of this preacher, and another that I am of that one, and others I am of Christ. He asked, "Were you baptized in Paul's name? Was Paul crucified for you?" We see the point there, friends. We are standing before God and the angels tonight. The Holy Spirit is witness through His word, and as we carry on this work, the Spirit makes intercessions for us with groanings that cannot be uttered. The church has no other institutions—it has no church institutions. The church is the only institution under high heaven that Christ is in, or that Christ has sanctioned. We as individuals can go out like Brother Dickey and build a book store, or like Claude McClung raise potatoes, or some others of you can run a store or an engine—that is our work of making a living while we tabernacle here below. But when it comes to a spiritual institution, Jesus built that, and it is the church. He did not build anything else that we can place a man at the head of, and say it is a church affair.

NO CHURCH INSTITUTIONS

We have no church institutions. Brethren can build any honest thing, and do any honest work, but we cannot say that it is a church affair. Sometimes our young people talk about a "church party." We do not have anything like that, because if it is a "church party" you can read about it in the New Testament. You can have a party, just so you do not do wrong, if you let the gospel principles guide you in the party, but call it "yours." Do not say that Glenwood church has a party for young people. The devil would not want a better thing than to hear God's people divide up and call every little thing a church affair, to where you do not know the difference between the church and human institutions.

Paul said, "Christ is the head of all things to the church, which is his body, the fulness of him that filleth all in all." (Eph. 1:22, 23). Our Bible school on Lord's day morning is the church at work. It is not a Sunday School with different organizations that we can go and join, and give our money to, and then go home before the church meets for worship. That would make an institution alongside the church just as literally as institutions we have fought through the years that seek to be connected with the church of the New Testament. We cannot have these as church institutions for it is the church that is to preach the gospel, care for the orphan and the widow, to help the poor and needy, and to keep itself unspotted from the world.

FAITHFULNESS, THE KEY TO HEAVEN

The church is to meet in worship, and to keep that holy array, and body clean, and so clean until after awhile we can pass inside the pearly gates, and lie around the eternal throne of God, in eternal happiness and joy, where there will be no old age or tears falling from any eye; where we will be the children of God eternal, in that home everlasting, where we can drink the waters of the river of life that flows from beneath the throne of God, and where we can pluck the fruit that grows on either side of the river on the Tree of Life, and where we can associate with Abraham, Isaac, and Jacob of Old Testament note, and with characters of the New Testament like Paul, Peter, James and John, Mary and Martha.

The people from Glenwood are passing on and in multiplied numbers as the years go drifting by. I am not alarmed, friends; I do not want to go back. I would not go back, if God were to give me a chance, to boyhood again and childhood's morning. I have lived a good life. It has been happy every inch of the way. There has been no time in my life that I have been in despair about anything for very long. I do not want to go back. There are too many hills yet beyond me. I want to go on. Over the hills, Brother Leslie (Freiley), until after while the towers of that fair city I see, and catch a glimpse of that glory-land, and hear the singing of the 144,000 that Brother Thomas (Campbell) mentioned tonight. Yea, that is far better than to go back and come again through forty years of earthly service. Give me strength, dear Lord, to press on over the hills, and to help as many people along with me as I can, and to touch as many hearts of boys and girls as possible, and to make people happy by the touch of divine power as I teach the word, the gospel, the truth of God Almighty.

Now, our time is up. I wish I could preach on to midnight. The way you are listening thrills my soul. Even Brother White is smiling back there. No better preacher has ever been among us, perhaps, than Brother L. S. White, and he is here tonight. God bless him, and help him through the years yet to come. I pray that every one of you people get to heaven. If you do what the Lord tells you to do in His book, you cannot miss it. All hell cannot rob you of your reward if you follow the teaching of God's word. John says that we cannot sin if the seed abides in us (I John 3:9), and Jesus said that the seed is the word (Luke 8:11). As long as you strictly obey the word of the Lord, you are not going to go wrong. If you go wrong, it is because you did not let the word of the Lord guide you. You let your old animal nature guide you, or your passion, or your pride, or something other than the Word of God. As long as you submit yourself to the leadership of God's word, you are submitting yourself to the leadership of the Holy Spirit. As long as you are under the leadership of God's Spirit, you are God's child and an heir, and a joint-heir with Jesus.

We are going to stand and sing an invitation song, if anyone wants to be nothing but a Christian, a member of the body of Christ, taking the Bible and the Bible only as your guide, we want you to come tonight. It would be a good time for somebody to make the confession and be baptized. Let us stand together and sing.

GROVER STEVENS

(A Biographical Sketch)

Grover Stevens was born in Caddo (Bryan County), Oklahoma on January 5, 1921. He was the fourth in a family of six boys and two girls. When about nine years of age he moved to Phillips, Texas, which is about two miles north of Borger, where his parents still reside.

After passing around among several churches he finally joined the Baptist Church. He became a Sunday School teacher, assistant Director of the Baptist Training Union, and a delegate to Southern Baptist Convention in 1939. On July 25, 1938, he "surrendered to preach" for the Baptists. He preached at Sanford, Texas, and substituted for the regular preacher at Phillips. He led several to join the Baptist Church through his efforts. Through the natural honesty of his nature and the faithful efforts of several gospel preachers he was eventually led to obey the gospel and be added to the church of the Lord.

After coming into the church of Christ he preached regularly for the church in Fritch, Texas, for five years, during which time he was married to Miss Katherine Miller of Kansas City. They now have two children—a girl five, and a boy two years old.

Brother Stevens attended Freed-Hardeman College in Henderson, Tennessee, and preached for the church at Bruceton, Tenn. Upon graduation in the spring of 1948 he began preaching for the church at Charlotte, Tennessee.

In disposition Brother Stevens is earnest, sober-minded and mild-mannered. He has held two public debates (with Church of God, and Baptists) and private discussions with several others.

His special interest is in teaching members of his former religious connection the way more perfectly. He is anxious for their souls and welcomes discussions, debates, or conversations with them.

Why I Left The Baptist Church

By Grover Stevens

It is a pleasure to me to be in Fort Worth and to have a part in this series of lectures. It is good to see old acquaintances and make new friends here. I appreciate the hospitality of the Vickery Boulevard congregation.

NO ANIMOSITY FOR BAPTISTS

I would like to say in the beginning that I have no animosity whatsoever against Baptists. Personally, I have no reason for leaving the Baptist church, but quite to the contrary, if personal reasons counted, I would never have left the Baptist Church, because personality is in their favor. Especially is this true of the congregation of which I was a member in Phillips, Texas. I believe that the Baptists are, for the most part, splendid people. I believe that most of them are honest and sincere. I believe that, if there are Baptists here tonight, most of them want the truth, and will consider the things that are said honestly and open-minded. However, sometimes, out of a sense of loyalty to that which we have become members of, we are prone to cast aside lightly any charges that might be made against us. I sincerely hope that that will not be the way you will do tonight. I beg you to hear what I have to say, study it carefully with an open Bible in hand, then, out of honesty to your own soul and to God Almighty, to embrace all that you find to be in harmony with the Bible. Believe it, not because I said it, but because you found it in the word of God. That is the only thing any of us would have you believe—the Bible, the word of God. In spite of all the accusations made to the contrary, we still preach only the Bible. Such expressions are idle, I suppose, in view of the fact that all "churches" claim the same thing. We know that *all* of them do not preach "only the Bible" for they are *many* and the Bible is *one*. The Bible does not teach contradictory doctrines. The Baptists hold the Bible up and say, "We preach the Bible". That is what we do.

So, what have I gained by telling you that we take the Bible and nothing but the Bible? Nothing, I suppose. I will just have to prove to you that we do actually stand on the Bible and nothing else, and that the Baptists do not. If they did, I never would have left them. I want you to consider the things that are said as honestly as you know how, tonight.

When I came into this world, I found it divided religiously. When I was old enough to notice things, I found a church on every hand. Here was one and there was another, all claiming to preach the Bible, yet wearing different names and teaching different doctrines. This sentiment prevailed, "It doesn't make any difference what church you are a member of, or what you believe, just so long as you are honest and sincere about it." Having grown up in an atmosphere like that, most of us just seem to accept it as the truth—as axiomatic, but it isn't. The Bible doesn't teach that. If so, where? Nevertheless, that is what we heard every day. Another thought akin to this is that everyone ought to go to church; everyone ought to be a member of some church. These things are preached by all denominational preachers. Hence, the general conception in religious circles, and the basis for all resentment toward the church of Christ, because we deny it.

BAPTISTS PREACH SOME TRUTH

I do not believe that everything they say is a falsehood or a lie. I believe that they preach a lot of truth. The part that they preach that is true, I am glad to accept, but the things they preach which are not the truth made me leave them. Let me illustrate my point. You will recall that in the Garden of Eden the devil preached truth along with a lie. He said, "Thou shalt not surely die." That is false doctrine. He also said, "For God doth know that in the day that ye eat thereof your eyes shall be opened and ye shall be as gods, knowing good and evil." That is the truth. This made the lie more deceptive. Did Adam and Eve sin when they believed and obeyed that? Why, certainly they did. It was half a truth and half a lie. If you say, "Well, I only stand for the things that are the truth", then I will reply, "Maybe that was what Adam and Eve thought too." "We'll just stand for half of it, and we'll tell the

Lord that we did not believe the other half." But it led them into error and condemnation just the same. Hence, what truth the Baptist Church preaches is perverted by the false. Then, too, they many times preach more against sin, moral sin or immorality, than gospel preachers do. I do not mean to say that we do not preach against immorality, but that they preach on it almost altogether, and we spend some time preaching doctrine and pointing out false doctrines. And we need to do that.

Upon attending the Baptist Church, one hears the Baptist preach against sin, and recognizes the fact that he is a sinner—that he is lost. Then being convicted of sin, and desiring to be saved and do what is right, we join the Baptist Church, or some other church. A person convicted of sin is ready to do anything he is commanded. For example, when I first became a member of the church of Christ, I wished that the Lord had left baptism out of the Bible. I said to myself, "Everything that the church of Christ teaches is fine, and I believe that most of the people in the denominations believe exactly what the church teaches, but when they come to baptism, they just seem to resent that. If the Lord had just left baptism out, then everything would be all right." I have learned since that that wasn't the trouble. People do not mind being baptized when they are convicted of sin. People wanting to obey God do not mind being baptized. They do not mind doing anything that God commands them to do. It is a matter of surrendering whole-heartedly one's own will to God's will. When that's done his attitude is simply, "Lord, whatever you want me to do, I'm willing to do it." Many, not realizing this, go on in rebellion against God, believing all the while that they are pleasing to Him. Hence, we join some church because we are convicted of sin, realize that we are lost, and because we believe that it is the right thing to do. That is the reason I joined the Baptist Church.

EARLY EXPERIENCE

I attended Sunday School at the Baptist Church in Caddo, Oklahoma, when I was a little fellow. After we moved to Texas, I didn't go much, if at all. By and by my mother started attending the church of Christ at Borger, Texas, so I began attending Bible study there. I attended there several months and was impressed with the way they studied the Bible. Then I took pneumonia and was out for about six weeks, so I lost interest and did not go back. After some time, I was encouraged to go to Sunday School at the Baptist Church by some of my friends. I became regular in attendance and made 100 in Sunday School right along. Our class was good to win the Banner. Those of you who know the Baptist grading system know that I had to stay for church to make 100. It wasn't long until I began to realize that I was lost and in sin, and needed to be saved. I wanted to be saved, so one Sunday night when the preacher was making propositions with folks, he invited any who knew that they were lost and "desired the prayers of the church" to hold up their hand. I knew that I was lost, so at this suggestion I raised my hand. It was difficult at first. It took all the strength I had to make that arm move, but after I got it started it wasn't so hard. As I held my hand up my face burned and my heart came up to my throat. When the preacher said, "God bless you, son," my face burned more and I was very self-conscious. Afterwards, several came to me and told me how proud they were of me and encouraged me. Then I felt more confident and was proud of myself. Of course, my Sunday School teacher and a few others encouraged me to join the church. I talked to my mother about it and was persuaded to wait awhile. She felt that I was being persuaded and didn't realize what I was doing. After some time I began to visit the Methodist Sunday School and church occasionally with a friend who was a Methodist. Finally I quit attending at all.

A little over a year later I made a speech at the Annual Boy Scout Father and Son Banquet. After the Banquet the Methodist preacher came by and asked me if I went to Sunday School or church anywhere. I told him that I didn't, so he urged me to come to the Methodist Church. Later the Baptist preacher approached me and was equally as urgent in his invitation as the Methodist preacher. (They had changed preachers at both places since the incident mentioned before). After some delay I began attending the Baptist Church. It wasn't long until I was under conviction again. I remembered the time before, so the Sunday morning I went up during the invitation and asked the preacher to pray for me. I felt just as I had before. I spent the afternoon trying to decide what to do. Late in the afternoon, some time before B. T. U. was to begin, I gathered up a change of clothes and went to the church building to see the preacher. He was in the auditorium talking with one of the men. I asked him if he would baptize me that night. He asked me, "Are you saved, Grover?" I said, "Well, I don't know; I guess I am." He took me into his office where we talked quite a while. When he heard of my former experience, he told me that I had been saved back then. I accepted that for I remembered how I had felt after they had prayed for me. That night I confessed that "God for Christ's sake has saved me from my sins, and I want to join the Baptist Church." Upon hearing that confession, they voted to receive me, and I was baptized into the Baptist Church that night. It was April 24, 1938.

ZEAL IN THE BAPTIST CHURCH

I took a personal interest in the work. I worked diligently. I was instrumental in leading several people to what I honestly thought was Christ, and they joined the Baptist Church. I was given a Sunday School class, made the assistant director of the B. T. U., and was licensed to preach. I preached once a month for a little congregation in Sanford, Texas, about twenty miles out, and filled in for our local preacher when he was away.

I had been preaching and working for some time, and nothing had challenged my attention pertaining to Baptist Doctrine. Then, one day my mother and oldest brother who had been attending the church of Christ, told me how the church of Christ preached the Bible. They urged me to attend a meeting starting in a few days. What I had heard about the church of Christ was told with contempt, so I had learned to feel that way toward them—at least, a little. However, I made up my mind that I would attend the meeting, listen to what was said and accept all that I could. I was determined to "give the devil his due." I wanted to learn what was taught whether I believed it or not.

A. G. Hobbs, Jr., was doing the preaching. Brother Hobbs

is a very plain preacher. He is very kind, but he never leaves a doubt as to what he is talking about. I went home and looked up some of the scriptures and found them right there. On many points I would say, "You know, I believe he is right about that," but on others, "Now, he just missed it there. If I could show him a few things in that connection, he'd see differently." I know that many of you will feel that way toward me before this lesson is over. You will think, "I wish I could tell him something." I wish you could, too, because I would like to remove every objection so that you could see your way to obey the truth. I learned that when I offered my objections to his position, that it was even more evident that he was right. That's the reason that the denominational preachers "don't believe in arguing." They do believe in arguing their side of it, but they don't believe in allowing a gospel preacher to examine their side. Suffice it to say that if I cannot sustain every point in this or any other lesson, I will apologize for it and retract it. Isn't that fair? I wish I knew everything that will come into your mind tonight, and I had the time to reply to it. I will do the best that I can out of a consciousness of what turned over in my mind as I listened to these things being presented. Maybe I can deal with the most of your objections.

MY ATTENTION CHALLENGED

The first thing that challenged my attention as I listened to Brother Hobbs was that there was just one church. I suppose there is nothing in the Bible more plainly taught, yet more disavowed. The Bible says that the church is the body of Christ (Eph. 1:22, 23). It says, "There is one body" (Eph. 4:4). The church is the body; there is one body; therefore, there is one church. Along with other proofs, I saw that there was just one church. Which one? So I began to study.

Other things challenged my attention as I studied. I wondered about God calling all preachers to preach. Does God call all preachers, then cause them to preach conflicting doctrines? Does God call Baptist preachers to preach, and then cause them to preach that immersion is the only kind of baptism, that only ordained Baptist preachers have the authority to baptize, the impossibility of apostasy, the miraculous operation of the Holy Spirit, and numerous other things? Then does God call a Methodist preacher to preach that sprinkling is baptism, and that you can fall from grace? Does God call both of them to preach these contradictory doctrines? John 17:20-23 and I Cor. 1:10-13 teach that he does not.

Why belong to a church? I told you that people, when convicted of sin will join one church or another, even though they do not know what it teaches or stands for. It is a church, they tell the story of Christ, and they were convicted of sin there, so they become members of it without questioning, or even knowing anything about its doctrines. When somebody criticizes it, the members of it resent it. Why? Because the criticism was true or not true? NO, we just don't like for people to criticize the church we are members of. Because of a sense of loyalty we resent it. That is human nature. We must overcome feelings like that and be ready to face facts.

Why become a member of a church? Because of parents, friends, relatives? Because of a nice building? Because it is conveniently located? Because they do a lot of good works? Because they teach some truth? Are these reasons we become members? For the most part, yes. The large majority of the people in the denominations join them without knowing what they teach, or stand for, hence they could not have joined because of their doctrine. I would say that 85 per cent or 90 per cent of the people in the Baptist Church do not know what the Baptist Church teaches. Some people say, "I know that they teach such and such a thing, but I don't believe it." Now look, first, you are a member of something that you do not even know what it teaches, and second, you are supporting a doctrine that you do not believe. If I were supporting a doctrine that I didn't believe, you'd call me a hypocrite.

THE SIXTY-FOUR DOLLAR QUESTION

Now here is the sixty-four dollar question. On the preceding basis, I want to know why you do not join all the churches in town? You have heard that question before, but I want you to consider it again. Why not joint the Methodist, the Baptist, the Presbyterian and the Adventist? I have friends in all of them. They all teach some truth. They all do many good works, they raise the fallen and they do benevolences. There are good people in all. They stand for morality. The reasons we give for belonging to one church could be given as reasons for belonging to all; so, why not join all of them? I'll tell you why. It would make me a hypocrite to be a member of more than one church. If you are a member of the Baptist Church, and you go next Sunday and join the Methodist Church, and then the following Sunday join the Presbyterian, folks will begin to say that you are not sincere, or that you are "not all there." At a place where I was preaching once there was a family that joined every church in town during the big meetings. The town and the churches were considerate—they just overlooked it. Their name is a synonym for being "a little off." Hence, joining all churches will give you a reputation for being a hypocrite or insane.

If it will make you a hypocrite for belonging to the Methodist Church and the Baptist Church at the same time—then why? Is it because of the good people in it? No. Is it because of the truth or the good they teach? No. Is it because they do a lot of good works? No. What is it then? The conflicting doctrines! The Baptist Church stands for immersion only, impossibility of apostasy and close communion. The Methodist Church stands for open communion, sprinkling for baptism and the possibility of apostasy—just the opposite. We are told that it is all right for one person to stand for Baptist doctrine, and another person to stand for Methodist doctrine, but it is not all right for one to stand for both the Methodist and Baptist Doctrines at the same time. To do so will bring the charge of hypocrisy or insanity upon you. If it will make me a hypocrite to belong to more than one because of the contradictory doctrines, then answer this question: *Is Jesus Christ a member of all churches?* Is he? Is Jesus Christ a member of the Baptist Church? If so, is he a member of the Methodist Church, too? Is he a member of both of them tonight—now? Is the Son of God standing for Baptist Doctrine of the impossibility of apostasy now, and at the same time over in the Methodist Church, is he standing for the possibility of apostasy? Is he doing that tonight? And if it will make me a hypocrite to do it, WHAT DOES IT MAKE THE SON OF

GOD? IS HE A HYPOCRITE? Does he endorse all conflicting doctrines? Is Jesus Christ a member of the Baptist Church, the Methodist, the Presbyterian, the Episcopal, the Adventists, the Mormons, and all of the different churches? Is he a member of all of them?

There is a good question in the Bible along this line, I Cor. 1:13. "Is Christ divided?" Just three words, "Is Christ divided?" The apostle Paul asked the question in condemning division. What is the answer to it? Will you answer it? Is Christ divided? The answer is in the question. It is a rhetorical question. "Is Christ divided? Was Paul crucified for you? Were you baptized in the name of Paul?" It was after considering things like these that I began to see that something was wrong—that the Baptist Church is not altogether the New Testament Church. Then I would try to justify the Baptist Church by looking to all the good they did, and the splendid people I had learned to love. I couldn't stand the thought of facing my friends and what they would have to say. It never occurred to me to rejoice in the truth and tell others who did not know. I guess I realized that they would not be glad to learn it.

I remember one day that one of the Baptist Deacons came to me in the store. We went back to the wareroom where we could be alone. He said "Grover, I heard that you are about to join the 'Campbellites'." There was that tone of contempt in his voice. He made it sound like that was the worst thing in the world. I stammered a little and said, "No, I have been attending their meeting, but I am not about to join." He said, "Well, I knew that you had better sense than to be led off by that bunch." I told him that they really knew and preached the Bible. He explained their ease in handling the Bible by telling me that the "Campbellites" only have ten sermons which they memorize and preach everywhere they go. He told me that the church was started by Alexander Campbell, that it was the most narrow-minded and bigoted bunch of people in the world, and they thought everybody was going to hell that didn't belong to their church. When he finished he left such a stigma that I thought, "Well, surely a fellow would be insane who would go with that group."

That helped for a while, as it eased my conscience to disregard what I had learned. It, very likely, was responsible for my not obeying the gospel before the meeting closed. However, the day the meeting closed, Sunday, that afternoon Brother Hobbs came to see me. He took my Bible, sat down beside me, and as I asked questions, he turned in the Bible and had me read the answers. When I didn't ask a question he had plenty of things to show me. We'll notice some of them in just a moment. He offered to talk to me in the presence of the Baptist preacher, or to talk to the Baptist preacher in my presence. He asked me to invite the Baptist preacher to meet with him or Brother Thomas McDonald, the local preacher for the church of Christ in my home town. I didn't want to ask him because I knew that he wouldn't. He took my Church Manual and showed me where Baptist Doctrine contradicts the Bible. I saw the truth very plainly. That night he insisted that I come and hear him. I made every excuse I could but he wouldn't hear them. I told him that I had a part on the B. T. U. program and couldn't get to Borger in time after that. We got out at 8:00 and his services started at 8:00. I thought that would end it, but it didn't. The only reason I could think of for not wanting to go is that I hated to face the Baptists and explain my absence from church which they would surely notice. Brother Hobbs said, "I'll be in front of the Baptist Church at 8:00 o'clock and take you to town." He preached on church history that night. He explained the origin of denominations and showed how the church of Christ stands for New Testament Christianity free from all denominations. When the invitation was extended I wanted to go. As I thought on what I should do, and what my friends in the Baptist Church would say, my head just whirled. I managed to stay in my seat, however.

PERSONAL STUDY

The meeting ended and I settled down to a long, hard study of things all by myself. I read the New Testament through and underlined the passages on baptism, the Holy Spirit, the plan of salvation, apostasy, etc. I copied each verse into a notebook on a sheet for each subject. When I had them all I studied them together. The more I studied, the more I realized that the Baptists were wrong, and the more it bothered me. I couldn't keep my mind on my work. I couldn't sleep. Phillips is a big oil field, and there is a big torch that burns day and night. I lay in bed and watched that torch and the lighted sky. The clouds reflected the red from its flames. I would lie there, sometimes till daylight, thinking, praying, studying, and wishing that something would happen. I prayed for the Lord to guide me. I asked the Lord to show me his will, the way He would have me go.

I struggled on until time for the Southern Baptist Convention which met that year in Oklahoma City; then, I decided to go to the convention and forget about the church of Christ. Here I was successful in forgetting my troubles and getting better established in the Baptist Church. I went with the local preacher and registered as a delegate. I returned, feeling much better, but not for long. Every time that I read my Bible I noticed those passages which I had marked. I still had my notebook, too. It wasn't long until I found myself spending sleepless nights again. I begged the Lord to show me what he would have me do. I prayed, "Thy will be done." This continued for nearly three months. Then one Sunday afternoon as I was studying and thinking, it suddenly dawned on me that the Bible is God's way of revealing his will to us. I realized that I had been praying, "Thy will be done," and as honestly and earnestly as I knew how, but that subsconsciously I had been holding out on the Lord in my desire to remain a Baptist. MY WHOLE STRUGGLE WAS REBELLION TO WHAT GOD WAS TELLING ME TO DO. The Lord was trying to guide me through the light of His word, but it didn't shine in the direction I wanted it to. Most of our struggles between right and wrong is not what is right and what is wrong, but surrendering our desires for what we want, to what we know is right. The Bible is God's way of telling us His will. He is doing everything He can to guide us by the Bible. When we refuse that, we "have not God." (II John 9).

After considerable study and prayer that afternoon, I gathered up my clothes and went to services at the church of Christ. When they offered the invitation, I went forward, confessed my faith in Jesus Christ and was baptized into him the same hour of the night.

The truth is what made me leave the Baptist Church. I now invite your attention to some of those truths. My first point is the most fundamental, and is the ultimate conclusion of every point I shall make.

THE BAPTIST CHURCH IS NOT THE NEW TESTAMENT CHURCH

The Baptist Church is not the church you read about in the Bible. Baptist preachers, and all other preachers, take the Bible and read the word "church," but they do not comment on it. They leave the impression that it refers to "their" church. The Baptist preacher will read a passage with the word "church" in it, and apply it to the Baptist Church. The Methodist preacher will read the same passage and apply it to the Methodist Church. The Presbyterian preacher will read the same passage and apply it to the Presbyterian Church. It cannot refer to all of them. If these passages refer to the Baptist Church, it cannot refer to the Methodist, because they are two different institutions. To which one does it refer then? I am affirming that out of the 112 times that the word "church" is used in the New Testament, not one time does it refer to the Baptist Church, or to any other denomination. It talks about "the church," "the church of God," "the church of the first-born," "the churches of Christ," etc., but most of the time it just says "the church."

Which church? Which one is it? When the Bible uses the word "church" it just refers to one. Now which one is it?

CHURCH THE "CALLED OUT"

First, the word "church" means "called out." "Called out" of what? What does it mean? The Baptists teach that you can be a Christian—you can be saved, and not be a member of any church, including the Baptist. Let us see. The word "ecclesia" translated "church" refers to the "called out" —to that body of people that have been called out of the world, out of sin, into Christ. That is the meaning and significance of the word "church" in the New Testament. It does not mean denomination. It does not have reference to the Baptist Church, not the Methodist, nor any of the rest of them. It simply means "the called out." The point is this: if you can be saved without being a member of any church, then it follows that you can be saved without being "called out" or a member of the "called out." You have to be called out of the world into Christ to be saved. The same thing that calls you out, that redeems you, makes you a member of the church or "called out;" don't you see? The Baptists do not use it that way. They talk about a person being saved and in Christ before he is a member of the church, and without being a member of any church.

I want to illustrate this point by substituting the terms "called out" and "redeemed" for church in a passage of scripture or two. Acts 2:47 says "the Lord added to the *church* daily such as should be saved." The Lord added to the *"called out"* daily such as should be saved. Now, see this body of people over here that are in sin and in the world, and the Lord added to this other body over here, the "called out," "such as should be saved." All of those who were saved were called out of the world into Christ. The process of *saving* and *calling out* are the same. "The Lord added to the *saved* daily such as should be saved." The Lord added to the *redeemed* daily such as should be saved.

In Acts 8:1 we read, "And at that time there was a great persecution against the *church* which was at Jerusalem." Now watch it, "At that time there was a great persecution against the *called out* which was at Jerusalem," "a great persecution against the *redeemed* which was at Jerusalem," "against the *saved* which was at Jerusalem." Do you see that? I do not see how you could miss it.

Acts 20:28, "Take heed therefore to yourselves and to all the flock over which the Holy Ghost hath made you overseers, to feed the *church* of God, which he hath purchased with his own blood." The *called out* of God which he hath purchased with his own blood," "the *saved* of God....., "the *redeemed* of God....." The church, the redeemed, the saved, the called out. This is the significance of the word "church," and is a far cry from the meaning Baptists give it. Remember they claim that a person can be saved, redeemed, belong to God and *not* be a member of the Baptist Church. The church is the Kingdom of God, the body of Christ, the family of God. When viewing the church as to its relationship to the world, it is the "called out"—called out of the world—the church. When viewing the church as to its government, it is a kingdom, the Kingdom of God. As to its organization it is the body of Christ. With reference to its relationship to each other, it is the family of God. Don't you see that the church in the New Testament is not and could not be the Baptist Church?

"CHURCH" NEVER REFERS TO BAPTIST CHURCH

If the word "church" never refers to the Baptist Church, then the Baptist Church is eliminated from the Bible. You know, of course, that the expressions "Baptist Church," "Baptist Churches," "Baptists," or "a Baptist" are not to be found in the Bible. We have now shown that the word "church" never refers to the Baptist Church. In as much as the Baptists admit that you can be a member of the New Testament Church, the kingdom of God, before and without being a member of the Baptist Church, then it follows that *the Baptist Church and the New Testament church are two different institutions, entered at two different times, by two different processes.* That is exactly it. This is according to the Baptists, themselves. Therefore the Baptist Church cannot be the New Testament Church.

Do I have to be a member of the Baptist Church to be saved? The Baptists say "no." If they should say "yes," then all the Methodists, Presbyterians, etc., would be going to hell because they are not Baptists. They say that they would not be that "narrow-minded." On page 17 of this little book, *Church Manual for Baptist Churches* by J. M. Pendleton, and published by the Sunday School Board, Southern Baptist Convention, Nashville, Tennessee, we read, "persons wishing to unite with a church give an account of the dealings of God with their souls, and state the 'reason of the hope that is in them'; whereupon, if, in the judgment of the church they 'have passed from death unto life', they are by vote of the church recognized as candidates for baptism, with the understanding that when they are baptized they are entitled to all the rights and privileges of membership." This simply says that a person desiring to join the Baptist Church must tell that he is saved. The Baptist Church then votes to determine whether the church thinks he is saved or not. They, deciding that he is, receive him into the church after baptism. Hence, he must confess that he is saved, that he is a member of the kingdom of God already, and then, he joins the Baptist Church. This being true, then it follows that a person can be a member of the kingdom of God, or body of Christ, or New Testament Church, before, and without belonging to the Baptist Church.

TWO DIFFERENT PROCESSES OF SALVATION

You had to confess that you were saved before you could join the Baptist Church. When I asked the Baptist preacher if he would baptize me, he asked, "Are you saved, Grover? We want saved people in our church." Then, at services that night I confessed that "God, for Christ's sake, has saved me from my sins" and I went to join the Baptist Church. I was visiting a Baptist Church one time and saw them do it this way: The preacher asked, "Do you believe that you were lost and that you are now saved for Christ's sake?" The reply was "yes." "Do you desire to join the Baptist Church?" "Yes," again. "You have heard the statement, what is your pleasure?" Then they took the vote. Once more I say that this proves, according to Baptists, that a person can be a member of the kingdom of God (saved) before and without being a member of the Baptist Church. *Hence, to be a Christian, to be saved, and a member of the kingdom of God, or the church you read about in the Bible is one thing, and to be a Baptist is another.* Friends, the conclusion is inevitable. THE BAPTIST CHURCH AND THE NEW TESTAMENT CHURCH ARE TWO DIFFERENT PROCESSES. This argument alone should show every honest person why you can't afford to be a Baptist.

THE "VISIBLE AND INVISIBLE" CHURCHES

Baptists teach that the church is used in two senses—a visible sense and an invisible sense. They claim that when you are saved, God adds you to His church, the New Testament Church, which is the invisible church. If you are regenerated, you are saved; God knows it, and you know it, but nobody else should pass judgment on you—that is, nobody except the Baptists; they vote it, you know. That makes you a member of the kingdom of God or the New Testament Church, which is the *invisible church*—to them. Then, you can go to the Baptist Church, relate your experience (tell them you are saved), let them vote on it to decide if you really are, then by baptism you become a member of the Baptist Church which is *a visible church*. They claim that all denominations are *visible churches*. They look upon the church of Christ as being just another "visible church" or denomination. That is the reason they think we are so narrow, that is, because they look at us as a church through *their* denominational, narrow, and erroneous conception of what the church is. They will say, "I think there are saved people in the church of Christ. I think their doctrine is wrong, but I think there are saved people in "their" church. Again, "I disagree with the Methodists, but I think there are saved people in the Methodist Church." This is because they think of a person being saved in the "invisible church" and then joining a "visible" one. This would be all right if the Bible taught it, but it doesn't.

Friends, the New Testament Church was a visible church. The Jerusalem church was a visible church. It met for worship every Lord's day, *yet was no denomination*. The church at Corinth met upon the first day of the week, sang, prayed, had preaching, took the Lord's Supper, and contributed of their means, yet it was no denomination. Paul called it, "the church of God" and "the body of Christ." (I Cor. 1:2; I Cor. 12:27).

WHAT MAKES A DENOMINATION?

I want to use an old illustration: Suppose that three denominations, the Baptists, Methodists and the Presbyterians have a union meeting. In the course of the meeting 400 people

THE BAPTIST CHURCH

are saved. Understand that I disagree with them on the way that they think they are saved, but we are waiving that point just now, in order to make another. These 400 persons, being saved, are members of the New Testament church, the Kingdom of God. When the meeting closes, they are told to "join the church of your choice." Suppose that 100 go into the Baptist Church another hundred go into the Methodist, and a third hundred join the Presbyterians. What made the first 100 Baptists? Now look, they were saved to begin with, already Christians, members of the Lord's church, then they joined the Baptist Church which made them Baptists. What was it that made them Baptists?! *It was the doctrines peculiar to the Baptist Church.* The doctrines that differentiate and distinguish the Baptist Church from the Methodist and all others. These doctrines are given in this Church Manual. If a Baptist Church didn't measure up to *this doctrine,* then it would not be a Baptist Church, but some other kind. Hence, Christians *plus the peculiarities of the Baptist Church make Baptists.* Christians (saved) plus the Methodist Discipline, the doctrines peculiar to the Methodist Church, make them Methodists. It is always Christian first, plus the creed containing the doctrine peculiar to the particular denomination that makes them members of the second church, the denomination. Two Churches? Why not? You are members of the Lord's church when you are saved—church number one; then you join some denomination—church number two. Hence, to be a Baptist is something in addition to being a Christian, and belonging to something in addition to the New Testament church. Where does the Bible teach us to join some denomination, the second church? The Bible teaches, "The Lord added to the church daily such as should be saved."

HOW NOT TO BE A SECTARIAN

But, what about the other 100? Suppose they couldn't make up their mind which church to join. As they study about it, it suddenly dawns on them, "we are saved aren't we? Our sins have been forgiven, haven't they? We are members of the New Testament church, are we not?" O, yes. "We are members of the Kingdom of God, aren't we?" Yes. "Well, suppose that we select a place, meet there upon the first day of the week according to the New Testament and worship God, and never join a denomination." Can they do that? If not, why not? Would that make them a denomination? If so, which one? They didn't join any denomination. They said, "We just want to be Christians, and Christians only."

This is exactly what the church of Christ pleads for. We ask people to be just a member of the New Testament church, and not of any denomination. I preach that a person must belong to the New Testament church to be saved. So do the denominations. I preach that a person does *not have to belong to any denomination to be saved.* Every one of them teach the same. When I teach the same thing that they do, they do not like it. Of course, they teach that you do not have to belong to any denomination to be saved, but that you ought to belong to one; and I teach that you do not have to belong to any denomination to be saved and that YOU OUGHT *NOT* BELONG TO ANY *because the Lord did not build them.* Yes, we are pleading with people to be a member only of the Lord's church, the New Testament church, the kingdom of God, and NOT *to be members of any denomination.* Be a Christian, and a Christian only.

DIVIDING THE KINGDOM OF GOD

Before I leave this point, I want to examine their claims from another angle. Baptists claim to be building up the kingdom of God when they, through their preaching, lead people to be saved. (I do not agree that they are saved, because, Baptists teach the wrong plan of salvation. We will notice that in a moment, but we are speaking in Baptist terms in order to make the point.) They claim that their greatest concern is simply to get folks "saved," then invited them to join the Baptist Church or some other denomination, *for they are* DIVIDING THE KINGDOM OF GOD. *When they lead you to be saved, that makes you a member of the kingdom of God. Then, when they encourage or allow you to join a denomination, that divides the kingdom of God into various denominations, draws you off, and fences you in.* The very name *denomination means divided.* *Denomination* and *denominator* came from the same root word which means *divide.* Division is condemned. (I Cor. 1:10-13; 3:1-4). Division is carnal, and to be carnal is sinful. Hence for a Christian to be a member of the Baptist Church, or any other denomination, is to divide the kingdom of God, and therefore a sin. Let me plead with you, friends, to leave the Baptist Church as I have done, and be a member only of the Lord's Family, the New Testament Church.

WHO IS IT THAT IS NARROW?

Just here, I want to call attention to this charge of being *narrow.* Usually about all the enemies of the church of Christ can say against us is "they are narrow minded." *Narrow* means *limited,* or *circumscribed.* We just noticed how the Baptists make Christians (?), members of the kingdom of God, then teach and encourage them to separate themselves from others in the kingdom of God by joining the Baptist Church, thus *limiting* and *circumscribing* themselves from all others whom they claim are members of the kingdom of God, too. Who is it that is narrow?!

Have you ever wondered just *why* we are called "narrow minded"? *It is* NOT *because we point out and condemn error, because all preachers do that.* The Baptists condemn the Methodists for sprinkling and infant membership, and the Methodists do not get mad and call them narrow-minded. Then too, the Methodists condemn the Baptist doctrine of the impossibility of apostasy, or once saved always saved, and the Baptists do not get mad and accuse the Methodists of being narrow-minded and bigoted. Yet, when I condemn the Methodists for sprinkling, and the Baptists for "once saved always saved," no more than they do themselves, they both get together and charge me of being narrow-minded. Why? I think I know why. When the Baptist preacher finishes condemning sprinkling, he tells them that it doesn't make any difference what you believe anyhow, and the Methodist preacher does likewise. But, when I get through pointing out that the Bible does not teach sprinkling for baptism, infant membership in the church, "once saved always saved", etc., and instead of telling the audience that it doesn't make any difference anyhow, I plead with them to accept and obey the truth, the word of God and turn from these false doctrines. This is why I am branded "narrow-minded", and it amounts to this: *A denominational preacher will preach for an hour and "wind up" by saying that it doesn't matter whether you believe what he has been preaching or not.* This makes him BROAD-MINDED. *But after I have preached for an hour, I "wind up" by pleading with you to accept it because it is the truth.* This makes me NARROW-MINDED. Isn't that the reason others are considered broad-minded and we are considered narrow-minded? I wonder what Jesus thinks, do you? Let's see, Mark 16:15-16 says, "Go ye into all the world, and preach the gospel to every creature. He that believeth and is baptized shall be saved; but HE THAT BELIEVETH NOT SHALL BE DAMNED". This is a never failing test for gospel preaching. When a preacher says that you do not have to believe what he preaches to be saved, he *is not preaching the gospel,* for Jesus said, "Go preach the gospel . . . . . *he that believeth not shall be damned."*

THE BAPTIST CHURCH IS UNSCRIPTURAL IN NAME

We have already said that the expression "Baptist Church" is not found in the Bible. John the Baptist, it is reasoned, baptized Christ and others, and since he was sent from God, that made Christ and all others Baptists. Well, that made Baptists before they ever had a Baptist Church. Did you ever hear of a Baptist that was not a member of the Baptist Church? Yet, they admit themselves that the Baptist Church was not established until the ordaining of the twelve. John was not called *Baptist* in the same sense that people are called *Baptist* today. The expression "Baptist" is found only 15 times in the Bible. Every time it is *"John the Baptist."* Mark 6:14 says, "John the Baptizer." The Greek is "John, he who baptizes," or "the man who baptizes." There is the passage that tells why John was called "the Baptist"—because he baptized people. This distinguished him from all other Johns. Do you know that in the book of John you cannot find the word "Baptist"? The Apostle John never called John the Baptist, "the Baptist." It is only found 15 times in the Bible, and every time "John THE Baptist." *The followers of Jesus Christ were never call-*

THE BAPTIST CHURCH

ed Baptists. The followers of John were never called Baptists. Is it not peculiar that if John's baptizing folks made Baptists out of them that not one was ever referred to as a Baptist then, or thereafter? Not one time is anyone ever called Baptist in the Bible except John.

Human names are condemned. (I Cor. 1:12). "Now this I say, that every one of you saith, I am of Paul; and I of Apollos; and I of Cephas; and I of Christ. Is Christ divided? Was Paul crucified for you? Were ye baptized in the name of Paul?" Again in Acts 4:12: "Neither is there salvation in any other: For there is none other name under heaven given among men, whereby we must be saved." Look at it, *"There is none other name."* Is it all right to use other names? Listen again, *"There is none other name."* Among human names (those not found in the Bible) I can think of none greater than that of *Paul*. Yet, if I were to present a check for my soul's salvation in the name of Paul at the judgment bar of God, he would have to say, "Not in the name of Paul, not in the name of Apollos, not in the name of Cephas, nor in the name of John the Baptist, for *salvation is in none other name than Jesus Christ."* *This is the only "name under heaven given among men whereby we must be saved."* This name exalts Christ. This is the name that we in the church of Christ are pleading for. Other names, or additional names are sinful. Wear the name of Christ and none other. (Phil. 2:9-11).

THE BAPTIST CHURCH IS UNSCRIPTURAL IN WORSHIP

They call Sunday the Sabbath day. Ex. 20:10 says, "Six days labor, but the *seventh is the Sabbath."* That would make Saturday the Sabbath day. In Acts 20:7 we learn that the disciples came together to break bread upon *the first day of the week.* Baptists teach that people ought to keep the Ten commandments, one of which commands the keeping of the seventh day, Sabbath. Yet, they will meet on *Sunday,* the *Lord's day* (Rev. 1:10), and teach that Sunday is the Sabbath day. This confuses the people. It confused me while I was a Baptist. The truth of the matter is, Sunday is not the Sabbath, nor is it the Christian Sabbath, but the Lord's Day. The old Law, the Sabbath included, has been "fulfilled" (Matt. 5: 17-18), "done away" (Ex. 34:27-33; II Cor. 3:6-14; Rom. 7: 1-7), "nailed to the cross" (Col. 2:14-16).

Baptists use mechanical instruments of music in their worship. I think a good bit has been said about that in other lessons, so just suffice it to say that the New Testament Church did not use mechanical instruments of music. David used them, but neither Jesus nor his disciples ever did. That is as good an argument as is needed. They had it to use, but did not use it. That is reason enough for not using it.

Baptists set aside the Lord's Supper and say that it makes it too common to take it every Lord's Day. The same passage that says for us to come together, says also for us to partake of the Lord's Supper. (Acts 20:7). They come together every first day of the week, they take a collection every first day of the week, and they have preaching... but to take the Lord's Supper every first day of the week makes it too common. Why is it not too common to *give* every first day of the week? Why is it not too common to *come together* every first day of the week? Why is it not too common to *have preaching* every first day of the week? They read in I Cor. 11:25, where Christ is quoted as having said, "this do, as oft as ye drink it, in remembrance of me," and conclude that they are left at liberty to take it when they are pleased to do so. The Bible plainly states, "upon the first day of the week..." (Acts 20:7). Every week has a first day. When God told the children of Israel "Remember the Sabbath day to keep it holy," they understood that they were to keep *every* Sabbath holy. Just so with us in regard to the Lord's Supper. The Lord said "Do this in memory of me," so we meet every first day of the week to remember the Christ in that humble and simple way, by keeping the Lord's Supper.

They have unscriptural means of raising money. In the first place they teach tithing. The Jews gave a tithe but we are taught to "lay by in store as we have been prospered (I Cor. 16:2), and as we "purposeth in our heart" (II Cor. 9:7), which will "prove the sincerity of our love" (II Cor. 8:8). Baptists will build an elaborate building, then go around begging the business men in town to pay for it. They want the bank to discount the notes. Various schemes and practices similar to these have given churches in general a "black eye." One can hardly get a bank to loan a church any money at all, because if they foreclose on a note it causes ill will toward the bank, and if they don't, they must suffer the loss. They just do not want to fool with it. Begging and hi-jacking business men and professional men to pay church debts is certainly not following the scriptures. Then too, they will use carnivals, suppers and other means of amusement to raise the money to support their churches. Let "every one of you lay by him in store" to support the cause of Christ and the work of the church.

THE BAPTIST CHURCH IS WRONG IN THEIR PLAN OF SALVATION

They teach that a person is saved by prayer. I could tell several incidents in which people were saved by prayer according to the Baptists. One Sunday night three boys, who were alien sinners, a preacher, and myself, all engaged in prayer until the boys arose and confessed that they were saved.

An alien sinner is not saved by prayer. John 9:31 says, "Now we know that God heareth not sinners, but if any man be a *worshipper* of God and *doeth his will*, him he heareth." It is God's will that we "obey the gospel" (II Thess. 1:8). The gospel commands us to be baptized into Christ "for the remission of sins." (Gal. 3:27; Acts 2:38). We have not done God's will until we have been baptized into Christ. Hear Isaiah, "Your iniquities have separated between you and your God, and your sins have hid His face from you, that He will not hear." (Isa. 59:2). We are to pray for the lost, that's true (Rom. 10:1), but the gospel, not prayer, "is the power of God unto salvation." (Rom. 1:16).

Paul says in II Cor. 5:11, "Knowing therefore the terror of the Lord, we persuade men." Some people try to persuade God to save the sinner, but Paul persuaded the sinner to obey God. God is willing to save all who will obey. (II Peter 3:9; Titus 2:11; I Tim. 2:4; Heb. 5:9). "God be thanked that ye were the servants of sin, but ye have **OBEYED** from the heart that form of doctrine which was delivered you, being **THEN** made free from sin, ye became the servants of righteousness." (Romans 6:17-18).

Baptists think that the "new birth" is a mysterious, mystical, operation performed by the Holy Spirit which produces some undescribable sensation to the flesh. They do not know *how* it happened, but they do know that a change has been made and their heart tells them that the change is of such a nature as to have come from God. Their pet passage is John 3:8, "The wind bloweth where it listeth, and thou hearest the sound thereof, but canst not tell whence it cometh, and whither it goeth: so is every one that is born of the Spirit." In the first place this would be carnal—a sensation to the flesh. A spiritual birth is of the spirit, not of the flesh. In the second place, the passage doesn't teach any such idea. It says, "so is *everyone*" not "so is the new birth," but "so is *everyone* that is born of the Spirit." MacKnight translates this passage, "The Spirit breathes where he pleases, and you hear the report of him, but know not whence he comes, or whither he goes; so is everyone who is born of the Spirit." We must hear the "report or Voice" of the Spirit—the inspired word of God. I John 5:1 says, "whosoever *believeth* is born of God." I John 4:7 says, "every one that *loveth* is born of God." I John 2:29 says, "everyone that doeth *righteousness* is born of him." We must take *all* that the Bible says. John 3:5 is plain enough, "except a man be born of *water* and of the *Spirit*, he cannot enter into the Kingdom of God." But if you have trouble with it and the others just mentioned, then the thing to do is to find some examples of how people were "born again" in the Bible. Nobody would question the fact that the people of Acts 2 were born again. After hearing Peter's sermon, they were pricked in their hearts (hence, believed, v. 37). Upon asking what to do, they were told to "repent and be baptized everyone of you in the name of Jesus Christ for the remission of sins, and ye shall receive the gift of the Holy Spirit." (Verse 38). Then in verse 41, "Then they that gladly received his word were baptized: and the same day there were added unto them about three thousand souls." Again, (Gal. 3: 26-27), "For ye are all the children of God by faith in Christ Jesus. For as many of you as have been baptized into Christ

THE BAPTIST CHURCH 77

have put on Christ." Notice that they were "children of God," therefore had been "born" into the family of God, but they were children of God by faith—by faith where—by faith *in Christ.* But, they were baptized into Christ, and thus "put on Christ." Hence, they were "born again" (made childen of God) by *faith* and *baptism.*

Baptists teach that sinners are saved by faith only. They say, "All you have to do is believe, and He will save you." Article 5 of their Declaration of Faith, page 48, says that justification is "solely through faith." James says just the opposite, "Ye see then how that by works a man is justified, and *not by faith only.*" (James 2:24). Their doctrine of faith only breaks down on the chief rulers of John 12:42-43. "Nevertheless among the chief rulers also many believed on him; but because of the Pharisees they did not confess him, lest they should be put out of the synagogue: For they loved the praise of men more than the praise of God." Were the chief rulers saved? If you say "yes," then you disagree with the Apostle John for he says, "every spirit that *confesseth not* that Jesus Christ is come in the flesh *is not of God.*" (I John 4:3). If you say they did not believe, then you disagree with the Apostle John again, for he says they *"believed on Him."* Sometimes Baptists try to dodge the force of this argument by saying they believed *on,* not *in* Him. The Greek is *"eis," the strongest expression in this respect in the Greek language.*

Many times they refer to Paul's statement to the Philippian jailor in Acts 16:31, "Believe on the Lord Jesus and thou shalt be saved," and argue that in as much as Paul did not mention baptism that it is not a part of the plan of salvation. According to this logic, we could eliminate *repentance, love* and *confession,* because they are not mentioned either. And did you notice that Paul said, "Believe *on* the Lord Jesus." Besides that, where do these go? "For by GRACE are ye saved through faith" (Eph. 2:8). "For we are saved by HOPE" (Rom. 8:24). "Moreover brethren, I declare unto you the GOSPEL which I preached unto you . . . . . by which also ye are saved" (I Cor. 15:1-2). "Wherefore lay apart all filthiness and superfluity of naughtiness, and receive with meekness the engrafted WORD, which is able to save your souls" (James 1:

21). "The like figure whereunto even BAPTISM doth also now save us....." (I Peter 3:21). So, we see that we are not saved by *faith only*) (James 2:24), but by grace, hope, the gospel, the word, and baptism also. But these are all made possible by Jesus (Matt. 1:21). Paul told the Philippian Jailor "Believe on the Lord Jesus and thou shalt be saved"—but do not stop here, let us read on—verse 32 reads, *"And they spake unto him the word of the Lord,* and to all that were in his house, and he took them the same hour of the night, and washed their stripes; and was baptized, he and all his straightway." Since faith is the first step taken toward salvation, Paul told the jailor to "believe on the Lord Jesus and thou shalt be saved," but when they "spake unto him the word of the Lord," he was baptized the same hour of the night, since the word of the Lord says, "He that believeth and is baptized shall be saved....." (Mark 16:16). Therefore, we are not saved by faith only, but by "faith which worketh by love" (Gal. 5:6).

Baptists make the wrong confession. They say "confess your sins," but Christ says in Matt. 10:32, "Whosoever therefore shall confess ME before men, him will I confess also before my Father which is in heaven." The confession is not made in baptism. Consider, (Rom. 10:9), "That if thou shalt confess *with thy* MOUTH the LORD JESUS and shalt believe in thine heart that God hath raised him from the dead, thou shalt be saved." The eunuch did not confess his sins, but did confess "that Jesus Christ is the Son of God." Who ever heard a Baptist preacher ask anyone to confess "that Jesus Christ is the Son of God?" Sometimes Baptists confess "that God, for Christ's sake, has pardoned my sins." This is the confession that I made and I have heard a number of others make the same confession. *This confession contradicts every verse in the Bible that speaks of baptism and salvation.* The Bible says we are made free AFTER we have obeyed the gospel. (Rom. 6:3-4, 17-18).

BAPTISTS DO NOT ADMINISTER BIBLE BAPTISM

John's baptism is out of date. In Acts 19:1-5 we find where Paul rebaptized twelve men who had received John's

THE BAPTIST CHURCH

baptism. Aquila and Priscilla took a preacher who knew "only the baptism of John" and "expounded unto him the way of God more perfectly." (Acts 18:24-26).

Baptists baptize people whom they claim already have received the remission of sins. "There is an actual, a real remission of sins when we believe in Christ—there is a declarative, formal, symbolic remission in baptism." (Baptist Church Manual, p. 13).

The Bible plainly states that baptism is FOR THE REMISSION OF SINS, (Acts 2:38), or to wash away sins (Acts 22:16).

Baptists do not baptize a person into Christ, but rather, *into the Baptist Church.* They say any such person is in Christ *before* baptism. Hear Paul, "For as many of you as have been BAPTIZED INTO CHRIST have put on Christ." (Gal. 3:27).

Baptist baptism must be on a confession that one is already saved. Bible baptism puts a person into Christ where salvation is. (I Cor. 12:13; Col. 1:18; Eph. 1:3; II Cor. 5:17; Rom. 6:4; II Tim. 2:10).

Inasmuch as Christian baptism is "for the remission of sins," or to "wash away sins," and to get "into Christ," or "put on Christ," and Baptists do not administer Christian baptism, as has just been pointed out, then it follows that those who obeyed the Baptist plan of Salvation have missed the Lord's plan of Salvation, and *they are therefore not members of the New Testament Church, the Body of Christ, have not had their sins remitted, and are not saved.*

Many will say, "Oh but I know I'm saved." "Well, how do you know it?" "Oh, I just know it. I feel like I am." "What makes you feel like you are saved?" "Because I'm saved," they will say. Saved because they feel good, and feel good because they are saved. Such people prefer their feelings to anything the Bible says. I am not opposed to a person's feeling good about being a Christian, but I am opposed to a person claiming to be a Christian just because he feels good. Feelings are based on faith. Hence the Catholic *feels* like the Priest forgave his sins—he feels forgiven, but he isn't; but *he feels forgiven because he* BELIEVES *that the Priest can forgive his sins.* I felt just as saved as you do, when I was in the Baptist Church. I had just as much feelings as any of them, and can tell just as good an "experience," but I finally learned that feelings were the result of what I believed. If you *believe* that something is going to go wrong, you will *feel* nervous as long as you believe that. When the children are out late, if you *believe* that they are all right, you will *feel* good; but if you *believe* that something is wrong, you will worry, fret, and maybe cry. *I feel saved because I believe that I am saved.* You ask, "Why do you believe that you are saved?" Because I John 2:3 says, "hereby we do know that we know him, *if we keep his commandments.*" I know that I am saved, and I feel like I'm saved because the Lord said that if I would obey his commands, then I would be saved. I have done that, therefore I know that I have the promise of God. Baptists would have this verse read, "hereby we do know that we know him, *if we feel like it.*" If you will study the scriptures with an open mind rather than through your feelings, you will then begin to feel different. You will feel that you should turn from the human organization, the Baptist Church and obey the gospel of Christ because the Bible teaches you to do that. *Don't follow your feelings.* FOLLOW THE BIBLE. FOLLOW CHRIST.

THE BAPTIST CHURCH IS UNSCRIPTURAL IN ORGANIZATION

The Baptist Church has a minister whom they call "Pastor," and deacons, but no elders. The truth of the matter is this: pastors, bishops, presbyters, and elders are all the same and take the oversight of the flock. The deacons are servants of the church. The preacher is a minister or evangelist, not "the pastor" of a congregation.

Baptist preachers call themselves and have themselves called, "Reverend." (There are a few exceptions to this, but very few). This word is used *one* time in the entire Bible and then in connection with the name of God. (Psalm 111:9). When you see the man you believe on a par with God, call him "reverend." This also violates the principle laid down by our Savior in Matthew 23:5-12.

THE BAPTIST CHURCH IS UNSCRIPTURAL IN DOCTRINE

They are wrong first in having a man-made doctrine at all. "This Declaration of Faith was framed many years ago by J. Newton Brown, D. D." (Baptist Church Manual, foot note, p. 43). Christ says in Matt. 15:9, "But in vain do they worship me, teaching for doctrines the commandments of men."

The Baptist doctrine contradicts the Bible in reason. Ask a Baptist preacher, "What is the Baptist Doctrine?" It is "what a church believes the Bible to teach." (Baptist Church Manual, p. 41). I have pointed out that it is the distinctive features of the Baptist Church that make it Baptist instead of some other kind of Church. Now ask, "Must I believe the Bible to be saved?" Answer, "Yes." "Must I believe Baptist Doctrine to be saved?" Answer, "No." Then, if I must believe the Bible to be saved, and must not believe Baptist Doctrine to be saved, then it follows that Baptist Doctrine is not Bible Doctrine. Jesus told the apostles to go preach the gospel and said, "He that believeth not shall be damned." When any preacher preaches things that you do not have to believe to be saved, you may rest assured that he is not preaching "the gospel," because you do have to believe "the gospel" to be saved. If a person can be saved without belonging to the Baptist Church and without believing Baptist Doctrine (that which is peculiar to Baptists), then why does the Baptist Church exist, and by whose authority? Baptists say they exist to save people, but how can this be, when a person can be saved and never hear of the Baptist Church? Friends, think about that seriously.

Baptist Doctrine contradicts the Bible in fact. "We believe that the salvation of sinners is WHOLLY of grace." (Baptist Church Manual, Article IV of the *Declaration of Faith*, p. 47). We are saved by HOPE, (Rom. 8:24), and Peter said BAPTISM saves us, (I Peter 3:21). If this is true, then we are not saved WHOLLY or ENTIRELY by grace, but by hope and baptism *also*. Then this article of faith is false.

In Article V on page 48, the Declaration of Faith declares that "justification, the pardon of sin, and the promise of eternal life...are SOLELY THROUGH FAITH." In the first place, this article of faith contradicts Article IV. How can salvation be WHOLLY of grace and at the same time SOLELY through faith? We have pointed out that we are saved by grace, faith, hope, the gospel, the word, repentance, confession, baptism, etc., but the expression "solely through faith" excludes everything except faith. The Bible certainly does not teach this. James 2:24 again, *"not by faith only,"* therefore, this article contradicts Article IV and also the Word of God.

Their doctrine of apostasy is false. "We believe that such only are real believers as endure unto the end." (Article XI, p. 54). This is the doctrine of "once saved, always saved" and if a person "falls from grace," then they claim that he was not saved to start with. Consider II Peter 2:4, "For if God spared not the *angels that sinned*, but cast them down to hell, and delivered them into chains of darkness, to be reserved unto judgment." Are these "real believers" more steadfast than angels?

Is it possible that Paul could be a cast-away? Paul thinks so, hear him, "But I keep under my body, and bring it into subjection: lest that by any means, when I have preached to others, *I myself should be a castaway.*" (I Cor. 9:27). Was Paul a "real believer?" Paul said, "Wherefore, let him that thinketh he standeth, take heed lest he fall.

Again, "Whosoever of you are justified by the law, *ye are fallen from grace.*" (Gal. 5:4). We are saved by grace. (Eph. 2:8). Therefore, people can fall from that which saved them.

Many Baptists do not believe this doctrine, but as long as they are Baptists they stand for it just the same.

BAPTISTS SUPPORT A DEMOCRACY, NOT A KINGDOM

The essentials of a kingdom are: a king, law, and subjects over which he rules. The king makes the laws, enforces the laws, and passes judgment on violators of the law. Officers are filled by appointment of the king. Since Christ has all authority in heaven and in earth and has been crowned

THE BAPTIST CHURCH 83

"King of kings," He makes the laws; He will judge all violators of His laws in the day of judgment.

A democracy is that form of government that the *subjects* by *vote* make the laws and elect their officers. I challenge you to compare the Baptist Church with these two forms of government.

"The government of a church (the Baptist Church) *is with its members.* The churches must say...whether music shall be led by choirs, *with the aid of instruments or not,* etc., etc." (Baptist Church Manual, p. 39). This very plainly shows that the Baptist Church is *democratic* in its nature, but Christ established a *kingdom.*

In John 4:24 we learn that we must worship God "in spirit and in truth." In John 17:17 Jesus said, "thy word is truth." In Rom. 10:17 we read that "faith comes by hearing the word of God." Our worship, then, to be "in truth" must be *as the truth directs.* In Leviticus 10:1-2 we have an example of two boys, Nadab and Abihu, worshipping God, but because they did so in a "strange" way "which he commanded them *not*," the Lord took their lives. Again in I Chron. 15:13-15, David says, in reference to the method of bearing the ark of the covenant, "...God made a breach upon us, *for that we sought him not after the due order."* Jer. 10:23 tells us "that it is not in man that walketh to direct his steps," and in Isa. 55:8-9, the Lord says, "my ways are not your ways, for as the heavens are higher than the earth, so are my ways higher than your ways." God *will not tolerate* PRESUMPTION. We, simply mortal men, cannot worship God any way WE see fit, but must "seek Him after the due order." Remember, Jesus said, "In vain they do worship *me,* teaching for doctrines the commandments (that is, following the precepts) of men." (Matt. 15:9). Which are you following, God or men?

Baptists take Christ's place in adding to the church. The scriptures say "the LORD added to the church daily such as should be saved." (Acts 2:47). But Baptists VOTE to receive people into the church. There is not one place in the Bible that teaches us to vote to receive people into the church, nor to put them out, either.

Baptists talk about "opening the doors of the church." No

man, whether he be the Pope of Rome, or a Baptist preacher, can "open the doors" of the Lord's Church. Those doors were opened by the Apostle Peter in the long ago, and they stand ajar to this good time, and shall ever be open until the trumpet shall sound and the Lord shall announce that time is no more. This is just more evidence that the Baptist Church is a human, man-made church. For if they can "open and close the doors" then it is of men and not of God. They cannot open, nor close the doors of the New Testament Church.

Baptists take the authority to change the great commission. Christ said in Mark 16:15, 16, "Go ye into all the world and preach the gospel to every creature. *He that believeth and is baptized shall be saved;* but he that believeth not shall be damned." Baptists teach, "he that believeth and is NOT baptized is saved already because of his faith." Thus, they promise the sinner salvation SHORT of the conditions upon which *God* promises it. Therefore, Baptists are standing on the promises and assurance of Baptist preachers and NOT ON THE PROMISES OF GOD. Which do you prefer to believe, Baptists, or Christ?

Indeed, this is the real issue—who is king? Who is head? Who has all authority? In whom do you believe? Let me illustrate. Many times the church of Christ is accused of "believing in water." No, we do not believe in baptism as such, but in Jesus Christ. We practice baptism for the remission of sins, because Christ, in whom we believe, and who is our King and God, commanded it. To refuse His command, or the purpose for which He gave it is nothing short of rejecting Jesus Christ—"we will not that he should reign over us"— at least in this respect. To simply follow Christ when you like it, is *not* to follow Him at all. You are your own King in such a case. That sets yourself above Jesus Christ, above His word. You sit in judgment over His Word, accept what you like and reject the rest if it is different from your feelings. Friends, such is not Christianity, but religious anarchy. You do not have a right to "believe as you please," to choose the way you like to serve Him, but simply to humbly submit to Him who is Kind and Love, and is the creator of heaven and earth, and before whom we must all stand in a little while.

THE BAPTIST CHURCH 85

Let me plead with you to renounce all denominational affiliations and humbly submit to Christ as Lord of lords, and King of kings. While we sing, just step out from your seat and come forward, confess your faith in Jesus as Lord, as you humbly repent of every sin, and be baptized for the remission of sins.

Addenda

As a reaction to Brother Stevens' visit to Fort Worth, and the lecture and tract which he distributed on the theme, "Why I Left The Baptist Church," a Baptist preacher of the community wrote the following letter to Brother Stevens. His reply also follows:

Fort Worth, Texas
November 12, 1948

Mr. Grover Stevens
Charlotte, Tennessee

Dear Sir:

I just finished your booklet on "Why I Left The Baptist Church," and after reading it and seeing what you believe, I would say the church left you.

In the first place all Christians ought to believe the word of God and be able to give it out without fear or favor. (II Tim. 2:15).

You stated that Paul baptized 12 of John's disciples. But Paul said in I Cor. 1:14 that he baptized none but Crispus and Gaius, verse 16, also the household of Stephanas. You say that baptism is part of the gospel. Verse 17 Paul plainly states he was not sent to baptize, but to preach the gospel.

Eph. 2:8. "For by grace are ye saved through faith, and that not of yourselves: it is the gift of God: Not of works (baptism) lest any man should boast. Why didn't you give all the scripture? In I Peter 3:21 you failed again. Why didn't you give all of the verse? "Not putting away the filth of the flesh but the answer of a good conscience toward God, by the resurrection of Jesus Christ." And not by baptism.

You said believers could fall from Grace and gave Gal. 5:4

as your scripture. All Bible students know that Paul was teaching them if they were justified by the Law, Christ is become of none effect. Just like you teach you are saved by baptism, and if you are, Christ is none effect, you are fallen from grace, as some of the Galatians were.

I know that he "that believeth and is baptized shall be saved." Just like "He that buys a ticket and gets on a train and sits down shall go to his destination," and I know also "He that buys a ticket (if he sits down or not) will arrive." No, you didn't leave the Baptist Church. (The church left you.)

When Christ said in John 10:28—what did He mean when He said, "I give unto them *eternal life* and they *shall never perish*"? Read I Peter 3:9. Verse 5 tells us that we are kept by the power of God. We don't and can't keep ourselves. You said in your booklet that Judas fell by transgression. John 17:12 tells us that he was the son of perdition that the scriptures might be fulfilled. Jesus said he was a devil from the beginning. Remember II Tim. 2:15.

You said God did not hear sinners' prayer when they pray. Luke 18:13 says God does hear sinners. Verse 14, "He went down justified." (And he was not baptized).

Mr. Stevens, answer this question: If a man can so sin as to be eternally lost after he is saved, is that man a lost believer or a lost unbeliever, and if he is lost, do you baptize him again, and if you don't baptize him again you don't believe what you preach.

Dear Brother, take the whole Bible plus nothing and minus nothing and stand on it, and you *would be a good Baptist.*

Yours in His Name,

BAPTIST PREACHER.

P. S. When I have time I will inform you on many more scriptures. Read Leviticus 17:11. It is the blood and not the water that makes atonement for the soul.

THE BAPTIST CHURCH

Charlotte, Tennessee
November 15, 1948

Baptist Preacher
Fort Worth, Texas

Dear ....:

Your letter of November 12th reached me today, which I am glad to receive and to have the opportunity of discussing the points of my tract with which you disagree. I admire your conviction which prompted you to write, and shall be very happy to discuss our differences. Judging from the introduction to your letter, you are an honest man and want to be governed by the Bible rather than sentiment. I would like for you to bear this in mind, that I do not have any hard feelings toward the Baptist Church nor Baptist people. I believe they are doctrinally wrong, and because I love them, I hope to teach them the truth. In order to make my reply as short as possible, my replies will have to be brief, but I assure you the kindest feelings prompted them. Now to your objections:

Paul did *not* say that he baptized none but Crispus and Gaius, etc., but "I baptized none of you (Corinthians), but Crispus and Gaius, etc." (I Cor. 1:14). However, even if Paul did not do the baptizing with his own hands, the fact still remains that 12 who had received "John's baptism" were re-baptized (Acts 19:1-7).

If baptism is no part of the gospel, then making Baptists is no part of the gospel for one must be baptized to be a Baptist. Inasmuch as Paul pronounced a curse on all who preach "any other gospel unto you than that which we have preached unto you" (Gal. 1:8), and since making Baptists is no part of the gospel, then it follows that all who make Baptists are accursed. If not, why not?

Your reasoning on I Cor. 1:17 is faulty. You say: "Christ sent Paul *to preach* the gospel, but Christ did not send Paul *to* baptize, therefore, *baptism* is no part of the gospel. This is erroneous. Here is the syllogism given and the correct conclusion drawn: Christ sent Paul to *preach* the gospel, but Christ did not send Paul *to baptize*, therefore "to baptize" (a verb, hence the act of baptizing) is no part of "to preach" (the act of preaching). They are two different acts. Paul preached baptism (Acts 18:8; I Cor. 12:13; Acts 16:14, 15; 30-34; Acts 19:1-5; Rom. 6:3-5; Gal. 3:26, 27; Col. 2:12). This is the gospel that Paul preached, which he certified was "by the revelation of Jesus Christ" (Gal. 1:12), and pronounced a curse on all who preach "any other gospel" (Gal. 1:8, 9).

You next quote Eph. 2:8, 9, and say "not of works (baptism)". In John 6:29 we read "this is the work of God that ye believe on him whom he hath sent." Hence, according to your own argument salvation is not of faith because it is "not of works" and faith is a work, therefore it is not of faith. Then too, there is more room to "boast" of faith than of baptism. Furthermore, baptism belongs to God's righteousness and not to man's (Rom. 10:1-3). Baptism is "the righteousness which is of God by faith" (Phil. 3:9).

I am surprised at your statement on I Peter 3:21. You say, "... by the resurrection of Jesus Christ. And *not* by baptism." Peter says, "... baptism doth also *NOW* save us," but you say "not by baptism"—the same as saying "baptism doth also *NOT* save us." You seem to think that the rest of the passage changes the meaning of the part that I quote. No, my friend, the passage still says, "... baptism doth also now save us." Do you believe that, Mr. ....? Or do you believe "baptism doth also *NOT* save us?" Which do you believe? And from what does baptism save us, Mr. ....?

Can a person fall from something he doesn't have, Mr. ....? We are saved by grace, yet the Galatians had "fallen from grace," therefore it follows that a person can fall from that which saved him (Eph. 2:8; Gal. 5:4).

You next try to eliminate baptism from Mark 16:16, "He that believeth and is baptized shall be saved," by giving a parallel (?) sentence. "He that buys a ticket and gets on a train and sits down shall go to his destination." Thus you make "buying a ticket" stand for faith, and "sitting down" stand for baptism. What about "getting on the train," Mr. ....? If we make "buying a ticket" stand for faith, and "getting on the train" stand for baptism, and "destination" stand for salvation, your own illustration will refute your position. However, I think that you meant to make "getting on the train" stand for faith, and "sitting down" stand for baptism, and "destination" stand for salvation. You then reason that a person does not have to "sit down (be baptized) to reach his "destination" (salvation). No, according to Baptist doctrine he wouldn't have time to "sit down" for the minute he "got on the train" (believed) he arrived at his destination (salvation). Not only that, but since one can travel other ways than by "getting on a train," it would follow that one does not have to "believe" (get on the train) to be saved. But enough of that. You say, "I know also, He that buys a ticket (if he sits down or not) still arrives." That is as much as saying, "I know also, He that believeth (if he is baptized or not) is still saved." Jesus said, "He that believeth and is baptized shall be saved," but you say, "He that believeth and is not baptized shall be saved." That is why I left the Baptist Church, Mr. ....

Next, you want to know about John 10:28. In the first place the Lord is talking about sheep who follow him. What about those who quit following, Mr. ......? We have eternal life in the sense that we have Jesus Christ (I John 1:2; 5:12). But having Christ depends on our "abiding in the doctrine of Christ" (II John 9). "They shall never perish" was said of sheep following the Lord. That a "brother" can "perish" is evident from I Cor. 8:11.

You want me to read I Peter 1:3-9 with emphasis on verse 5, which reads, "Who are kept by the power of God through faith unto salvation ready to be revealed in the last time." First, notice that we are kept "through faith." I Tim. 5:12 says that some have "damnation because they cast off their first faith." You say, "We don't and can't keep ourselves." Jude says, "Keep yourselves in the love of God, looking for the mercy of our Lord Jesus Christ *unto* eternal life." (verse 21). Now back to I Peter 1:5. Notice next that the salvation is ready to be revealed in the last time. But according to Baptist doctrine it has already been revealed. Then I Peter 1:9, "Receiving the end of your faith, even the salvation of your souls." But according to Baptists one receives the salvation of his soul in the beginning of his faith.

It was Peter who said that "Judas by *transgression* fell," Mr. ...... (Acts 1:25). Judas himself said, "I have sinned." (Matt. 27:4). Was Judas a free moral agent, Mr. ....? If so, he betrayed the Lord by choice, and if not, then God is responsible for the act.

The Publican in Luke 18:13, Mr. ...., was a Jew and therefore a child of God under the law. Nobody but the Jews were allowed in the temple.

It is possible for a believer to quit believing (I Tim. 5:12; 4:1). Will there be unbelievers in heaven, Mr. ....? The Bible tells us of believers who are lost (John 12:42, 43). Hence the answer to your question is, it is possible for a man to be a lost believer (John 12:42, 43), and it is also possible for a believer who was saved to quit believing (I Tim. 5:12).

No, I do not baptize "him" again, and I believe and practice what I preach, too. I preach that baptism is for the remission of *alien* sins (Acts 2:38; 22:16).

How could I take the whole Bible plus nothing and minus nothing and be something that is not even mentioned in the Bible? Nobody can follow the Bible and nothing else and be a Baptist, nor a member of the Baptist Church, for it is nowhere found in the Bible. That is the reason I left the Baptist Church.

I believe in the blood of Christ, Mr. .... How do we contact the blood of Christ? Rom. 6:3 says that we are baptized into His death. Christ's blood was shed in his death (John 19:34). Hence, we contact the blood of Christ and get the benefit of it when we are "baptized into his death."

Mr. ...., it is my sincere prayer that you will open your eyes to the truth and leave the Baptist Church which is nowhere to be found in the Bible, and turn to the Lord and His Church. We must both stand before our Maker and give an account, therefore, with a view to the judgment before God, let us be honest with our own souls for their salvation's sake. I shall be very happy to hear from you as often as you can write.

In Christian Love,

GROVER STEVENS

CLAUDE B. HOLCOMB

(*A Biographical Sketch*)

Claude B. Holcomb was born in Williamson County, Texas, December 14, 1906, and has lived in the state all of his life. His formal education began in a one-room, one-teacher country school in Wichita County, to which he walked three and one-half miles each way. He graduated from Denton High School in 1924, and in the fall of the same year enrolled as a freshman at Southwestern University in Georgetown, Texas. The following year he returned to Denton and entered North Texas State Teachers College. His father died when he was fifteen years of age, and since that time he has had to support himself, paying his way through school by working in the printing business. Altogether he spent about twenty-three years in the various departments of printing, the last few years of which were in publishing religious books, periodicals, and pamphlets. It was while engaged in this work that he became interested in serious Bible study, and finally came to a knowledge of the truth, renounced Methodism, and obeyed the gospel of Christ.

With the help of a devout father-in-law, R. A. McCurry, and other able men in the church, he has acquired an unusually good library. He has spent many hours at the feet of Brother R. L. Whiteside, one of the greatest thinkers and commentators of our time, who lives in the same city.

Brother Holcomb's public work in the church began with teaching a large class of college students at the Pearl Street congregation in Denton, which he continued for about five years. During this time he was called upon several times to preach in the absence of the regular preacher, and this lead to regular work as county evangelist in Denton County. Since 1942 he has served congregations in local work at Lake Dallas, Justin, and Denton; and has been engaged in evangelistic work in Texas and other states. He is greatly aided in the Lord's work by a devoted wife.

Why I Left The Methodist Church

CLAUDE B. HOLCOMB

Thank you, Brother Campbell. I am glad to be here on this occasion. I am grateful to the brethren who are in any way responsible for my receiving the invitation to be here tonight and speak to you on the subject announced. We are grateful to God for his divine Providence in all things, for the opportunities afforded, and for the blessings to be derived from meetings of this kind.

ONLY THE TRUTH WILL SAVE

I do not know anything very colorful, or particularly interesting to you with respect to my leaving the Methodist Church; nevertheless, I am glad to have the opportunity to engage in this service with you. We are interested in the truth only. I am quite certain, as I am sure you are, that this series of lectures has been designed not merely to gratify any lust for excitement or sensationalism, nor to provide an occasion to carry on a tirade of vilification toward any person or group of persons. But it has been designed to bring to light the truth of God. That is why we are here tonight. We are interested in the truth. Jesus said, "Ye shall know the truth, and the truth shall make you free." Jno. 8:32. Not only will the truth free men and women from the bondage laid upon them by reason of ungodliness, but it will free them from the shackles of error, into which so many have fallen through the devices of Satan. The only field in which the devil has to work is the minds of men. It is through men, therefore, that Satan has advanced his cause upon the earth. As a result, the religious world is plagued with a maze of confusing doctrines, commandments of men, and myriads of traditions. This is the devil's work. God is not the author of confusion, but of peace. It is supremely important that we be made free from the traditions of men and the shackles of error, for I remember that Jesus said in his day that there was a certain class of people that had made void the word of God by their traditions (Matt. 15:6). He said concerning them, "This people honoreth me with their lips but their hearts are far from me. In vain do they worship me, teaching for their doctrines the commandments of men." We want to avoid that, therefore, for certainly we want to worship God in an acceptable way. So we are here in the interest of truth. God would have all men to be saved and come to a knowledge of the truth. Christians have an innate desire to see the will of God done upon the earth, and, therefore, we, too, would have all men to come to the knowledge of the truth. All spiritual truth is derived from the word of God. Jesus said, "Thy word is truth." To the word of God, therefore, we must go, because "it is not in man that walketh to direct his own steps." (Jer. 10:23). Realizing that our welfare upon the earth, and the destiny of our souls when we come to die, are contingent upon conforming our lives to the truth of God, we ought to desire the truth in religion above all things else. David said, "The steps of a good man are directed by the word of the Lord."

I am persuaded to believe that thousands of people now engrossed in error are honest and sincere in heart. I am persuaded to believe also that as soon as they are convinced of their erroneous position that they will renounce it and accept the truth. It takes an honest and a good heart to do this. The narrow-minded person is the one who rejects the truth when he sees it. The broad-minded is the one who gladly receives the truth and cherishes it in his heart. There are still multitudes of good and honest people if we can only reach them. It must be remembered, however, that the truth has no inherent power by which it can advance itself. Truth will prevail in our world only so long as it has champions to advance its cause, and to defend it against error. That is our work as Christians. Christians are the light of the world, holding forth the word of truth. Not only through exemplary lives according to its principles, but also through teaching that truth constantly "in season and out of season." And so we are here tonight to advance the cause of truth by exposing one of the systems of error that stands in the way of its progress. We trust that God may be pleased with such an effort as we strive for his glory in this service.

PROPHECY FULFILLMENT REPEATS ITSELF

Just here I should like to read a few verses taken from Isaiah 59. The prophet said, "Behold, the Lord's hand is not shortened, that it cannot save; neither his ear heavy that it cannot hear: But your iniquities have separated between you and your God, and your sins have hid his face from you, that he will not hear. For your hands are defiled with blood, and your fingers with iniquity; your lips have spoken lies; your tongue has muttered perverseness." Now if the reader were not aware of the fact that the prophet in this place, and the following verses, had in mind primarily the condition of Israel at the time he lived, I believe that if he knew the conditions which exist in certain religious groups tonight, that he could well be persuaded that the writer of these words was describing such groups. The reader might think that he was describing conditions such as prevail in that organization about which I am to speak tonight. The prophet goes on to say, "None calleth for justice, nor any pleadeth for truth; they trust in vanity and speak lies; they conceive mischief, and bring forth iniquity. They hatch adders' eggs, and weave the spider's web: He that eateth of their eggs dieth, and that which is crushed breaketh out into a viper. Their webs shall not become garments, neither shall they cover themselves with their works: their works are works of iniquity, and the act of violence is in their hands. Their feet run to evil, and they make haste to shed innocent blood: their thoughts are thoughts of iniquity; wasting and destruction are in their paths. The way of peace they know not; and there is no judgment in their goings: they have made them crooked paths; whosoever goeth there shall not know peace. Transgression and lying against the Lord, and departing away from our God, speaking oppression and revolt, conceiving and uttering from the heart words of falsehood. And judgment is turned away backward, and justice standeth afar off: for truth is fallen in the street, and equity cannot enter. Yea, truth faileth; and he that departeth from evil maketh himself a prey: and the Lord saw it, and it displeased him that there was no judgment."

A METHODIST FOR TWENTY-NINE YEARS

As has been announced, it is my assignment to tell you why I left the Methodist Church. Now this might suggest a rather personal aspect in the minds of some of you, but as far as I am concerned, I am forgetting that part of it. And though some references may be made to my own experiences, let us think of every personal reference made in a comprehensive sense; as applying in principle, at least, to every one who might find himself in similar circumstances. I was a Methodist for twenty-nine years. I suppose I would have been recognized during most of that time as a full-fledged Methodist, by anyone's standard; and all of that time as at least an acceptable member of the Methodist Church. I have in my hand a church certificate made out to me: "The bearer hereof, Claude B. Holcomb, has been an acceptable member of the Methodist Episcopal Church, South, in Denton charge, North Texas Conference." This is dated "June 15, 1936" and signed by D. E. Hawk, pastor in charge. I suppose, therefore, that I was recognized up to this time as an acceptable member of the Methodist Church. I think that after I have told you a few things with respect to my own experience, that you will see that I was by anybody's standard a "good Methodist." Now this certificate is only good for twelve months after it is made. So you can very well see that I am no longer a member of the Methodist Church. This is not a demit either. I suppose that you are aware of the fact that every child born into a Methodist family becomes a member of that institution when he is a baby—in a sense, at least. I was sprinkled when I was a baby. The truth of the matter is, I was sprinkled three times that I know of, including the time when I was a baby. Two of these I asked for myself. Being just a lad and calling upon no one to guide me in the matter, and having no one to restrain me, after I heard the appeals of certain preachers, and when they "opened the doors of the church," I decided that meant me, and I walked forward, answered all the questions, and was sprinkled as a boy about six years old. Then after a few years I sat in another revival meeting, I heard the appeal of the preacher, and was moved by it. So I thought maybe I had better do that again, and I went forward, and they went through the whole process again. In this process I committed myself to support the Discipline, and all Methodist institutions —as all who join that organization do.

ZEAL FOR METHODISM

Throughout all my younger days I attended the services of the Methodist Church regularly. When I came to be of high school age, I spent five hours every Sunday in services at that church. There was the Bible school on Sunday morning, then the morning service. In the afternoon around 3:00 o'clock there was the Intermediate Epworth League. Then one hour before the evening service, the Senior Epworth League, then the evening service. I was always there; I never missed. This was in addition to the meetings through the week. Not only that, but in both of these Epworth Leagues that I attended on Sundays, I played the piano for their song services. I did that for a number of years in the Methodist Church in Denton, Texas.

DARK HOURS BEFORE THE DAWN

After graduating from high school I went to a Methodist University, and here was the beginning of the dark hours before the dawn. In 1924 I enrolled as a freshman in Southwestern University at Georgetown, Texas. There the faith I held up to that time was undermined through the influence of evolutionary and modernistic teachers in that institution. I made mention of this fact not so many months ago to a friend of mine, and he expressed surprise at that, because he said that he thought that Southwestern University was the stronghold of Methodist orthodoxy in Texas. That may be true to a certain extent, particularly when compared with that institution's big sister over here in Dallas, Texas (Southern Methodist University). It may be the bulwark of faith as far as Methodists are concerned, or a stronghold of Methodist orthodoxy, but the modernistic influence was there at that time just the same. That was back, remember, in

1924. It was there, maybe not to the extent that you will find it in many places, but it was there nevertheless. It was not long until I learned that the head of the Science department of that institution was an out-and-out evolutionist. He was not at all reluctant to preach the evolutionary theory to all that came to his class. I had a number of arguments with some of my friends concerning these things. We had sessions in the dormitory, one of which I remember lasted all night long. We left the room and went to the breakfast table the next morning. All night long we argued upon this very point —evolution. I remember another occasion that I sat in another room in that dormitory and discussed these things with a number of boys until 4:00 o'clock in the morning. There were numbers of other sessions.

Well, you can understand some of the thinking that went on in my mind at that time. But that was not all. I learned, too, that the head of the Government and Economics Department (they were combined at that time; I do not know whether they still are or not) was what we call a "Modernist." He denied the Virgin Birth, and the miracles of Christ, and other fundamental facts of the Bible. At the end of the school year, after having had so many discussions concerning these things, and after having learned that so many "greats" among the Methodists held to such ideas as these that I had heard in that institution, I returned to Denton. I was downcast and downhearted with respect to spiritual things.

The next year I enrolled at the Texas State College at Denton and did the rest of my college work there, but during that time I did not go to the services of the church much. I did not go much when I was in Georgetown. I just drifted along, and for several years it was only on rare occasions that I went to church services at all. After a few years I moved to Wichita Falls, and went to work there. I placed my membership, or certificate, with the Floral Heights Methodist Church of that city. I did not go there very much—just on rare occasions. A few years later I moved back to Denton, and moved my certificate with me, and put it back in the church there. Then, in the course of a few years, it so happened that the work in which I was engaged at that time led me to do the proof reading on a number of religious publications—most of which were for the Fundamentalist Baptists. We printed John R. Rice's weekly paper for a number of years. We printed all the literature for Sam Morris, and other men. We did a great deal of printing for J. Frank Norris. I read all these things and knew that I did not believe all of them, but at the same time it revived a spark down deep in my heart, a spark of religious feeling that had been there all the time. I had done my best to smother it. Then I began to study a little bit. Then it was—well, you know how those things are—I met a young lady that had the most fascinating smile I ever saw! I kept company with the young lady regularly for quite a while, and became acquainted with her family. Through their insistence, I attended a gospel meeting that was conducted at the Pearl Street congregation at Denton in which J. Early Arceneaux did the preaching. Now J. Early Arceneaux has done a lot of preaching in Fort Worth—I know that. There are quite a large number of you that are acquainted with him and his preaching. You are assured that at least I *heard* what the New Testament teaches with respect to salvation, and with respect to the church. I heard the truth. It made a rather deep impression on me, but I did not accept it at that time. However, it set me to thinking. I will tell you what I did—I would go to work and read the articles that the Fundamentalist Baptists would print; then I would go to the home of this young lady I told you about, and I would argue with her father on these things. Sometimes I would think I had some good arguments, too.

STUDIES TO DEFEND METHODISM

Then I decided to study Methodism to see what I could learn about that. As a matter of fact, I set out to defend Methodism. So I began to study, and, of course, that was fatal to the cause. I tried. I did my very best to defend the Methodist Church and its teachings, and that led me to do some earnest, sincere, hard study—not only from some books that I had procured from my friends, but of the Bible itself; here is where I spent most of my time. I was trying to show that the Bible would support the Methodist Church in principle. That is what I started out to do. I studied earnestly. Many of you in this audience tonight know many of the things I learned as I studied Methodism, and you also know what I learned when I studied the New Testament. I learned the truth. But I did not obey it at once. I was beginning to see that there was no way for an individual who was sincere and honest, as I believed I was deep down in my heart, to escape these truths that were plainly revealed in the New Testament. I began to attend the services of the church of Christ. I began to attend the Bible classes. I studied and continued to study. I talked to some of my Methodist friends. I argued with them concerning some of these tenets of Methodism. I went on, and more and more I could see that the longer I studied the more I was losing with respect to my Methodist faith.

OBEYS THE GOSPEL

Then one Sunday afternoon, after I had been to the worship of the church of Christ that morning, I was sitting out on the running board of my automobile and thinking these things over. I was deeply impressed; I was concerned; I was in dead earnest. I wanted to go to heaven when I came to the end of the way. I believed in God, and I believed that Jesus Christ was the Son of God, and the Savior of men. I believed that with all my heart, but I couldn't believe that my sins were forgiven. I began to think those things over that afternoon as I sat on the running board of that automobile, and the thought came to me all at once: "You do not have a single thing to which you can cling, not one." I got up and went into the house where the company of people were at the time. In a little while we drove out home, and I went in and told my wife: "Get a change of clothing ready. I am going to be baptized." That made her very happy, of course. I walked down to the church building that evening, and went up to the preacher. I asked, "Is the baptistry ready?" "No," he said, "but we can get it ready mighty quick." I said, "That's fine; let's do so. I want to be a Christian, just a Christian and a Christian only." And so it was in the month of June, 1936, the same date as this certificate, that I was baptized into Christ.

THE METHODIST CHURCH

JOHN WESLEY—NOT CHRIST—FOUNDER OF METHODISM

Now with respect to the Methodist Church, you know already that I learned that John Wesley was its founder, and nearly every Methodist will agree with that. I have found only one person in all of my experience that argued with me that the Methodist Church is the church of Christ, and that Jesus himself built that church. I found only one, but her argument did not last very long. In McTyeire's History of Methodism on page 14, we have this statement: "The history of Methodism cannot be given without a biography of John Wesley. To him belongs the distinction of Founder. Great men by a natural law come forward in groups; but to insure the success and unity of a movement, there must be a solitary pre-eminence" Notice that. There must be a solitary pre-eminence to insure the success and unity of that movement. I believe that. "While Charles Wesley, George Whitefield, John Fletcher and Thomas Coke were mighty auxiliaries, it is around John Wesley that the religious movement of the eighteenth century called Methodism, centers." I believe that, too. Here is the difference between this and the New Testament Church: in the church of Christ pre-eminence is given unto Christ and unto him only. (Col. 1:18). In the Methodist Church it is admitted here that pre-eminence is ascribed to John Wesley. Not only that, but in this paragraph we see that "to John Wesley belongs the distinction of being the founder of the Methodist Church." The New Testament Church was built by Christ himself. (Matt. 16:18). This he did on the first Pentecost after his resurrection from the dead, through his holy apostles unto whom he had given the keys of the kingdom. Now this is one reason why I left the Methodist Church. I learned these things. I found out that the Methodist Church did not have the scriptural founder. It was the only safe thing to do, to be in a church that had a scriptural founder.

METHODIST CHURCH 1700 YEARS TOO LATE

I learned, too, that the Methodist Church began 1700 years too late to be the church of the New Testament. I read from Nathan Bang's History of the Methodist Episcopal Church,

Vol. I, pages 39 and 40: "In 1729 Wesley attended the meeting of a small society which had been formed at Oxford, in which were included his brother Charles, and Mr. Morgan, for the purpose of assisting each other in their studies and consulting how they might employ their time to best advantage..... It was about this time, that the society above named, having attracted some attention from the regularity of their lives, and their efforts to do good to others, that some of the wits at Oxford applied to the members the name of Methodists, a name by which John Wesley and his followers have ever since been distinguished." From a study of the New Testament, I came to realize that this is an unscriptural name, but this is the name that has been ascribed to John Wesley and his followers ever since 1729.

METHODIST NAME ANTI-SCRIPTURAL

God gave unto his people through his Son Jesus Christ, the name Christian, and that name glorifies the name of Christ every time it is spoken. We learn from I Peter 4:16 that, "If any man suffer as a Christian let him not be ashamed, but let him glorify God in this name." Give glory unto Christ by the name that you wear. I could not do that by the name "Methodist." I came to realize that, and that is another reason why I left the Methodist Church.

Brother Claud McClung is sitting over here on my left. He is a very consecrated Christian man, and a fine gospel preacher. I have been associated with Brother McClung in two gospel meetings in which he did the preaching, where I was working regularly. He told me that he was conducting a meeting in a certain place one time, and he met a lady in one of the stores there at the time of the meeting. During the course of the conversation the lady said to Brother McClung, "I am a Methodist." Brother McClung said, "You are?" "Yes." "Well, I am a Christian," said Brother McClung. "Oh, but I'm a Christian, too," said the lady. "Well," he said, "what did you tell me you were a Methodist for?" That set the lady to thinking. If I remember correctly, he told me that he baptized that lady during the course of that meeting. Yes, Brother McClung says that is right. People just need to stop and think about these things. If we could just reach them and get them to thinking and studying, as I studied and hundreds of others have studied.

I learned that the Methodist Church began at an unscriptural time—seventeen hundred years too late. You know, if the time and the place had not been designated by the Lord, that possibly would not have made so much difference. This is an argument that Methodists make, "It doesn't make any difference when the church started." But the prophet said, "The mountain of Jehovah's house shall be established on the top of the mountains." When? "In the last days ... when the law goes forth out of Zion, and the word of the Lord from Jerusalem." (Isa. 2:2, 3). And all of you who know your Bibles know that according to the promise of Jesus Christ, he sent the power of the Holy Spirit upon his apostles on the first Pentecost after his resurrection from the dead, and the church was established upon that day through them, "and the Lord added daily to the church such as should be saved." The time has been designated, A. D. 33. The Methodist Church began in 1729. That is too late.

WHOLE SYSTEM UNSCRIPTURAL

So we have found that the Methodist Church has an unscriptural founder, unscriptural name, began at an unscriptural time and an unscriptural place. The very groundwork, the whole system, is unscriptural. It is wrong. But that is not all. Its whole structure is also unsciptural, if it may be said that it has any structure. The Methodist Church has an ecclesiastical system of organization that is second only to that of the Roman Catholic Church. From the book known as the Methodist Discipline, I learned that the highest authority in the Methodist Church inheres in their College of Bishops. That is their high court. These are the ones who have the last word. On page 264 of this book, we find the beginning of a series of articles that are known as the Decisions of the Bishops—Bishops' Decisions. On page 287 I read, "The church cannot appeal from the decision of its own court." That's the Bishops. There are 118 of these articles up to this time, Bishops' Decisions, imposed upon the Methodist Church. The Bishops are assigned, each one, to his own district. They look after the affairs of the church in that district, and preside over the conferences, district conferences and quarterly conferences. He is the one who has the rule, and he rules as he pleases in his assigned district. We find duties assigned to that bishop in this book (Discipline). We find duties assigned to the presiding elders who are subordinate to him. As we read on we find duties assigned to preachers-in-charge, traveling deacons, traveling elders, supernumeraries, superannuates, local preachers, exhorters, stewards, trustees, and so on *ad-infinitum.* Now where in the Bible can you find anything about such a system as that? There is nothing. Therefore, the whole system is unscriptural, non-scriptural and anti-scriptural. Have you ever stopped to think that under God's arrangement the church of the Lord Jesus Christ grew faster in thirty years time than any religious movement that has been known before or since? Even in our time, the church is growing faster proportionately than any religious group on earth. Now if you doubt that you can ask your friend and my friend, Jeff D. Ray, a scholarly man. (Fort Worth Star-Telegram Newspaper Writer of Religious Articles, an aged Baptist preacher). He wrote an article last year concerning this very thing in which he said that the church of Christ is growing faster than any religious group of our time. He gives as the reason the fact that we are not at all reluctant to teach what we believe, and we constantly teach it. We believe in indoctrinating the members. We believe in bringing the truth to light.

"WHAT IS METHODISM?"

"What Is Methodism?" That is the title of a little article that is printed in this paper known as the Methodist Messenger. This is the official organ of the Methodist Church in Denton. I receive it every week through the mail. Here is a little notice that is printed in this issue: "Two groups in the church within the last week have asked the pastor to talk to them on the Methodist Church. The young people are wanting to know the rules of the church." (Don't know anything about it). "The Bungalow class are wanting to know what Methodism stands for." (They have been Methodists for years, perhaps). "Methodists as a rule do not talk much about Methodism, as little, perhaps, as any, does it indoctrinate." This is wise. It is better not to indoctrinate when the doctrine is weak. The strength of the New Testament church lies in the fact that it indoctrinates its members. That is because the doctrine comes from the right source, and therefore, it is right. This simply means that God's plan will accomplish the ends that God has designed for it, if God's people will work the plan.

METHODIST CREED CONTRARY TO NEW TESTAMENT

Now then, as we look further into the Methodist creed, we find that it is in itself anti-scriptural in many points. It is also inconsistent with itself, as are all humanly devised creeds. Human creeds are objectionable for many reasons. They are written by men, and therefore, are not infallible. God's word is. Human creeds do not meet humanity's needs, and they are insufficient. They are constantly in need of amendment, and the same authority that makes them amends them at will. The gospel contains the mind of God, and is not subject to amendment. Human creeds are constantly in need of amendment, and are therefore imperfect. "The law of the Lord is perfect converting the soul." (Psa. 19:7). Human creeds disagree with one another, and therefore they cannot all be right. Not only that, but all human creeds at some point conflict with the plain teaching of Christ, and therefore they are all wrong, and that includes this one (Methodist Discipline). Yet, it is the very constitution of Methodism. Most of the members do not know what is in it. Some of them do. Yet, they have all vowed to support it, as I did when I became a member of the Methodist Church. There are some members of the Methodist Church who have told me that they do not believe the things that are printed in the Discipline, and yet, they took an oath when they became a member of that body to support the Discipline. Here it is on page 371. When they come to join the church, to submit themselves for sprinkling, the question is asked by the preacher: "Will you be subject to the Discipline of the Church, attending upon its ordinances, and support its institutions?" Here is the answer: "I will endeavor so to do, by the help of God." Some do not realize this. There are others who have taken the vow, and they realize that they have taken such a vow, but it doesn't mean much to them, and they do not profess to keep it.

LACK OF CONVICTION AMONG METHODISTS

A few years ago, I went up to the radio station for a broadcast, and there was a man there who was a Methodist minister. He was the father of the announcer of the radio station. After we had been introduced, this man said to me, "My son got me out early this morning just to come up here and hear you." I said, "Well, that's fine. I am glad you are here. However, I do not want you to think that this is a frameup, because it just so happens that my lesson this morning is directly opposed to Methodist doctrine." He smiled and said, "That's quite all right; I will hear you." So I went into the studio and gave my lesson on the subject of "Salvation By Faith Only," a scriptural study. After the lesson was completed I went back into the other room, and this man said, "You know, my son and I were trying to decide where you might think that you and I would be at odds on what you had to say this morning." I said, "Well, you heard the lesson, didn't you? 'Salvation By Faith Only' is one of the cardinal doctrines of the Methodist Church, and you are a Methodist minister." He said, "Yes, but I believe just as you do about it." I said, "You do?" He said, "Yes." I said, "Well, you know you read in your Discipline that 'the doctrine of salvation by faith only is a most wholesome doctrine and very full of comfort?" "Yes," he said, "I know that's there, but, you know, all Methodists do not believe alike." You know, friends, all honest religion is based upon conviction. If there is no conviction in it, then it cannot be honest religion.

Last Sunday evening I was talking to a friend of mine at the railroad station in Denton. He was a Methodist. He wanted to ask me a question concerning the church, and, of course, I was glad to hear it. After I had answered the question to his satisfaction, I said, "Now, I would like to ask you a question." "All right." I said, "Why are you a Methodist?" I have known him for a long time, and we are good friends. He

THE METHODIST CHURCH

reflected a moment. He did not answer at once, but directly he threw out his chin and stepped out and said, "Because my mother and daddy were Methodists. That is all the reason I can give you." I said, "Well, that's a fair, frank and honest answer." Then in the course of that conversation I told that man that I had been a Methodist. I think he knew that already. But I said, "I studied long enough to find out that I was not a Methodist, and truly had never been." He shook his head and said, "I am not either." Yet, he holds membership in a Methodist Church.

Just this past week there was a lady in one of the stores in Denton talking to one of our sisters. She said, "Why, you know Methodists do not care what you believe." No conviction! Another woman that I heard of said, "I don't read my Bible very much, because I know what I believe without reading it." She was right about that. She did!

There are many things that we could point out in this book (Discipline) tonight if we had the time, that would show you the inconsistencies, the weaknesses, the unscriptural positions taken in so many places by the leaders of the Methodist Church. As far as I was concerned, there was the matter of baptism. First of all, as to the necessity of it, I had always been taught that you did not have to be baptized—not even sprinkled if you did not want to be. You could be saved anyway. After studying my New Testament, of course, I learned otherwise. (Acts 2:38; 8:12, 38; 9:6; 10:48; 16:31-33; 18:8; 19:5; 22:16; Mark 16:16; Rom. 6:4; Gal. 3:27; I Peter 3:21). I learned that it was a commandment of the Lord. I could not disobey any commandment of the Lord without being disobedient in the heart. As long as I refused to be baptized in the scriptural manner and for the scriptural purpose, that meant that my heart was filled with all the rebellion that it could hold. Therefore, I changed. I left the Methodist Church.

FALSITY OF METHODIST BAPTISM

Then there was the matter of what baptism is. We can turn to page 369 of this little book (Methodist Creed), and there we read that "the minister shall take each person to be baptized by the right hand, and placing him conveniently by the font according to his discretion shall ask the name, and then shall sprinkle or pour water upon him, or if he shall desire it, shall immerse him in water." You know, I began to study that one time, and I saw that they had that thing just in reverse. In one instance they take the element and place it upon the subject, and in the other instance they may take the subject and place him in the element. Something wrong somewhere. I noticed that in my study. That was one of the things that I began to think about in regard to baptism before I left the Methodist Church.

Then I came to the matter of the sprinkling of infants. I had always thought that it was all right. I talked to a lady in Denton one time who told me this experience: She had been a Methodist all her life, until she was married and a baby was born to the family. She insisted on having the baby sprinkled, but her husband was a member of the church of the Lord and he would not agree to it. So this lady went to her pastor and said to him, "Brother Pastor, my husband is rather a peculiar fellow, and he has to have scripture for everything that he believes and everything he does religiously. Now I want to have my baby sprinkled and I want you to give me the scripture, so that I can go and show it to him, and we can have our baby baptized." Well, Brother Pastor said, "Now, Sister Stover, there is no passage of scripture that I can give for the sprinkling of babies. That is just one of our church ordinances. It is in the Discipline." Sister Stover told me that she began to think about that, and she said to herself, "Well, perhaps there are some other things which are not in the scriptures." She began to study, just like I did. It was not very long until she obeyed the gospel.

Babies are not subjects of baptism to begin with. They may be subjects of sprinkling according to some people's standards, but according to the scriptures only believers can be baptized, and babies do not have that capacity. So I am not willing to trust my soul's salvation upon a flimsy foundation like that. If it has nothing to do with the saving of the soul, then God has no use for it, and neither do I. What can the purpose be?

METHODISTS ARE TURNING MODERNIST

Now there are a number of reasons why I left the Methodist Church. I would not be able to give all of them to you in this discourse tonight. But here are just a few things that I would like to call to your attention. There are many people in the Methodist Church who do not realize that such things as these are going on. There are fewer people, I believe, in other religious bodies that know about these things. Of course, the preaching brethren here, and a few of these others know something about it, but the things that I have here will startle you. The Methodist Church has been taken over by "Modernists." These are men who have denied the fundamental facts of the Bible. A young lady asked me not very long ago, "What is a Modernist?" I did not have this statement before me at the time. I gave her a definition in my own words. But here is a good definition of a Modernist: "The Jesus of the Modernists is not the Lord Jesus Christ of the New Testament..... Every cardinal doctrine concerning the Lord Jesus Christ is denied. Especially do they attack his virgin birth, his miracles, redemption by the blood of his cross, and his bodily resurrection. Their evolutionary creed will not allow them to admit of any supernaturalism. So, therefore, the virgin birth is discarded as a biological impossibility. Jesus worked no miracles because a miracle is contrary to nature and natural laws, and the resurrection of our Lord's body is flatly denied. The only resurrection they admit of is that his spirit and influence live on. Comparable to the song we used to sing, 'John Brown's body lies a-mouldering in the grave, but his soul goes marching on.' The blood of Christ shocks their cultured sensibilities, so they do not preach salvation through his blood, but flatly deny the fact of his substitutionary atonement." I found this statement to be true in the Methodist Church. The beginning of it was back in 1924 when I attended Southwestern University; but I have learned much more with respect to it since then.

PROMINENT METHODIST LEADERS DENY DIVINITY OF CHRIST

First of all, let us get a statement or two from the most prominent among them, and then we can see what some of the lesser lights think about it. Here is a statement from Bishop Francis J. McConnell, a statement which he made in an article which he called "The Christ-like God": "Some ardent teachers would almost make Jesus the First Person, as did one celebrated Methodist theologian who once spoke of Jesus as God Almighty. Some students can hardly explain their resentment of the tendency to deify Jesus, since the tendencies seem to rob him of his supreme value of a human ideal. Is not their tendency to deify Jesus more heathen than Christian? Are we not more truly Christian when we cut loose from a heathen propensity and take Jesus simply for the character that he was and the ideal that he is?" Now listen to this: "Back in the early days of the church there were some, probably only a few, thinkers who taught that Satan had a claim on the souls of men which only the death of the Son of God could satisfy, and that God met the obligation by sending the Son to the Cross. As an intellectual construction this theory arouses only amused pity today."

Here is another statement from Dr. Ivan Lee Holt. This was contained in an address that he made before the Methodist young people's conference, January 7, 1936. This address was recorded in the Christian Beacon, August 15, 1940. Listen to this: "He defended the Soviet Union from attack. He declared that the aims of the dictatorship of the proletariat in Russia 'was the establishment of a better life'. The Russian Government does not purport to do this through exploiting someone else, but through raising the general level of all." Now, here is the statement that I want you to get: "It is difficult to find youth anywhere in this world more devoted to the cause of Christ than you will find in the youth of Russia devoted to Stalin and his new Social order." That is modernism. That is in the Methodist Church.

Here is another great Methodist. Dr. E. Stanley Jones in his book, "Christ's Alternative To Communism", page 224, makes this statement: "When the western world was floundering in an unjust and competitive order..... God reached out and put his hand on the Russian Communist to produce a juster order and show a recumbent church what it has missed in its own gospel...... I am persuaded that the Russian experiment is going to help—and I was about to say force—Christianity to rediscover the meaning of the Kingdom of God on earth." Do you believe it?

The Methodist pastor in Denton is on the radio five days a week. We have taken quite a few notes with respect to some of the statements he has made on these radio broadcasts, and I would like for you to know some of the things that are being taught in the Methodist Church there. That is the reason that this friend told me last Saturday night that he was not a Methodist either. This same friend told me that one Sunday morning this preacher opened the doors of the Methodist Church, and extended an invitation to come and join the church. In extending that invitation he had this to say: "Perhaps you do not find it in your hearts to believe in Jesus as your Savior just now, but come on and join our church anyway, and perhaps the rest will come later." That is why this friend did not believe in the doings of the Methodist Church, but he was still a Methodist, he said. Here are some other statements from the same man. This is what the Methodists are feeding upon in Denton. These are some of the reasons why I'm glad I left it. "Yes, I have heard," he said, "that everything works together for good to them that love God, and I know where it is. It is in the Bible; but that is not a pure statement. It is not a premise. Jesus made no statement that would uphold this, and wherever Jesus and St. Paul conflict, go to Jesus. There is no sense to that statement. You can't make sense out of it. Give me a God where sense is." And further, "We are not concerned now with what the will of God is, but where it is. What I believe might not help you immediately. Some other belief might be better for you." I listened to him again as he made this statement—I think he must have been talking about us then: "You say there is only one way. You would confine us to a single channel of religious thought—to a Book. Tell me, what kind of God do you serve?" (I told him over the radio the following Sunday morning). "Nothing is made up for us if we are strong. It is up to us to create our own way. I cannot see that, no matter how blind I am, the way is already appointed for me." Here is something else: "It isn't full maturity to think only as Jesus did. The pattern of my religious life can never be the pattern of Jesus' religious life as he lived on the earth, or if he were living now."

Many of you, I am sure, are informed of a Methodist young people's movement known as the "Wesley Foundation." The Methodist student movement in Texas is a very strong organization among the youth of many colleges of our state. In all of the larger colleges you will find an organization known as the "Wesley Foundation." That is made up of Methodist young people. Some of you have read the comments made by Mr. Lynn Landrum in the Dallas News, criticizing some of the work of the "Wesley Foundation" in Austin, and the University of Texas. With respect to this comment of Mr. Landrum, in another issue of this official organ of the Methodist Church in Denton, this man has this to say concerning the "Wesley Foundation": "The Wesley Foundation movement is as solid as the Methodist Church itself; and the Methodist Church is as solid as Christianity. The Methodist Church is sane, not fanatical; it is comprehensive, not tangent-like in its excitements; it deals with all areas of thought, and deals with them sincerely, carefully and soundly." I am not going to be able to read to you all the things these young people are being taught by their leaders, but I am going to take the time to read just a few.

Here is the complete address, stenographically reported, made by Dr. Ehrensperger before the Texas Methodist Students Conference in 1939. This is what that man had to say to those young people: "The Christian goal of life is commonly called the Kingdom of God, which today I would like to call the Blessed Community . . . . . . Like all great attributes of human nature, imagination comes by long cultivation. It is a process of growth, of feeding, and of cultivation that enables it to reach a state where it functions adequately in the process of living. It permeates all life and is fundamental to religion." (Imagination). "If we are to understand the background of our

Christian religion we must have this kind of imagination, for the poets wrote much concerning it." Now I read all that to give you this "Man was made in God's image. God imagined man. It will take imagination to get back to God. It is imagination that we need in the worship services of our church, in the observance of rituals and sacraments, in the celebration of the feast days which often times have become so meaningless for us. Imagination should be the spur to make us seek the kingdom of heaven and to find God, for we must get to God if we are to be brothers in the blessed communion of Christian life." Do you know what the Bible says concerning imaginations of men? We are to cast down imaginations and every high thing that exalts itself against the knowledge of God, and bring every thought into captivity unto obedience of Christ. (2 Cor. 10:5). That's scriptural teaching. Here is something else. They are teaching the young people this now: "In religious thought there is no blueprint for the Christian. There is no revelation which is systematic description. Revelation is not knowledge about God, it is knowledge of God. It is not information; it is event. Theological students are constantly enrolling in a course on doctrine of God and expecting to find Him by way of terms, but God must be found through persons and experiences. The Bible is not revelation, but records of and comments on revelation."

SUMMARY

I am going to have to sum things up very quickly, but here is one that I can't pass over. The young people of the Methodist Church are having this constantly instilled in their minds: "A Christian's attitude toward a pagan's religion should be one of interest in enlarging understanding about religion. Pagan religions should not be destroyed but merged with our religion. Since centers of power change, religions change; and there is no way of predicting future religions." Now then, listen: "The traditional attitude that there is only one God and that all religions must give way in place of this belief is inadequate and not necessarily true . . . . . . The best religion would be one which could assimilate the good points of others rather than destroy older traditions. It will be one that can gather up areas of meaning value, goods from struggles in all the world, and yet be more sensitive and more flexible." That is the best religion, they say. "The traditional attitude that there is only one God is inadequate and not necessarily true." Verily, the devil has transformed himself into an angel of light. Infidelity has donned the garb of religion and taken its place in many pulpits of our land, and has propagated these miasmatic doctrines over the radio, through the press, and by every means available to man in this day and time. Who can fail to see the fulfillment of New Testament predictions that many false teachers have gone out, and that the spirit of antichrist does work even now, and prevails in our religious world? They are here, all around us and many of them are harbored by Methodism! That is why I left the Methodist Church.

Even if I were to concede that the members of the Methodist Church were Christians, I still would not want to be a member of it. It is too far removed from the glorious church Jesus built and died for. Jesus loved the church "and gave himself for it that he might sanctify it, having cleansed it by the washing of water with the word, that he might present it to himself a glorious church, not having spot or wrinkle or any such thing, but that it should be holy and without blemish." The church of the Lord Jesus Christ is the bride of Christ, and that is a tremendous appeal for its purity. Christ loved the church infinitely more than any man can love his bride, because his capacity to love is so much greater. And he wants her to be holy and without blemish. The frills and trappings conceived by men fall so far short of the beauty and simplicity of the New Testament pattern, that they are too cheap, much too cheap, to be dragged into it. The church of the Lord Jesus Christ is resplendent by the effulgence of its own glory, and anything added by men only mars its beauty, darkens its light, and neutralizes its influence and its power to shed abroad the gospel of salvation through the Lord Jesus Christ. She must be kept holy and without blemish as the precious bride of Christ! And when this is done, she stands amidst the nations of the earth with a glory and a grandeur that transcends all the highest concepts of splendor that can occupy the thoughts, or even the imaginations of humankind. May God bless her and keep her, and strengthen her through the love of Jesus Christ who dwells in the hearts of the saints who compose that body. How happy I am tonight to be free from the shackles of denominationalism, and to be a member of the church of the Lord Jesus Christ, which is his bride! There is where God dwells among his people. We are builded together for an holy temple in the Lord. Each several building is fitly framed together for an holy temple in the Lord. And ye also are builded together for an habitation of God in the Spirit. There is where God is —in the church of the Lord Jesus Christ. It is his body of the redeemed; purchased by the blood of Christ. It is the family of God, and God has no children outside his family. I must be in it, friends, and you must be in it, if you want to be in that great company of the redeemed, who by the hands of ministering angels shall at last be ushered through the portals of glory into the presence of the Ancient of Days—there to behold the superior excellence of his glory and bask in the sunlight of his love throughout the ages of eternity. You must be in the church of the Lord Jesus Christ; that is, the body which he purchased with his blood. That is what he shed his blood for —to redeem the church. Let us be more solicitous, therefore, of the purity of the church. Let us throw off all the shackles of error; let us renounce all error which we might have held throughout all our life, just to be a member of that glorious body, the church of the Lord Jesus Christ. Is that your desire tonight? If you are here and not a member of that church, we want you to know that we are earnestly concerned about your welfare. We want you to know that we would like to see you become a Christian. And the Lord in his grace is offering you further opportunity tonight to become obedient unto him and to renounce all false ways. If that's your desire tonight, will you not come and let your wishes be made known to us, while we stand and sing.

WAYMON D. MILLER

(A Biographical Sketch)

Waymon D. Miller was born at Mayflower, Arkansas, on April 26, 1918. He remained on the farm until about four years of age, when his family moved to Conway, and after a year to Little Rock. He received his public school education in North Little Rock, and was graduated from high school there in 1937. He was studying to be a professional artist at his conversion, and when he decided to devote his life to preaching the gospel. Before beginning his preaching career he was also an amateur radio musician, with regular programs on numerous stations.

In the fall of 1937 he entered Harding College, Searcy, Arkansas to further his preparation to preach the gospel. While in Harding he was elected president of the freshman class, and won state debate championship in the junior college division. Later he attended Ouachita College, and did extention study with the University of Arkansas. While in Harding he formed acquaintence with Miss Naomi Holt, whom he later married. The Millers also have a daughter, Mary Lee, five years of age.

Brother Miller has preached in many states, and is now working regularly with the North Side congregation in Fort Worth. He has a special interest in writing, and has contributed many articles to gospel papers. He is a staff writer for the Gospel Record. He has written and published a book on the theme of this lecture, "Why I Left The Nazarene Church." He has engaged in a number of public and written religious debates. At present he is writing another book for future publication, "Modern Holiness Doctrines," which is an exhaustive study of these modern religious errors.

Why I Left The Nazarene Church

WAYMON D. MILLER

I am deeply grateful tonight for the honor that has been conferred upon me. This is a rare type of lectureship program, very unusual in its nature, and one that the presence of such a great audience attests remarkable interest. I feel keenly sensible tonight of my inability as I stand before you. I have been informed that all the preceding speeches have been excellent ones. I have therefore a very high mark set before me by these other capable brethren, to which I feel doubtful that I can attain. But we are genuinely grateful for the interest you express by your presence in the theme of the evening assigned me, "Why I Left The Nazarene Church."

I was reared in the Church of the Nazarene. I attended the Church of the Nazarene first when about six years old. At my home in North Little Rock, Arkansas, my older brother and I were playing in the front yard one day. The pastor of the Nazarene church drove by and saw us. He stopped, and asked, "Are you boys members of any church? Do you attend church anywhere?" We replied in the negative. He then got out of his car, went to the door, knocked, and asked our mother if she would permit us to go to Sunday school the next Sunday if he would come and get us. To this she gave her consent. That was my first inducement to attend the Church of the Nazarene.

My grandfather was an invalid for eight years before his death. He was bedfast when I started attending the Nazarene church. Shortly after my brother and I started attending the Nazarene church, my mother also started going. And soon the Nazarene people (I pay tribute to them here for their zeal) were conducting cottage prayer meetings in our home for the benefit of my grandfather. This was a source of joy and inspiration to him as long as he lived. At about the age of six years, soon after I started attending the Nazarene church, my mother, my two brothers and I all became members of that denomination. I was a member of the Church of the Nazarene for approximately ten years, or until I was about sixteen years old. I must say that at this early age, while in my formative years, some of the impressions made upon me by the Nazarene people were ones that will be retained as long as I shall live.

It was rather unusual that I became a member of the New Testament church. For about a year prior to my obedience to the gospel I became dissatisfied with the teachings of the Nazarenes. Many reasons were involved in that, too numerous to discuss just now. But I stopped going to church anywhere, and for a period of a year hardly darkened a church door. About a year after my leaving the Church of my own free will and personal dissatisfaction, I was urged to attend the church of Christ in North Little Rock.

Perhaps just here I should return to some events even earlier in my life, and connect some experiences that have a bearing upon my religious life. I was born in a rural village, Mayflower, Arkansas, which is twenty-two miles north of Little Rock. In the fall of 1921 two gospel preachers, W. W. Still and J. C. Mosley, came through this little town on their way to Fort Smith to attend a "preacher's meeting." At that time there were a few Christians, but no established New Testament church in Mayflower. These brethren investigated the possibilities of holding a gospel meeting there when they returned from Ft. Smith. The school house was obtained, and Brother Mosley preached for about two weeks, baptizing seventy-five persons. My mother and father obeyed the gospel in that meeting, and a thick layer of ice was broken on the gin pond to provide a place of baptizing. Brother Mosley is now very aged, but still living in Whitwell, Tenn. I have long since lost all contact with Brother Still. I was about three years old when the above meeting was held. My family then moved to Conway, Arkansas for a year, and then to Little Rock. My mother and father did not attend church regularly, and soon lost almost all interest in the truth. Being left in its infancy, and without qualified leaders, the newly-established church in Mayflower withered away. But the church there has since been re-established. It was after my mother and father had grown indifferent to the church that we started going to the Nazarene church, my father excepted. Before the elapse of much more time, after our becoming Nazarenes, my father was restored to the truth, and assisted in the establishment of a church in North Little Rock. He was one of the charter members, and one of the first deacons, of the New Testament church in North Little Rock. And it was through his insistence that about eleven years later I started attending the church of the New Testament.

At first I was not too well impressed with the idea of attending the church of Christ. It did not appeal to me very much. I did not know too much about the church of Christ, but what I did know was not very favorable. I had heard people talk so disparagingly about "Campbellites" that I had a repulsion for them. I had been taught to avoid them, and had regarded them as narrow and bigoted. To me they appeared the most reproachful of all the more distasteful religious sects. They seemed to be just fanatical rabble-rousers with a Pharisaical spirit. Everything that I had heard about the New Testament church was unfavorable propaganda, which had almost completely poisoned my mind against it. It seemed that to believe as "Campbellites" was the next thing to having no religion at all.

But the first time I attended the church of Christ, to my great surprise, I was deeply impressed with the service. It was so simple and unpretentious. The sermon especially attracted my attention. There was something about the ring of it, the first time I heard a true gospel sermon, that aroused my curiosity. I began to wonder what was the difference between the way that fellow preached, and the manner of preaching to which I had been accustomed as long as I could remember. I spent considerable time in meditation upon this first gospel sermon. In it I had found something strangely different. Though I had intended to be indifferent to it, my heart was troubled and my conscience was stirred over it. I had supposed it would be insensible and unattractive, though I found it to be strangely appealing. And it finally dawned upon me that the real difference between the preaching of this man, and that to which I had been accustomed, was that in every single point, however insignificant, he had the scripture to verify his teaching. I had never been used to anything like that. I had never been used to a religion that could sustain every phase and aspect of it by the simple word of God, without injecting into it any of the traditions, speculations and theologies of men. So that appealed to me very much.

I will not say that it was easy to leave the Nazarene Church. It is never easy to depart from error. In this point members of the New Testament church, who have never been members of a sectarian denomination, cannot wholly sympathize with those in error. But, my friend, if you are present as a member of a human institution, I can by personal experience sympathize with you for sacrifices you may make in accepting the truth. You may say tonight, "I am not a member of the true New Testament church, of which you now speak. I am hesitant to accept what you now teach because I am abiding in the religion of my youth, which has many sentimental and endearing attractions to me." I could once say the same thing! You say, "It is the religion of my friends, and if I depart from it, I would risk the loss of all my friends of this life." I had to do the same thing! You say, "If I abandon my present views, I might even make personal enemies." I had to take the same chance for the truth of Christ! You say, "If I depart my present religion, I would go into an institution to which few, if any, of my relatives belong." I did exactly the same thing. I can count on this hand, and have two fingers to spare, all of the relatives I have who are members of the Lord's church. And so I can completely sympathize with any of these sentiments that might disturb you tonight. But if we are not willing to submit to sacrifices, we cannot be disciples of the Lord.

On September 15, 1935, I obeyed the simple gospel of Christ, just as I can read it from this Book. I was baptized by Brother Clem Z. Pool. My younger brother, Orlan, obeyed the gospel upon this occasion with me. He now is a gospel preacher having preached for the past seven years. He is now attending Abilene Christian College. Brother D. H. Perkins, now of Denver, Colo., who followed Brother Pool in North Little Rock, is most responsible for my beginning to preach the gospel. Since I started preaching, no other has rendered more assistance than Brother E. R. Harper, now of Abilene.

THE NAZARENE CHURCH

I should like to add an interesting side light to my obeying the gospel. When I was a member of it, the Church of the Nazarene occupied a building at 6th and Olive in North Little Rock. They presently outgrew that building, and erected a new building in another location. When they moved into this new building, our brethren bought the building at 6th and Olive, and in this building they still meet. Hence, I prayed "through" at the Nazarene mourner's bench, and obeyed the simple gospel of Christ in the same building! I shall not speak disparagingly tonight of the Nazarene people, many of whom are yet my intimate friends. To this day I hold these Nazarene people in highest esteem. I have not set myself against them, but rather oppose the erroneous doctrine which they hold. I can truthfully say that the Nazarene people are among as conscientious, zealous and sincere people as can be found. And I did not leave them because of a lack of these qualities, but because I knew that conscientiousness, zeal and fervency alone were not sufficient. A person may have all of these, and still not be obeying God. This is illustrated in the life of the Apostle Paul, in his persecution of the church before his conversion. (Acts 23:1; 26:9-11).

It is impossible tonight to relate to you all of the reasons why I left the Nazarene church. It would be impractical to array before you every tenet, even every cardinal doctrine, that the Nazarene church holds. But I would like to supply for your consideration a few doctrines of the Nazarene church. They are doctrines I could not reconcile with the scriptures when I began studying my Bible. In presenting these matters I shall not have time either to give every scripture which refutes them. I shall just give a specimen of simple scriptural denial of them. I've found this, in my study of the Bible, that God does not have to say a thing a thousand times for it to be true anyhow. When God states a truth in one place, in simple, unequivocal terms, it is just as much true if he had said it a million times! So if we can find just one simple scripture which contradicts in an unmistakable way these cardinal teachings of the Nazarene church then we shall have amply disproved them.

ORIGIN AND FOUNDATION OF NAZARENES

First, I shall relate a brief history of the Nazarene church. Near the close of the nineteenth century was begun in America what is now known as "the holiness movement." The "holiness movement" in this country was an outgrowth of the Wesleyan "holiness movement" in England, which swept all Europe like wildfire. I have before me tonight the official manual of the Nazarene church from which to quote. I did not wish to misrepresent any detail of their teaching. The manual provides the following historic data: "On May 12, 1886, a number of the brethren in Providence, Rhode Island, interested in promoting the Wesleyan doctrine and experience of entire sanctification, organized and held weekly religious services." (Manual, page 15) The Nazarene church is an outgrowth of that "holiness movement." I quote further: "In October, 1895, a number of persons, under the leadership of Rev. Phineas F. Bresee, D. D., and Rev. J. P. Widney, LL. D., formed the First Church of the Nazarene, at Los Angeles, California, with one hundred and thirty-five charter members." (Manual, page 17) There it is, acknowledged and claimed by the Nazarene church Manual, the official creed of that church, as to exactly when, and surrounded by what circumstances, the Nazarene church was established. For these reasons I could not be a member of the Nazarene church any longer.

You may ask, "Why? What is elicited by these statements that caused you to see that you could not continue with them?" There are three reasons drawn from the above quotations. In the first place, the Nazarene church was founded for the wrong purpose, and upon the wrong foundation. I read to you very definite statements that this movement was instigated for the specific purpose of promoting "Wesleyan doctrine." It was established, therefore, to promote the peculiar theology of John Wesley. As I studied my Bible I came to see that any organization founded upon human ideas and opinions in religion, was established upon the wrong foundation. The Apostle Paul declared, "For other foundation can no man lay, than that is laid, which is Jesus Christ." (1 Cor. 3:11) Our Lord Jesus Christ is then the foundation of the New Testament church. No other foundation is acceptable. No other can be laid, than that which is already laid, which is Jesus Christ! So I could not continue with an institution founded upon Wesleyan doctrine. The foundation of the true church, of which we can read in this Book, is Jesus Christ, and Him only. "For other foundation can not man lay!"

Then secondly, the Church of the Nazarene was the wrong church to be the New Testament church. In consulting this manual, which is their church creed, and expresses their doctrines, that the Church of the Nazarene was established in 1895 by two preachers, and one hundred thirty-five charter members, in the city of Los Angeles, California. Yet when I referred to my Bible in the second chapter of Acts, I found that the New Testament church was established in the city of Jerusalem. It is the distance around the world from Jerusalem to Los Angeles, California! The New Testament church was established in 33 A. D.; the Nazarene church in 1895. Too much difference there for it to be the church which Jesus died to redeem and purchase! (Eph. 5:25; Acts 20:28). The Nazarene church is admittedly of human origin, being founded as we have already quoted from their manual. But Jesus said, "Upon this rock I will build *my* church..." (Matt. 16:18) Jesus is the divine Builder of the true church, and not these men mentioned in this manual! So I could not accept Nazarene doctrine further, for it was founded in the wrong place—Los Angeles instead of Jerusalem; it was founded at the wrong time—1895 instead of 33 A. D.; it was founded by the wrong persons—the men I named instead of Jesus Christ. In these three vital tests, the Nazarene church cannot be identified with the New Testament church.

And then, thirdly, the Church of the Nazarene was established for the wrong purpose. It not only rested upon the wrong foundation, but was conceived for the wrong purpose. I have read from this manual that it was established for the purpose of promoting Wesleyan doctrine—established solely for the promotion of the peculiar theologies of John Wesley! As I studied my New Testament I saw that such would not do, that such is not acceptable to the Lord. Jesus emphatically stated, "For in vain they do worship me, teaching for doctrines the commandments of men." (Matt. 15:9). That is exactly why the Nazarene church was established, to "teach for doctrines the commandments of" John Wesley! But Jesus said those who do that, those who pursue such a course, would be worshipping Him in vain. Then I considered Paul's warning in this matter: "Though we or an angel from heaven, preach any other gospel unto you, than that which we have preached unto you, let him be accursed." (Gal. 1:8). What is it, Paul? If anything else is preached than that which has been declared by inspiration, both the preacher and the recipient will be condemned thereby. I could not, therefore, further subscribe to the doctrines of John Wesley, because they were not preached by any divinely inspired preacher of apostolic time. The peculiar theologies of John Wesley were never proclaimed by divine authority, and therefore I could not continue in them. While the Nazarene church was founded to promote the teachings of Wesley, the New Testament Church was established, and exists today, for the express purpose of proclaiming and promulgating the simple gospel of Christ. (Eph. 3:10). For no other reason was the divine church established, for no other reason does she exist today, except to preach the Word of God, and that alone, unmixed and uncontaminated with human theologies.

HEREDITARY TOTAL DEPRAVITY

Perhaps the most important peculiar doctrine of the church of the Nazarene is that of hereditary total depravity. Now, that is an expression as long as a yardstick—so long I can hardly pronounce it some times. But it really has a simple, yet diabolical meaning. Of course the term "hereditary" means "by inheritance, by birth." The term "total" means "absolute, or complete." "Depravity" means "wicked, corrupt, estranged from God, a state of spiritual condemnation." Now, here is what we have, adding these together, that by birth one is completely wicked and abandoned of God; he is of such spiritual condition at birth, or by inheritance, that he is wicked in heart and estranged from God! It will be well here to notice other terms by which this doctrine is also called. Some times it is called "inbred sin," "inherent sin," "the old man," "the Adamic nature," or "the carnal mind." I cannot emphasize too strongly the importance of this teaching in reference to "holiness" doctrines. Were it not, I say, for this one doctrine alone, all other so-called "holiness" doctrines could not stand, nor would there be any need of them. This is the one doctrine that supports all of the other peculiar beliefs, and I shall show you why as we study further.

Let us then consider what Nazarenes teach about this doctrine. On page 27 of the church manual, under the heading "Original Sin, or Depravity," is found the following expression: "We believe that original sin, or depravity, is that corruption of the nature of all the offspring of Adam, by reason of which every one is very far gone from original righteousness, or the pure state of our first parents at the time of their creation, is averse to God, is without spiritual life, and is inclined to evil, and that continually; and that it continues to exist with the new life of the regenerate, until eradicated by the baptism with the Holy Spirit." This, my friends, is the unscriptural, anti-scriptural and nauseous doctrine of hereditary total depravity. This doctrine, as we trace it back through history, evidently originated with Augustine in the fourth century. As far as I have been able to determine, he was the first to assert this doctrine. It was not taught then very extensively until the time of John Wesley. The doctrine appealed to Wesley, and he further developed it and amplified it. And the teachings of John Wesley on inherent sin have become the basis of all "holiness" sects. Now, I want to call your attention to this, that this one false doctrine, conceived in the mind of Augustine in the fourth century, and amplified by Wesley in his day, paved the way for a number of other unscriptural doctrines. You know, that is always the course of error. When one innovation, or unscriptural practice, is introduced, usually other unscriptural practices must be invented to accommodate it.

What did Wesley teach about this doctrine, which served as the basis of modern "holiness" doctrines? Wesley said, "Every man born into the world now bears the image of the devil, in pride and self will; the image of the beast, in sensual appetites and desires." (*Wesley's Sermons*, Vol. II, page 266).

I quote further from Wesley: "We are condemned before we have done good or evil, and under curse ere we know what it is." (*Original Sins*, Wesley, page 340) Original sin, or depravity, as I mentioned, fostered several other false doctrines. If a man were born totally depraved, Wesley then conceived that nothing short of a miracle of God could save him, hence the doctrine of the direct operation of the Holy Spirit. It also developed the unscriptural doctrine of sanctification, the "second blessing," which "eradicates" this depraved nature. This also promoted the unscriptural doctrine of Christian perfection, the result of having the "image of the devil" removed by the Holy Spirit. All of these doctrines are intimately related, interdependent one upon the other, and all reposing upon the unscriptural doctrine of hereditary depravity.

Now then, what does the Bible teach about that? Does the Bible teach that because Adam sinned, then all men are born in sin, bearing "the image of the devil," and "condemned before we have done good or evil?" Why, surely not; The Apostle Paul wrote in this matter: "Wherefore as by one man sin entered into the world, and death by sin, so that death passed upon all men, for that all have sinned." (Romans 5:12) But this scripture is not worded so as to favor Wesleyan doctrine. The verse says, "So that *death* passed upon all men, for that all have sinned." If Nazarene doctrine were true, the verse would have to read like this: "So that *sin* passed upon all men, for that *Adam sinned.*" But that is not what it says, is it? Or, again: "The image of the devil passed upon all men, for that Adam sinned." It doesn't say that either, does it? If you follow the thoughts Paul develops in this fifth chapter of Romans, especially noticing verses seventeen and eighteen, it will enlighten our study upon this subject. He here argues that Adam brought sin and death into the world, and that Jesus came to offset these evil consequences through the redemption of man. Jesus came to abolish death, and bring life and immortality to light through the gospel. (II Tim. 1:10). Now, let us examine the matter critically. If all men were born in sin because of Adam's transgression, then since the death of Christ all men are born redeemed, since Christ's work was to destroy the effect of Adam's sin! We are forced to accept one of the two horns of that dilemma—either total depravity or universalism!

Let us see if all men are born so engrossed in sin as Wesley imagined. Luke informs us that Christ himself was a descendant of the fleshly lineage of Adam. (Luke 3:38). Luke here traces the genealogy of Christ back to Adam! Now, according to Nazarene theology, this would mean that our Lord Jesus Christ, the Prince of heaven, the sinless Son of God, came into this world bearing "the image of the devil" and therefore under divine condemnation! This conclusion they must accept if they maintain their doctrine of hereditary sin, or accept the Catholic doctrine of Immaculate Conception. This Catholic doctrine claims that while all men inherit sin from Adam, that God miraculously purified the Virgin Mary before the birth of the Savior. But this is simply another doctrine of Catholic forgery. Let us remember that Christ was in the flesh a descendant of Adam, yet Peter said that he "did no sin" (I Peter 2:22), hence the doctrine that sin is inherited from Adam is false!

Let us examine a few more scriptures which deny such an absurd and unscriptural doctrine. The Word of God positively declares: "The son shall not bear the iniquities of his father." (Ezek. 18:20). I do not know how much plainer scripture would have to read to deny this false doctrine. Nazarenes claim that sin is transmitted all the way from Adam down from father through son unto us. But Ezekiel affirmed that *"the son shall not bear the iniquity of the father!"* If that be true, how could sin be inherited? Nazarene doctrine asserts, as we have seen, that one is born in sin, inclined to evil, and that continually. Does the Bible say whether this is so? It positively denies it! Ezekiel again proclaimed, "Thou wast perfect in thy ways from the day thou wast created, until sin was found in thee." (Ezek. 28:15). What is that? You were first perfect, until sin was later found in you. Nazarene doctrine reverses that order. It claims that we are born in sin, which remains until you are both saved and sanctified, and then you are perfect! The Apostle Paul contended that one is a sinner because of his own wickedness, and lost because of his own sins. And the Lord knows this is enough! Our own sins are sufficient to eternally damn us, and enough for us to bear, without ladening us with the sins of Adam, or anyone else! Paul said, "And you who were sometimes alienated and enemies in your minds by your wicked works." (Col. 1:21). Paul, alienated from God by Adam's transgression? No, by "your wicked works!" My friends of the Nazarene Church cannot accept this scripture, with its undeniable implications. Paul here contends that one is separated from God because he has personally sinned. I formerly believed that I was separated from God because of Adam's sin; that his sin was transmitted father to son down to me, that I was held accountable for Adam's transgression, that I was born "bearing the image of the devil," as Wesley contended.

Let us consider this matter of depravity from another point of view. Truly the rule is a poor one that will not work both ways. It has been asserted that the son inherits "the image of the devil" from his father. But what if the father has already been to the mourner's bench, "prayed through," received the "second blessing," and had the "image of the devil" eradicated from him before the child was born? He is then regarded as sinlessly perfect, according to Nazarene theology. The child cannot therefore inherit "the image of the devil" from his father, because the father's sinful nature had been destroyed! Furthermore, if we can inherit a sinful nature, why cannot we inherit a righteous nature? If a child is born of a Nazarene parent who has had sin "eradicated," and is in a state of sinless perfection, why cannot that child inherit this sinless nature? Is damnation the only thing to be inherited from the parent? If moral character were hereditary, it would be as easy to inherit salvation as damnation! Further still, if moral character were hereditary we would frequently witness an even more complicated situation. If one parent were sanctified (perfect), and the other parent still retained "the image of the devil," then the child would be a spiritual enigma—half saint and half devil! But I'm sure Nazarenes would not accept this conclusion. Yet this logically demonstrates that moral character is not transmissible.

SANCTIFICATION

The second doctrine we shall examine here is that of sanctification. This is the second step taken in following the course of Wesleyan "holiness." The doctrine of sanctification, as we mentioned, became necessary because of the first doctrine, inbred sin. If one were born bearing the "image of the devil," there must of necessity be some means of removing this image before one could obtain heaven. To fulfill this need, the "holiness" advocates produced the doctrine of entire sanctification, which is also called "the second blessing," "the experience of grace," "the fulness of the blessing," and many such kindred expressions. According to Nazarene theology, a person goes to the mourner's bench to pray away his past, personal sins. (And I remind you, my friends, that I am speaking from personal experience. I sometimes say that I "cut my teeth" on a Nazarene mourner's bench!) This is the first "blessing," the first "helping" of salvation. But God hasn't completed his work in this first experience, and they must return again to seek the "second blessing." The first experience at the mourner's bench prays them "through" to salvation from *their* sins, and then they have to return to the "bench" for God to pardon them of *Adam's* sin! That is sanctification in a nutshell, according to their concept of it. I quote again from the Nazarene manual: "We believe that entire sanctification is that act of God, subsequent to regeneration, by which believers are made free from original sin or depravity, and are brought into a state of entire devotement to God, unto the holy obedience of love made perfect. It is wrought by the baptism of the Holy Spirit, and comprehends in one experience the cleansing of the heart from sin, the abiding and indwelling experience of the Holy Spirit, empowering the believer to life and service." (*Manual*, page 29) Now, let us consider the complications of such a theory. According to this doctrine a person is first "regenerated" and then later "sanctified." Before obtaining this "second blessing" this would make one a child of God, regenerated, but still bearing "the image of the devil!" According to the theory, one is a believer while still possessed of "original sin or depravity," since this experience "eradicates" these from the believer. I suppose we are to look upon the regenerate, who has not yet obtained sanctification, as a "depraved believer!" The doctrine also has a person regenerated, not having as yet his heart cleansed from sin. But there is no such idea in the scriptures as a regeneration which does not cleanse the heart from sin! Furthermore, the theory avers that sanctification empowers the believer to life and service. I suppose then that before sanctification one is a believer without life or service! These are ridiculous and absurd, as well as manifestly unscriptural. The Bible denies and refutes such theological concoctions. I again charge this doctrine to be but a figment of John Wesley's imagination! There is not a single syllable of scripture that suggests such a doctrine.

The English verb "sanctify" is translated from the Greek "hagiazo." Thayer, a peerless and universally accepted Greek scholar, defines "hagiazo" in this manner: "To render sacred or holy, to consecrate, to render or to acknowledge to be venerable, to hallow, to separate from things profane and dedicate to God, to purify by expiation, to purify internally by a reformation of the soul." (*Greek-English Lexicon*, Joseph H. Thayer, page 6). Personally, I prefer the expression, "to separate from things profane, and dedicate to God." That is a most appropriate definition of sanctification, as the idea is used throughout the Bible. Surely the Bible teaches the sanctification of God's children, but not at all according to Wesley's ideas. As people of God we are separated, a peculiar people, a holy nation. (I Peter 2:9). Most assuredly we are separated from the world, and dedicated to the service of God. We must separate ourselves from defilement, and touch not unclean things, for God to accept us. (II Cor. 6:17). This matter is stressed with great force in the Bible. But this is far removed from Wesley's ideas of sanctification.

The Bible explains how we are sanctified. Sanctification is effected by the offering of the blood of Christ. (Heb. 10:14). The Bible nowhere teaches that we are sanctified by a baptism of the Holy Spirit, as Nazarenes claim. The Holy Spirit never appeared directly to anyone to save or sanctify them, but Nazarenes assert that He does both. Let us consider another scripture: "Know ye not that the unrighteous shall not inherit the kingdom of God? Be not deceived: neither fornicators, nor idolators, nor adulterers, nor effeminate, nor abusers of themselves with mankind, nor thieves, nor covetous, nor drunkards, nor extortioners, shall inherit the kingdom of God. And such were some of you; but ye are washed, but ye are sanctified, but ye are justified in the name of the Lord Jesus, and by the Spirit of our God." (I Cor. 6:9-11). What happened, Paul? You were once in sin, engaged in these worldly practices, but now you are washed, sanctified and justified. Notice that order. That is not the Nazarene order of washing, sanctification and justification. The Nazarene order is: (1) Pray at the mourner's bench; (2) then you are justified, and (3) later, at a second "experience," you are sanctified. The divine order is: (1) "Washed" in the blood of the Lamb of God, (2) "sanctified," or set apart for God's service, and (3) "justified" or accepted with God. The apostle further shows how this separation from sin and dedication to God occurs. "God be thanked, that ye were the servants of sin, but ye have obeyed from the heart that form of doctrine which was delivered you. Being then made free from sin, ye became the servants of righteousness." (Romans 6:17-18). You were once the servants of sin, but obeyed from the heart the gospel of Christ, which *then* (not later) set you apart (sanctified you) unto the service of God. That is simple sanctification as expressed in the Bible.

SINLESS PERFECTION

The next doctrine in order is sinless perfection, which we have already defined. Simply speaking, sinless perfection is the product of sanctification. When one receives sanctification it enables him to live a sinlessly perfect life, according to Nazarene theology. Recently I heard of a Nazarene preacher who professed never to commit a sin. He claimed, "Since I have been sanctified, every impulse or desire to sin has been completely erased from my heart!" This is a claim which is consistent with Nazarene doctrine. They claim that their desire to perform sin is removed by sanctification. Yet the Nazarene church manual prescribes discipline to be exercised upon ones who live such "perfect" (?) lives, but who are found committing sin! Such a gross inconsistency! Every Nazarene preacher who is ordained must first experience sanctification, have all sin removed from his life, and testify that he is living sinlessly. But the manual also reveals how a Nazarene preacher can be disfellowshipped if he walks in sin! But, if in sanctification the "Adamic nature" is removed and I have absolutely no impulse to sin, if I do sin after that, then with what nature do I commit sin? It cannot be the Adamic nature, for that has already been "eradicated." It must therefore be my Christian nature which led me into sin! Yes, Nazarenes withdraw fellowship from those whose "Adamic nature" has been removed, and who have absolutely no desire, no impulse, to commit sin, but are guilty of sin anyhow! Such inconsistencies cannot be compatible with the scriptures.

What does the Bible teach in the matter of Christian perfection? There are numerous different senses in which the term "perfect" is used in the Bible. The term is used at times to signify absolute perfection, and at other times to suggest a relative perfection. When absolute moral perfection is meant, the term is always applied to God and never to man. When the term is applied to man, it is invariably suggestive of a relative perfection. The idea of man's absolute moral perfection, or sinlessness, is foreign to the Bible. In the matter of perfection, God is our flawless example which we cannot fully duplicate, but after Whom our lives are to be patterned. (Matt. 5:48). Paul used the term in both these senses. He disclaims absolute perfection (Phil. 3:12), but claims a relative perfection (Phil. 3:15). This is the only intelligent interpretation of these two passages. The term "perfect" is also used in still another manner in the Bible, to refer to spiritual maturity. Paul urged the Hebrew brethren to lay aside the first principles of the doctrine of Christ, and to go on unto perfection. (Hebrews 6:1).

The Bible denies that man can achieve absolute moral perfection in this life. As already cited, Paul disavowed perfection in the absolute sense. (Phil. 3:12). The writer of old claimed, "For there is no man that sinneth not." (I Kings 8:46) And further, "There is not a just man upon the earth that doeth good, and sinneth not." (Eccl. 7:20). These ought to

THE NAZARENE CHURCH 133

be conclusive. Yet Nazarene preachers claim, "I do good, and never have any impulse to sin!" But the Bible teaches that there is no such person!

How does one obtain perfection, or holiness? I would like to answer this with a personal experience. Last year I preached in a meeting in Oregon. One night at the close of the service a lady shook hands with me, and said, "Preacher, you do not believe in holiness, do you?" My reply was, "Surely, I do." She asked again, "Do you believe in the holiness of the child of God?" Again I replied, "Yes, I believe that." The next night there was submitted a written question which asked how a person received holiness. For an answer I turned to Ephesians 4:24, and read, "And put ye on the new man, which is after God created in righteousness and true holiness." This new man is created after God according to *true holiness,* and not the imaginary, hypothetical type for which Wesley contended. How does a person receive this holy nature? Paul said, "By putting on the new man." The apostle further instructed us as to how this "new man" is put on. (Romans 6:3-6). In this passage the apostle discusses water baptism as the consummating act of conversion, from which one arises "to walk in newness of life." In this completion of conversion, the old man is crucified, and one is raised to live unto God. (Verses 6, 10). Christian holiness is not therefore a "second work of grace," but is imparted at conversion. Holiness is received by putting on the "new man;" the "old man" is discarded, and the "new man" is received in conversion. Hence, holiness is received at conversion. There is therefore nothing mysterious in the meaning of holiness. It is synonymous with righteousness or godliness, which none would deny are received in conversion.

THE MOURNER'S BENCH

The last doctrine we shall review with you is that of mourner's bench salvation. Remove the mourner's bench from the Nazarene church and with this stroke you would inflict a mortal wound to their "holiness" doctrines. The mourner's bench cannot be divorced from all vital "holiness" doctrines; they are all dependent upon it. At the mourner's bench most of their vital spiritual transactions occur. It is at the mourner's bench they receive everything worthwhile in the "holiness" religion. It is there they "pray through" to salvation. It is there that they get the "second blessing." It is at the mourner's bench they pray for divine healing. It is at the bench that they pray for the salvation of their friends. It is there that they pray for a "spiritual revival"—great emotional demonstrations. Hence the mourner's bench is indispensable to "holiness" doctrines. If in closing we can show the impropriety of the mourner's bench, then all of their other doctrines shall fall with it.

The mourner's bench is without question the most ridiculous and absurd feature of the "holiness" religion. Let me illustrate how this is true. The preacher will preach for an hour or so. He injects all the vigor and vitality of his system into his sermon, convincing sinners, who stand perilously upon the brink of eternal doom, that if they will only decide to accept God that he will immediately save them. After the hour of persuasion, he finally convinces the sinner that he should be saved, and that God is willing to immediately save him. Sinners come in assurance of the fact that God is willing to save them, but they get to the mourner's bench only to find out that God has changed his mind! Instead of God saving them instantly, then now they must pray, scream, cry, and beg God to do what the preacher assured them He was already willing to do. When the sinner is out of the notion of being saved, and the preacher does all he can to get him into the notion of being saved, God is in the notion of saving the sinner. But when the sinner finally takes a notion to be saved, he then finds that God has changed His mind; he has now backed out! God, who was at first willing to save the sinner, must be begged to change his mind again, and return to a willingness or notion of saving the sinner! Such is the glaring absurdity of this doctrine.

To impress the unscripturalness of such a doctrine, I wish to file a number of charges and indictments against the mourner's bench system of salvation. (1) God has nowhere required the unregenerate, or alien sinner, to pray for the forgiveness of his sins. If anyone will confront me with just one verse of scripture which teaches, suggests, intimates, infers or implies that God has required the alien sinner to pray for the pardon of his sins, then I'll go back to a Nazarene mourner's bench! (2) Of all of the cases of conversion in the New Testament, especially in the book of Acts, no inspired gospel preacher ever urged a sinner to pray his sins away at a mourner's bench. Gospel preachers many times informed inquirers what to do to be saved. On Pentecost three thousand were saved. (Acts 2). But there is no record of a single prayer being uttered on Pentecost! The procedure was simple. The gospel was preached (verses 14-37), the hearers were exhorted to believe that Jesus is "both Lord and Christ" (verse 36), and they were commanded to repent and be baptized for the remission of their sins (verse 38). Those who did so were saved, and added unto the Lord's church. (Verse 47). Our "holiness" friends often pray for a reinactment of Pentecost, but they are not willing to follow these Pentecostal precedents. There was no mourner's bench there! (3) The mourner's bench places all the responsibility of salvation upon God, whereas man is responsible for accepting God's will. (Acts 2:40). Man is responsible to God for hearing and obeying the truth. The mourner's bench represents man as being passive, while God is active in conversion. This idea is foreign to the New Testament. Man is required to "save himself"—take an active, responsible, obedient part in his own conversion. (4) The mourner's bench represents God as being a respecter of persons. The Bible declares, however, that "with God there is no respect of persons." (Romans 2:11). God treats all men with equality; what he does for one, he will do for all.

I could not begin to estimate the number of times I have seen a Nazarene mourner's bench swarmed with "seekers" for salvation, and usually as many would go away not having found God as those who claimed to have found him there! I still read the Nazarene church paper, *The Herald of Holiness*. Nazarene preachers report to that paper the achievements of their revival meetings, and many times their reports indicate that there were more left "seeking" salvation at the mourner's bench than found it. Under the dispensation of grace, God does not refuse to save any who earnestly apply for the salvation He offers. The mourner's bench is therefore inadequate. It will not save all who need to be saved! The divine plan of salvation is offered to "all the world" and "every creature." (Mark 16:15).

(5) The mourner's bench, in a similar connection, implies that God is unwilling to save all who come to him. As already seen, many turn away from the mourner's bench disappointed and filled with despair, feeling that God will not save them. We have been cited a case in Tennessee where one man, after repeated and unsuccessful attempts to obtain "salvation" at a mourner's bench, went totally insane, and was committed to a state institution. The thought that God would not save his miserable soul was too much for this poor man. But whether it leads to this unusual extreme, the mourner's bench does nevertheless argue that God is not willing to save all who seek salvation. The Apostle Peter strongly denies this idea when he contended that the Lord is "not willing that any should perish, but that all should come to repentance." (II Peter 3:9). This can never be reconciled with the teaching of the mourner's bench.

(6) Saul of Tarsus was commanded to cease his fasting and prayer and complete his obedience to Christ. If God ever intended to teach that prayer and mourning obtains our salvation, the case of Saul would have offered the best opportunity in all the Word of God. But after having spent three days in fasting and prayer, he was asked by the inspired, Spirit-led preacher, "And now why tarriest thou? arise, and be baptized, and wash away thy sins, calling on the name of the Lord." (Acts 22:16). Had Ananias been a modern "Holiness" preacher, he would have said, "Pray on, Brother Saul, and you will 'get it' after while!" I have never known a Nazarene preacher instruct a mourner to do precisely what Ananias required of Saul! In the case of Saul, God amply demonstrated that he does not save by the mourner's bench method.

(7) The mourner's bench disregards the fact that it is useless to call upon the Lord without obeying him. Jesus asked, "And why call ye me, Lord, Lord, and do not the things which I say?" (Luke 6:46) Since the mourner has not completed his

obedience to the Lord (Acts 22:16), his tarrying in prayer is useless.

(8) Finally, the mourner's bench does not comply with God's plan of salvation. It is rather a system conceived as a substitute for obeying God's divinely revealed will to the sinner. In sending the apostles forth into all the world with the gospel, Jesus charged that they preach the gospel to every creature. He also gave the provisions of the gospel, commands for the sinner to obey: "He that believeth and is baptized shall be saved.—" (Mark 16:16) On the day of Pentecost, Peter commanded that countless throng: "Repent, and be baptized every one of you in the name of Jesus Christ for the remission of sins.—" (Acts 2:38) According to these revelations of inspiration, God requires the sinner to believe in Jesus Christ, repent of his sins, and be baptized for the remission of sins. Any system that does not incorporate these divine requirements is not of God but of men. Since the mourner's bench does not include all of these divine requirements, it is not then God's means of saving the sinner.

As we bring this lesson to an end, we deeply appreciate the undivided attention given us. You have listened most kindly and patiently, and I trust that your heart will be receptive to whatever truths it stands in need of. We are happy now to tender to you, my sinner friends, the invitation of Jesus Christ. Will you not at this time yield your hearts to the crucified Savior in obedience to the simple terms of the gospel. He is both ready and willing to save you; he will not turn you away! Dear friends, if you have never obeyed the truth of God, let it make you free tonight. Will you not thrust aside the shackles of sectarian bondage for the freedom of the truth. You may tonight be led out of the dismal, dark abyss of error, and into the marvelous, radiant light of the truth. Have you the courage just now to lay all aside for Christ, regardless of the cost? Will you not be unashamed to confess your Lord, though others may scoff and scorn you for doing so? The only unquestionably safe course for your soul is to take your station upon the simple teachings of the word of God, and forever reject the wisdom and councils of men in religion. If you'll live for Christ tonight by obeying him, he'll wash your soul from sin in his own blood, make you a new creature, a citizen of the kingdom of Christ, and give you hope of that blessed eternal inheritance in the celestial city of God.

CLAUDE A. GUILD

(A Biographical Sketch)

Born in Buffalo, Montana, May 9, 1916. He is the son of Mr. and Mrs. Charles A. Guild, Albany, Oregon. He attended the College of Idaho and Abilene Christian College, Abilene, Texas. He has a B. A. degree from the latter. He was a member of the Lutheran Church, Norwegian Synod. He obeyed the gospel of Christ under the preaching of J. C. Bailey, Radville, Sask. He was married to Sammie LaRue Lacy, Altus, Oklahoma, March 22, 1939. (She was a student of A. C. C.) They have four children. He has done evangelistic work in Washington, Oregon, California, Idaho, Wyoming, Colorado, Montana, New Mexico, Texas, Okla., Alaska, British Columbia and Saskatchewan, Canada.

At the present time he is laboring as evangelist for the church of Christ in Riverside, Fort Worth, Texas.

Why I Left The Lutheran Church

CLAUDE GUILD

Let me say it is good to be here, see this house filled, have part in this series of lectures, and to speak to you especially upon this subject assigned videlicet; "Why I Left The Lutheran Church."

BOOKLET ON "WHY WE LEFT"

The little booklet which Brother Campbell announced is entitled "Why We Left The Lutheran Church", and already some have made inquiry as to the "We." By that I mean my immediate family: my father and mother, myself and my brothers and sisters. And it's a pretty good crowd because there are ten children in our family.

INTRODUCTION

Tonight, in our study together, I think it well that we read a passage of scripture as an introduction to our lesson, and I would have you listen, please, as we read from 1st Peter 3, beginning with verse 13: "And who is he that will harm you, if ye be zealous of that which is good? But even if ye should suffer for righteousness' sake, blessed are ye: and fear not their fear, neither be troubled; but sanctify in your hearts Christ as Lord: being ready always to give answer to every man that asketh you a reason concerning the hope that is within you, yet with meekness and fear; having a good conscience; that, wherein ye are spoken against, they may be put to shame who revile your good manner of life in Christ. For it is better, if the will of God so will, that ye suffer for well-doing than for evil-doing."

SETTING FOR CHANGE MADE

I think it well, before we enter into the doctrinal differences, and some of the major differences why we left the Lutheran Church, that I give you a little historical background to the setting of the change we made. The only regret that I have about a lesson like this is that the personal pronoun has to be used. But I know, of a necessity, that when a subject like this is assigned, that it just has to be, so we will go ahead and use it. My mother's people were Norwegians. That's no reflection on my mother either, I'll have you know. The Swedes might disagree with me. But, anyway, her father and mother and oldest brother and sister were born in Norway. They came to America and settled in Minnesota, and while there, she, with other children, was born into the family; and, of course, coming from Scandinavian countries, they being wholly, almost so, Lutheran people, they inherited, so to speak, their religion. While they lived in Minnesota, they were members of the Lutheran Church, and in particular, of the Norwegian Synod. When mother married father, he wasn't anything religiously, but she was zealous after her father's religion, or her parents' religion, and she was determined that father would become a Lutheran. Hence, he consented to read before the minister for eighteen months before becoming a Lutheran; then he became a member of the Lutheran Church. After that, they moved westward to the state of Montana, where they homesteaded, and to that union were born ten children. While we lived then in Montana, we were still in a Norwegian community, and we were still in the Norwegian Synod, and my mother for a long time was superintendent of this particular Lutheran Church, in its Sunday School work.

MOTHER'S DISSATISFACTION

But to bring the historical setting for our lesson tonight, just as briefly as we can, to its climax, I'll tell you this; while we were living there, that is, in Montana, my mother became seriously ill and was taken to the hospital. Those months that she stayed—nine in number—in the hospital, she read her Bible. Not only did she read her Bible, but she called the minister of the Lutheran Church several times for confession. Each time she called him for confession, there were a number of questions she would ask him. The thing that she was primarily interested in was, not only her own soul (since seven doctors said she couldn't live), but in her little children left out on the homestead. She wanted to know that she had done the right thing by us. And I'll name in our lesson tonight some things in particular which she had in mind. I name just one of them now and that is this: We had all been sprinkled when little babies, at the age of eight days, and she wanted to be sure that she had done the right thing. And in her conversing with the Lutheran minister about these things in Lewistown, Montana, in the hospital, he answered her the very best he could—and he has my sympathies, because I speak the truth and lie not, he did the very best he could with what he had. But in answering my mother, it brought no satisfaction, because his answer would usually end up something like this: "Now, that's all right. I know, I know it's confusing to me, too, but after a while, when we all get over yonder, these things will be made plain." But mother was not satisfied to wait until she got over there to make it plain. She thought that perhaps she could understand some of these things while she lived and while she had an opportunity to do something about it. On the third visit from the minister to my mother in the hospital for confession, she was still reading the Bible. When she wasn't able to read it, father would read it to her. She was seeking and searching for the things that were of interest and that were perplexing to her. On the third visit of the minister for confession, she ask him again questions relative to the things that disturbed her. His answer was this (this was the last time he visited her): "Good woman, if you don't quit reading that Bible, you are going to go crazy." Well, having been in the hospital several months already, and under the condition she was there, finding no religious satisfaction, seven doctors saying she couldn't live and leaving us little children out on the homestead, made my mother determined more than ever to live. And she put up a determined fight. It wasn't long after that till she made a turn for the better, and she began to get strength, and stronger day by day. Finally she was dismissed from the hospital and came back out to the homestead where we were. Though not able to do her work, she was able to be about a little, and all the time here at home she prayed.

J. C. BAILEY INSTRUMENTAL IN CHANGE

Brother J. C. Bailey, who came from Saskatchewan to preach the unsearchable riches of Christ to us in Montana, related this in the Abilene lectures and in Corsicana last winter, when he was there; how my mother told him, as I have heard her say many, many times, the reason she would leave the house and walk along the timberline in the foothills that bordered our pasture, our land, was to pray earnestly that somehow, somewhere, we might learn the truth and what's right with reference to God and things religious. And you'd have a hard time persuading my mother, and I join ranks with her, to believe that God did not hear nor answer her prayers. I am of the conviction tonight, that as surely as God heard and answered the prayer of Cornelius in Acts the tenth chapter, he heard and answered the prayers of my mother.

UNUSUAL PREACHING

That fall, there was a call that came on the old country telephone that there was going to be preaching down in the schoolhouse. They didn't know just what stripe or color or kind it was, but it was different to anything we had been hearing, and they were sending the invitation around. Mother and father would not let us children go the first night, for they wanted to see and hear for themselves. The first night my parents heard something that they had never heard before. They heard the gospel preached in an unadulterated way, just as it is written in the word of God. And, at the end of the first service, my mother went to Brother J. C. Bailey, and asked him about infant baptism, and said she'd like to know if there is any passage in the Bible that would authorize it. He said, "Good woman, you go home tonight, and you search your Bible. If you can find infant baptism in your Bible and show me just one passage, one will satisfy me, I'll be sprinkled and be a Lutheran preacher the rest of my life. If you can't find it in your Bible, I'll show it to you in the catechism; and in turn, I'll want you then, when it is not found in the Bible, to be immersed for the remission of sins and become a Christian."

SEARCHING THE SCRIPTURES

My folks had searched the Bible, not only that night, but many nights before that, and months before that, but this was the first time that it had ever dawned upon us that there were contradictions between these two books, the Bible and the Lutheran Catechism. We had been taught to believe that this book simply made the Bible plain, that you had to understand the Bible through reading of this volume. To memorize the articles of the Catechism was essential to the understanding of the word of God. This was the first time that it had dawned on us that the two might conflict, or contradict each other. At the close of the second service, Brother Bailey showed the conflict between the two volumes, and with which contrast tonight, I hope I can satisfy your minds, too.

OBEDIENCE TO THE GOSPEL

The next night, after my mother heard the third gospel sermon, she came forward and made the good confession. A man living in the community by the name of C. V. Barnhart took a triple-bed wagon box and dammed up the creek so there could be water for immersion. While the water was rising, and during the time she was being baptized, my mother's father—my own grandfather—her own brothers and neighbors, who had religious affiliation with the same institution, rode on horses around the baptismal scene and cursed and swore. But my mother continued in the baptismal, was baptized by Brother Bailey in the name of the Father, the Son and the Holy Spirit for the remission of sins, and has never given up the faith to this good day. She is strong and living to this good night. Thank God for that.

EFFORT TO SAVE OTHERS

After that, Brother Bailey wanted to see my father become a Christian too. He said, "Listen, I didn't get to make up my mind the first time. She led me before the minister and I had to read before him eighteen months to become a Lutheran, and this time I'm going to make up my own mind." I may be a little of the disposition of my father, but, anyhow my father was going to make up his own mind in this thing. He was running coal mines. Brother J. C. Bailey took off his white collar, went into the coal mines with my father and mined coal for six weeks. But he had other things in mind beside mining coal by tonnage and making a wage. While he mined, he preached to my father; and after six weeks he baptized him; and along with baptizing my father, he baptized my oldest brother and sister and myself. Since that good day, including my baby brother who was baptized into Christ just about ten days ago, my entire family—father and mother and the ten children—all have been baptized into Christ. And there, if you please, is just a little historical background to the reasons why we left the Lutheran Church.

REASONS FOR CHANGE MADE

But this is not sufficient. I know that. I believe that I need to give you tonight some one-two-three reasons why we made the change that we made. We firmly believe that in the change we made we came from darkness into light. And the things I am saying tonight, I am saying with all the kindness I can command toward those who are still in darkness. I believe I can sympathize with the disposition of heart with people who are still in error, who have never heard the gospel preached purely, as it is written. And that people tonight has my sympathies; but along with that, let me say: I fear no contradiction of anything we may have to say tonight. We have preached these same things from Ketchikan, Alaska, to Corsicana, Texas. I have preached it with Lutheran preachers on the front seats. It would be my humble prayer, my earnest request, that all Lutherans who would be interested in a lesson like this, be present, and if anyone has anything to say, or wants to take issue with anything we have to say tonight, I believe it would be fair, Brother Campbell, to open the house and give them any amount of time they want after the lecture. And that bargain stands good tonight, and it will stand good tomorrow night, or a week from tomorrow night, or just any time you want to arrange the meeting. We have no fear of anything I have to say, nor am I ashamed of anything I have to say.

HUMAN FOUNDATION OF LUTHERANISM

Here is reason number one why we left the Lutheran Church: The foundation of Lutheranism is human and not divine. If you can't understand that language, let me say it in a little different way: The foundation of Lutheranism is on humanity, rather than on Jesus Christ the Son of God. It was founded on a human being, an individual by the name of Martin Luther, rather than on the foundation of Jesus Christ. Listen to me, there never was heard of, or read of, a Lutheran Church until All-Saints Day on October 31, 1517, in Whittenberg, Germany. To be specific, there never was a Lutheran Church until 431 years and two days ago from tonight. There never was. But I note that New Testament language reads like this: "Upon this rock I will build my church," said Jesus in Matt. 16:18. The Lord spake this language in the year 32 A. D. Then I go to Acts 20:28, Paul to the elders of Ephesus, down at the sea-shore of Miletus, said: "Feed the church of the Lord which he has purchased with his own blood." Two things in that verse make me believe that the church was in existence in the year 60 A. D., the time that Paul spoke this to the elders of Ephesus down at the sea-shore of Miletus. One reason, Paul said, "Feed the church," and you can't feed something that doesn't exist; the other reason is, Paul said, "Which he has purchased with his own blood." It was a thing of the past; it had already been purchased. Somewhere between 60 A. D. and 32 A. D. the Lord Jesus had built his church.

INSTITUTION OF LORD'S CHURCH

I then take you to the language of Acts according to the historian, Luke, in the second chapter, verse forty-seven: "And the Lord (watch it) added to the church daily such as were being saved." There, if you please, is the first time the church is spoken of as an existing institution. And that took place on the first Pentecost after the resurrection of Jesus Christ, in the year A. D. 33. And when we search the scriptures, we find what the word of God teaches as to the establishment of the Church. Jesus Christ established his church in the year 33 A. D., on the first Pentecost after the resurrection. And more than that, he is the foundation of it. In 1 Cor. 3:11, Paul says: "Other foundation can no man lay than that is laid, which is Jesus Christ." And since the apostle Paul says that Jesus Christ is the foundation of the church, I am persuaded that no human institution, bearing a human name, including the institution that I had my affiliation with, viz., the Lutheran Church, could be the New Testament church.

"LUTHERAN" AN UNSCRIPTURAL NAME

The second reason why we left the Lutheran Church was because it is unscriptural in its name. In Acts 26:28, 29, when Paul preached before Agrippa, Agrippa said: "Paul, almost thou persuadest me to be a Christian." Paul answered: "I would to God, that not only thou, but all men were even as I am except these bonds." In other words, Paul wanted all men to be what he was; and what was he? A Christian. Peter, the one from whom we got our text tonight, declared in 1 Pet. 4:16: "If any man suffer as a Christian, let him not be ashamed, but let him glorify God in this name." And I dare tell you that in Sunday school, and up until the time of confirmation for me (and had I prolonged my life in the Lutheran Church any longer), to every time I heard individuals called Christians, I could name a hundred times they were called Lutherans, or a proportion of 100 to 1. You never hear people in sectarianism talking about, "I am a Christian," or "We are Christians." But rather you hear, "I am a Lutheran." or "I am a Baptist." or "I am a Methodist." "Whatever you do in word or deed, do all in the name of the Lord Jesus." Col. 3:17. And the name that individuals wore in New Testament time was Christian.

SCRIPTURAL DESIGNATIONS

The church itself, in a local sense, as a local body, the "called out," was called the church. But with reference to whose church it was, it was called "the church of Christ." Rom. 16:16. Paul said: "The churches of Christ salute you." In Acts 20:28, he said: "Feed the church of the Lord which he purchased with his own blood." And Jesus, confessed by Peter to be the Christ, the Son of the living God, said: "Upon this rock I will build MY church." Hence, it is the church of Christ. It is not the church of Luther. It is not the church of any man, or any group of men, or any group of men and women, but it is the church of Jesus Christ. You know this is true; I say it without fear of contradiction. If tonight we would destroy the Lutheran Church, though it is not in our power to do that but some day every foreign plant which our Father has not planted shall be rooted up, for Jesus said: "Every plant which my heavenly Father hath not planted shall be rooted up." The way to do it, I believe with all my heart, would be to destroy the creed of the institution. If you would want forever to lose the name Lutheran in the religious world, you destroy the Lutheran Catechism. Because it is in this volume that you read the name Luther and the name Lutheran, and it is not in THIS VOLUME, the Bible. That is one of the things that perplexed us; we were continuously disturbed about that thing. Who is Luther? What is the name Lutheran? As we would search the sacred record, there was not anything there that would indicate the wearing of any name likened unto that. It was the name of Christ that needed to be honored. I dare to say it again: if you, tonight, would destroy Lutheranism, it would be by the destruction of the creed that bears the name, the name that is not in this volume here, the Bible.

MAN-MADE CREED OF LUTHERANISM

The third reason why we left the Lutheran Church is because it walks by a man-made creed. So that you may not think I am misrepresenting Lutheranism, I brought with me a volume, presented to those in confirmation into the Lutheran Church, published by a Lutheran publishing house. The author of this book is Dr. Schramm, and it was published by a Lutheran book concern in Columbus, Ohio. The title of the book is "What Lutherans Believe," and this is it, as it is stated on page 14: "We who are Lutherans prize our Catechism as one of the crown jewels of our church. It is a summary of heavenly truth presented in a most desirable manner. It is simple, yet profound. While it is adapted to the mind of the child, it also meets the needs of the mature Christian. Only eternity will reveal the service which this priceless book has rendered to the kingdom of God." Now are you listening? Listen to this: *"It is intended as a help to understand the Bible.* It is a systematic arrangement of Bible teaching. Because these doctrines are presented in groups, they are easy to lay hold of. Thus, the work of the study is simplified." And we read another statement from Dr. Schramm on page 14: "It is intended (that is, the Catechism) as a help to study and understand the Bible." Friend of mine, I am persuaded to believe that when people—whether an individual who speaks as the voice for the church or the church speaking for itself—make a declaration like this which I have read tonight, viz., that a catechism has to be written to help people understand the Bible, it is an insult to God Almighty. Now, I'll have to explain what I am explaining. I believe this, my friends, that God is the author of this volume. Not only God is the author of this volume, but God is the Creator of this, his creation, humanity, mankind. God made our minds, and he made the Book, the Testament, the Bible. I believe that God made a volume that we as people can understand. And for a group of people to get together in a council, or convention, or synod, and write a catechism to make the Bible plain is an insult to God Almighty.

ALL-SUFFICIENCY OF THE SCRIPTURES

Now, I'll tell you another reason why I just can't accept a statement like this, that we need a man-made creed to make the Bible plain. Listen to Paul in II Tim. 3:16, 17: "Every scripture given by inspiration of God, is profitable for teaching, for reproof, for correction, for instruction which is in righteousness: that the man of God may be complete, furnished completely unto every good work." The Bible will furnish you completely unto every good work. I remember the language of Isaiah, Isa. 35:8: "And an highway shall be there, and a way, and it shall be called the way of holiness; the unclean shall not pass over it; but it shall be for the redeemed, the wayfaring man, yea fools, shall not err therein." Yet, I find folks saying, "We need a human creed, a catechism, to make God plain, so that we will be able to understand what God says." There is just one thing wrong with that—it's just not so. Listen to the language in 2 Cor. 2:17: "For we are not as the many, corrupting the word of God; but as of sincerity, but as of God, in the sight of God, speak we in Christ." And, if an individual speaks in Christ, he is going to have to speak according to the word of God, and not according to the catechism. John declared, "Whosoever goeth onward and abideth not in the teaching of Christ hath not God." And then he said, "if you abide in the teaching, you have both the Father and the Son." 2 Jno. 9. That's another reason we left the Lutheran Church, because they walk by a man-made creed.

TEN COMMANDMENTS MISAPPLIED AND VIOLATED

The next reason why we left the Lutheran Church was because they misapply and violate the Ten Commandments. According to Article 21, in Questions and Answers of the Catechism, I read: "What is the moral law? Answer: The moral law is the law which sets forth our duties to God and man as briefly comprehended in the Ten Commandments." Now the answer to question number 22, "What is the Moral Law?" "The moral law is the Ten Commandments and it is binding on all men." Now to show you that that is exactly the position, Dr. Schramm says on page 17, in "What Lutherans Believe": "It is a common thing to speak of this law as having been given by Moses on Mount Sinai some 35 centuries ago. As a matter of fact, the first giving of the law took place in the Garden of Eden. When God created our first parents, he wrote his law upon their hearts. It was not necessary for Adam to learn the Ten Commandments." Dr. Schramm says, "Our first parents had the Ten Commandments." They didn't have to learn them because God wrote them on their hearts! I am persuaded, because of inspiration, that Adam never had the Ten Commandments; they were never given to Adam and I'll tell you why, because Moses said he never had them. Deut. 5:2: "Jehovah God made a covenant with us in Horeb (speaking to the Israelites); he made not this covenant with our fathers but with us, even us, who are all of us here alive this day." Again, Ex. 20:1, 2: "I am Jehovah thy God who brought thee out of the land of Egypt, out of the house of bondage." Then, beginning with the third verse, he gives them the Ten Commandments: "Thou shalt have no other gods before me. Thou shalt not make unto thee any graven images. . . . ." And on and on and on.

Notice again, to whom were the Ten Commandments given? To those who were in the land of Egypt, to those who were in the house of bondage. Adam was never in the land of Egypt; he was never in the house of bondage. Noah was never there, Abraham was never there, Isaac was never there, Jacob was never there. It was not until the Israelites were brought out and made a nation that the Ten Commandment law was given. So Lutherans misapply the Ten Commandments, and say that it is for all men—meaning that we are to keep it. And that is what they taught us.

To teach that we are to keep the Ten Commandments today is a misapplication of the Ten Commandments. Listen to God's prophet, Jer. 31:31: "Behold the days come saith the Lord, when I will make a new covenant with the house of Israel and with the house of Judah, not acording to the covenant that I made with their fathers in the day that I took them by the hand to lead them out of the land of Egypt." God promised through the prophet Jeremiah that he would make a new covenant with his people. (The same language is found in Heb. 8:8). If he was to make a new one, how long was the old one to last? Listen to the language of Paul in Gal. 3:19: "What then was the law? It was added because of transgressions until the seed should come." Hence, we know that the law was to last till the seed should come. Who is the seed, then? In the sixteenth verse of the same chapter of Galatians, Paul says, "Now unto Abraham were the promises spoken, and to his seed. He said not, And to seeds, as of many; but as of one, And to Thy seed, which is Christ." Hence, the law was to last till the seed should come, but the seed was Christ. So, the law was to last until Christ came. When Jesus came, what did he say about the law? In Matt. 5:17, he said: "Think not that I am come to destroy the law, or the prophets: I am not come to destroy, but to fulfill." Jesus said when he died on the cross, "It is finished." And I am persuaded one thing he had in mind was the Old Law. Its purpose was accomplished, fulfilled, finished, because Col. 2:14, says: "Having blotted out the handwriting of ordinances that was against us, which was contrary to us, and taking it out of the way, nailing it to his cross." The Law, which included the Ten Commandments, was nailed to the cross. Hence, it is not for all peoples. The Ten Commandments were not observed by Adam and Eve in the beginning. They have been nailed to the cross, and we were given a covenant that was a better covenant, not a national testament, but an international testament. The Great Commission says, "Go teach all nations."

SPECIFIC VIOLATION

Not only do they misapply, but they violate the Ten Commandments. Notice, Lutherans teach that you are to keep the Ten Commandments. But they have misapplied it when they teach people in this dispensation to keep them. But just assume that we are to keep the Ten Commandments. If they are to keep them, they violate the fourth commandment, because it says: "Remember the Sabbath day to keep it holy." "Six days shalt thou labor and do all thy work, but the seventh day is the Sabbath of the Lord." How many Lutherans today are keeping the seventh day? You will not find them doing it. And it can't be a Christian Sabbath, changed from the seventh day to the first day of the week. But I insist, if the Lutheran people are going to keep the Ten Commandments, let's see them keep them. I have more respect for Seventh-Day-Adventism than I do for Lutheranism. They insist that the law must be kept, the Ten Commandment law; and they are, at least, consistent in this point and are keeping the Sabbath. Lutherans are not keeping the Ten Commandments; they are misapplying them and violating them.

INFANT BAPTISM AND SPRINKLING

The next reason why we left the Lutheran Church was because they teach infant baptism and sprinkling. According to Dr. Schramm on page 136: "We recognize any mode of baptism in which water is applied in the name of the Father, Son and the Holy Spirit, whether it be by immersion, or pouring, or sprinkling." Now, that's exactly the position taken by Lutherans. They recognize any mode of baptism. This is the thing in paticular that disturbed my mother. Was she sure that she had done the right thing by her children in having them sprinkled? The Lutherans teach that you can have any one of the three modes of baptism, sprinkling, pouring or immersion. But listen, the first thing that worried us was the word "mode." We just didn't read the word "mode" in the Bible. There is no such thing, according to inspiration. The Bible doesn't suggest, nor intimate, nor is there an inference, that there can be "modes" of baptism. Note the language of Paul in Eph. 4:4, 5: "There is one body and one Spirit, even as you are called in one hope of your calling, one Lord, one faith, one baptism, one God and Father of all, who is over all, in all and through all." Since Paul said, There is ONE, we became distressed, because the Lutheran Church was offering three.

When it came to infant baptism, this disturbed us, because we read Mk. 16:16: "He that believeth and is baptized shall be saved." A baby eight days old is not old enough to believe that Jesus Christ is the Son of God. But he has to be old enough to accept testimony, or reject testimony; and finally when he becomes old enough to accept testimony and becomes a believer, then Jesus says he can be baptized. Acts 2:38 disturbed us, because it says, "Repent and be baptized every one of you, in the name of Jesus Christ, for the remission of sins." That baby has to be old enough to know that it is turning from sin, if it is a sinner. And we understand that a baby eight days old is not old enough to turn from sin. Acts 8:12 disturbed us, because it says, "When they believed Philip teaching the things concerning the kingdom of God and the name of Jesus Christ, they were baptized both men and women." If, in all inspiration, there was to be a convenient place for infant baptism to be taught, there is where it ought to have been recorded. And it would read: "When they believed Philip teaching the things concerning the kingdom of God and the name of Jesus Christ, they were baptized, men, women and infants." The word "infants" should have been inserted, if the Book taught it, but it's not there! It says, "both men and women."

We had some trouble, so we came to Matt. 28:18-20. Jesus says, "All authority has been given unto me." He then is the authority, has the authority in heaven and on earth. He said, "Go teach all nations, baptizing them." Baptizing whom? The ones who have been taught. After they had been baptized, they were to be taught "to observe all things whatsoever I have commanded you." Infants are not old enough to receive instruction.

John 3:23 was another passage: "John baptized in Aenon, near to Salem, because there was much water there." As long as we were in the Lutheran Church, they taught that you could have sprinkling, pouring or immersion, but we never one time saw a baptism by immersion. It was always applied by sprinkling.

Another thing that caused us to disbelieve in infant baptism was the statement of Rom. 6:4: "We were buried by baptism into death, that like as Christ was raised up through the glory of the Father, we also might walk in newness of life." So baptism, described by Paul, is a burial.

INFANT MEMBERSHIP IN THE ROOM OF CIRCUMCISION

But now I need to tell you the very reason they taught infant baptism. Dr. Schramm tells us on page 141 in his volume on "What Lutherans Believe": " In the Old Testament, circumcision was the sacrament of initiation. It was administered to the boy babies when they were eight days of age. If God could make a covenant with a baby in the Old Testament, certainly he can and does the same things in this new dispensation. Accordingly, we conclude, that since baptism has taken the place of circumcision, babies should be baptized." Now I want you to note with emphasis, this language: "If God could make a covenant with a baby in the Old Testament, certainly he can and does the same things in the New Dispensation." I want to ask Dr. Schramm, or any of his cohorts tonight, Where is the chapter and verse for it? The thing that disturbed our immediate family was this: Dr. Schramm says that circumcision was aptly applied to the boy babies in the Old Testament and that baptism has taken the place of circumcision. We ran into some difficulties, because of the ten children in our family, six of them happened to be girls. Then to add injury to insult, the Lutheran preacher sprinkled my sisters as well as my brothers. And if infant baptism is to take the place of circumcision in the Old Testament, where is the authority for sprinkling girl babies? And that's one reason why we left the Lutheran Church!

TOTAL DEPRAVITY

Most of the denominational world tonight practices infant baptism. But why? Because, before the practice of infant baptism there came the cursed doctrine upon the earth that an infant was born totally depraved, that it was born in sin, having inherited it from its father or its mother. Sin is inherited? I remember a proverb that Israel was using and that God rebuked them for having. In Ezk. 18:1, 2, God says through his prophet: "You will have no more occasion to use this proverb in Israel any more." What was the proverb they were using? It was the same that the Lutherans are using with reference to inherited sin. The Israelites were saying: "The fathers have eaten sour grapes and the children's teeth are set on edge." God says that you will have no more occasion to use this proverb in Israel. How many of you have eaten sour grapes? Did you ever eat sour grapes and go home and find your children's teeth set on edge? That's not the way the grapes I ate did our family. But God says, mark it friend of mine, that you will have no more occasion to use this proverb in Israel. To capitalize on it, in the 20th verse of the same chapter, God declares: The son shall not bear the iniquity of the father, nor shall the father bear the iniquity of the son. But the righteousness of the righteous shall be upon him, and the wickedness of the wicked shall be upon him." That is plain enough for those tonight who are sincerely seeking the way to heaven.

If sin is inherited, does it come through the flesh? If it comes through the flesh, watch out! You make Jesus Christ a sinner because he was born of the flesh. Jno. 1:14 says, "The word became flesh and dwelt among us, and we beheld his glory, as of the glory of the only begotten of the Father, full of grace and truth." Whatever was full of grace and truth was the word that became flesh. But in the 17th verse of the same chapter, he says: "The Law came by Moses, but grace and truth came by Jesus Christ." Jesus Christ was grace and truth, but grace and truth was that which became flesh. Since Jesus Christ became flesh, if sin comes through flesh, is handed down from parent to child, you of necessity make Jesus a sinner when you teach your doctrine of inherited sin. But if you say, "No, preacher, it comes through the spirit," watch out, for I read in Heb. 12:9, where Paul says, "should we not much rather be in subjection to the Father of spirits and live?" God is the Father of our spirits. And if sin comes through the spirit, it makes God a sinner. And this is another reason why we left the Lutheran Church.

FALSE TEACHING ABOUT LORD'S SUPPER

We left the Lutheran Church because they misinformed us about the Lord's Supper. Hear from the Lutheran Catechism, page 19: "What is the sacrament of the altar? Answer: It is the true body and blood of Jesus Christ, under the bread and wine, given unto us Christians to eat and drink as it was instituted by Christ himself." Dr. Schramm will show you a little further on this thing. Isn't this peculiar? They had to write the Catechism to explain the Bible, but then they had to have Dr. Schramm to write "What Lutherans Believe" to explain what the Catechism says. I don't know if they are ever going to get explained what they are going to explain. But this is what Dr. Schramm says about the Lord's Supper: "We Lutherans insist that both the bread and wine, and the body and blood of Christ be received by every communicant at the Lord's Supper." That is, with the bread and wine, you receive the body and blood of Jesus Christ. They tell you that the doctrine of consubstantiation is scriptural. It is a primitive hangover from Catholicism.

The Catholics teach transubstantiation, which means that when the bread has been blessed, it actually becomes his body, and when the cup has been blessed, it actually becomes his blood. Luther didn't like that, so he, rather than say that it actually becomes the body and blood, said, "With and under the bread is the body, and with and under the cup is the blood." And in the Lutheran Church to this day, there is a great division in the body of Lutheran people, some wanting to hold to the doctrine of transubstantiation while others are resorting to the doctrine of consubstantiation. Really, the only difference in the teaching of Catholicism and the teaching of Lutheranism is this: The Catholics come out and say that it is his body and his blood, but Lutherans say that with and under it is his body and blood. The Catholics say that it really is; the Lutherans say with and under. They make a sandwich out of it. Now listen, my friends, that's amusing, but you can't laugh the truth of this down.

Though Jesus said in Matt. 26, Mk. 14, Lk. 22, and Paul stated in 1 Cor. 11 that "this is my body", people just fail to understand the simplicity of the language of the Son of God as it is used in personification. If you can't understand that, how are you going to understand John 10? Jesus said: "I am the door." Did Jesus mean that he was made out of two-by-fours? I read John 15:1-6 where Jesus said: "I am the vine." Are you going to take him literally? Do you believe that he meant that about this season of the year he was going to lose his leaf, be barren for the winter, then each spring leaf out again and bear fruit? You can understand that he used concrete things for persons. In other words, he personified the language, when he saw the cup, the fruit of the vine, and the unleavened bread and said, "This is my body; this is my blood." We were misinformed with reference to the Lord's Supper.

THE CONFESSIONAL BOX

Next to the last reason why we left the Lutheran Church, we had to make a confession to the pastor. It, too, is a primitive hangover from Catholicism. Listen to the Catechism, page 18: "What is confession? Answer: Confession consists of two parts: the one is, that we confess our sins; the other, that we receive absolution or forgiveness through the pastor as of God himself, in no wise doubting, but believing that our sins are thus forgiven before God in heaven." And three times during those long, long months while my mother was in the hospital, the preacher came and she made confession through him, as through God himself, believing that she received the absolution, or forgiveness, of her sins.

THE LUTHERAN CHURCH

When we came into the marvelous light, we learned the truth on this subject from such passages as I Jno. 2:1, 2: "My little children, these things write I unto you that you sin not; but if any man sin, we have an Advocate with the Father, even the pastor." Is that what it says? Not at all! John says "we have an Advocate with the Father, even Jesus Christ, who is the propitiation, not only for our sins, but also for the whole world." Who is our Advocate? Who is our Intercessor? It is Jesus Christ, the Son of God. We ceased that foolishness, then, of going to confession to the pastor, confessing to him and expecting to receive the forgiveness of sins as from God himself.

FALSE TEACHING ABOUT CONVERSION

Here is the last reason, and then we are through. We left the Lutheran Church because they did not teach the truth on conversion. They taught us conversion was "justification by faith only." Listen to Dr. Schramm again: "The Lutheran Church has always, quite properly, given a great deal of prominence to this doctrine, viz., justification by faith only." And he didn't just state it mildly; he stated it in full. I dare tell you that this is right, that in the Lutheran Church they do give a great deal of prominence to the doctrine of "justification by faith only." They teach, like they do in the Baptist Church, that as soon as you have mentally consented to the fact that Jesus Christ is the Son of God, by faith alone you become a child of the King. We left the Lutheran Church because that doctrine is not true.

It is not true because James says: "Ye see, then, how that a man is justified by works, and not by faith only." (Jas. 2:24). Then in the last verse of the second chapter, James says: "As the body apart from the spirit is dead, faith apart from works is dead also." And listen to the language of Jesus, Matt. 7:21: "Not everyone that saith unto me, Lord, Lord, shall enter the kingdom of heaven, but he that doeth the will of my Father who is in heaven." Jesus said that there is something that you need to do. Listen to Jesus as he spoke to Paul, when Paul asked him what he would have him do: "Arise and go into the city and there it will be told thee what thou must do."

Why didn't Jesus say, "Why, Paul, you believe that I am the Christ the Son of God; why, bless your heart, you are saved; just go to preaching, that's all you need to do." Not at all! He said, "Go to the city and it will be told thee what thou MUST do." And the last word that we use was the language of the revelator in Rev. 20:12: "The books were opened and another book was opened, which is the book of life, and the dead were judged out of the things written in the books, according to their works." Your works are going to have something to do with it, friend of mine.

FROM DARKNESS TO LIGHT

And just to show you more concretely, I read again for your benefit a verse we have used, to show the things we did when we came from darkness to light. True, we believed that Jesus Christ is the Son of God, but, in addition to that, we repented of our sins, for Lk. 13:3 says, "Except ye repent, ye shall all likewise perish." And having made the good confession, (Rom. 10:10) we were baptized for the remission of sins, to be saved, because Jesus said: "He that believes and is baptized shall be saved." Mk. 16:16. We rejoiced, having come out from under creeds, out from under humanism, out from under everything that is foreign to the word of God, to stand upon the word of God and it alone. And I would beseech you tonight that you come out from under bondage into light. If you are a subject to the invitation, would you come? We rise and sing.

LUTHER BLACKMON

(*A Biographical Sketch*)

Luther Blackmon was born March 24, 1907 at Bald Prairie in Robertson County, Texas. His parents were members of the church and taught him the truth at an early age. He obeyed the gospel when young but afterward fell away and for some years remained out of duty.

In 1926 he moved to Houston, Texas where he eventually, through the persuasion of some of his friends, started attending church and was restored. This was under the preaching of Flavil Colley who was instrumental in encouraging Bro. Blackmon to preach.

For the past 15 years he has preached continually. His labors have been chiefly in Texas but he has held meetings in a number of other states. From October 1941 to December 1943 he lived and preached in the Verde Valley of northern Arizona. During the most of his preaching life he has lived in Houston. The first local work he did was with the 26th and North Shepherd Drive congregation in that city. The last two years he spent in Houston was with the Norhill church where Roy E. Cogdill preached. In 1946 Brother Blackmon and Brother Cogdill both moved to Lufkin where they now live.

Why I Left The World

By Luther Blackmon

When Brother Caskey and Brother Campbell first mentioned to me about preaching in this lectureship on this theme, I thought it was a little unusual, but it seems that the interest in the subject vindicates their judgment and their decision to have someone speak on it. I appreciate the presence of all of you and especially those who have come from a distance. I am glad of the opportunity to speak at Vickery Boulevard. My association with the Christians of Fort Worth has always been pleasant and this fine audience leaves little to be desired for this occasion, as far as my part in it is concerned. The theme of this lesson, like those that have preceded it, sounds rather personal. But I would like for you to think of the principles of truth involved rather than the person. Apply these truths to your own life. Why should anyone come out of the world and turn to Christ? It is my purpose to discuss the subject tonight under three headings: 1. What is the world? 2. What is the Christian's relationship to the world? 3. Why I chose Christ instead of the world.

THE WORLD DEFINED

Jesus said in Matt. 16:24, "..... If any man will come after me, let him deny himself and take up his cross and follow me. For whosoever will save his life shall lose it; and whosoever will lose his life for my sake shall find it. For what is a man profited if he shall gain the whole world and lose his own soul? Or what shall a man give in exchange for his soul?" In reading the New Testament you cannot but be impressed with the fact that the world and whatever the world stands for is generally used in antithesis to the kingdom of heaven. But, even so, there is a sense in which this is not true. Jesus said of his disciples, "..... I have chosen you *out of the world.*" (John 15:19). But he said in his prayer to his Father, "And now I am no more in the world but these are *in the world.*" (John 17:11). *In* the world but not *of* the world is the idea. We, as Christians, are citizens of a heavenly kingdom, but we cannot escape the fact that we live in a material, physical world in which we do some things and sustain some relationships that are not directly a part of our Christian life and duties, nor are they of the dominion of Satan. Sitting in a cafe one day eating lunch, I was talking with a friend about playing golf. A lady listening in on the conversation asked me if I played golf. I answered that I tried to play the game sometimes. She was almost horrified. "Don't you think it is wrong for a Christian to play golf?" she asked. I admitted that I didn't think it was wrong and asked her why she thought so. She said, "It is of the world, and we are not to partake of the world." This is typical of the attitude of many. They entertain the idea that everything that the Lord allows or approves is in the church and that everything else belongs to the devil.

CIVIL GOVERNMENTS NOT OF THE DEVIL

I think it was some such notion as this that gave birth to the idea that all earthly governments belong to the devil. Some sincere brethren believe that. I was reading just recently Brother David Lipscomb's comment on Romans 13. He believed that all earthly governments are headed by the devil. Brother Lipscomb was one of our great pioneer preachers, and, undoubtedly, a scholar of no mean ability. The writings of the pioneers have been of inestimable worth to me in the study of the Bible, among which writings is Brother Lipscomb's work; but I am under no obligation, morally or spiritually, to believe anything any of them taught just because they were great men. I do not believe that God ordained government for the good of his people and then turned it over to the devil. Brother Lipscomb argued that if man had obeyed God's law, civil government would never have been—would not have been needed—that human governments were needed because man would not obey God's government. Well, if man had never disobeyed God, a lot of other things would never have been; the church for an example. The law of Moses was given be-

THE WORLD FOR CHRIST

cause of sin, Paul said in Gal. 3, and although it was a theocracy, it was, nevertheless, civil law, in part—six of the ten commandments dealing with man's relationship to man. But one would hardly say, as Brother Lipscomb said of earthly governments, that the law of Moses was an "instrument of wrath, ordained for the children of wrath."

Some say that we cannot logically be citizens of two kingdoms at the same time; therefore, we are not citizens of any earthly government—that "our citizenship is in heaven" and we are simply sojourners here, that we sustain a relationship to this government similiar to a foreigner who comes here to make his home but never becomes naturalized. He pays taxes for which he receives the protection of the government, the benefits of the schools, etc., submits to the laws, but has no part in making or executing them. But Paul claimed his Roman citizenship as protection against the scourging he was about to receive. (Acts 22:25). If not, what did he mean by "one who is a Roman?" He let the centurion think he was a Roman anyway. Being a citizen of an earthly government does not align one with the world as we are talking about the world tonight.

BIBLE USE OF WORD "WORLD"

The Bible refers to the physical universe as the "world." "He was in the world and the world was made by him and the world knew him not." (John 1:10). Again, "God who at sundry times and in divers manners spake in time past unto the fathers by the prophets, hath in these last days spoken to us by His Son, whom he hath appointed heir of all things, by whom also he made the worlds." "Worlds" mean physical universe. The human family is referred to as the "world." "..... sin entered into the world." (Rom. 5:12). "God so loved the world....." (John 3:16). But the sense in which we are speaking of the world in our lesson tonight is that spiritual dominion over which Satan actually has control. Satan does have a kingdom. It is a spiritual affair, antagonistic to everything for which the Lord and his kingdom stand. Paul said in Eph. 6:12, "For we wrestle not against flesh and blood, but against principalities and powers, against the rulers of the darkness of this world, against spiritual wickedness in high places." The devil is called the "Prince of this world." (John 16:11; 14:30; 12:31). In II Cor. 4:4, he is called the "god of this world." Christians are in the physical universe, of course, and are of the race of mankind; but we are not of, and cannot take part in, the affairs of the world as they relate to that spiritual dominion over which Satan is head. This brings us to:

THE CHRISTIAN'S RELATIONSHIP TO THE WORLD

The Christian's relationship to the world is both positive and negative. On the positive side he is "the light of the world," the "salt of the earth," and "letters known and read of all men." God's plan for saving the world includes human agency. "It pleased God by the foolishness of preaching to save them that believe." "The manifold wisdom of God" (the gospel) is to be made known through the church. (I Cor. 1:18; Eph. 3:10). The Lord doesn't have any other medium through which to preach the gospel, except the church; and just to the extent that the church of the Lord carries out her part of the divine program, just to that extent will the scheme of redemption accomplish that for which it was designed. My obligation to the world then is the same as was that of my Savior, to save the world. To the extent that I fail, He fails. I speak reverently. He will not save the world in a miraculous burst of divine power; only by the gospel. The gospel will not be preached without the church; only by the church. The church will not function without personal efforts of people like you and me. Do you believe that? Do you act as if you believe it?

On the negative side of the ledger we must "keep ourselves unspotted from the world." "Friendship with the world is enmity with God. Whosoever, therefore, will be a friend of the world is the enemy of God." (James 4:4). Some members of the church have a hard time finding the line between the church and the world, and still a harder time trying to stay on the right side of it. The trouble (whether they will admit it or not) is that they want to see how far they can go without going too far; how bad they can be without being too bad; how much they can get by with. Such people aren't really interested in going to heaven; they are interested only in staying out of hell. They would be willing to sell out their interest in the glory-world pretty cheap, if they could figure out some way to keep out of the other place. Such people usually turn out like Demas, of whom Paul said, "Demas hath forsaken me, having loved this present world." They are more concerned about what they have been "separated from" than what they have been "separated into." John said, "Love not the world, neither the things that are in the world. If any man love the world, the love of the Father is not in him." But who is the man who loves the world? John doesn't leave us in doubt on this point. "For all that is in the world, the lust of the flesh, and the lust of the eye and the pride of life, is not of the Father, but is of the world." (I John 2:15-17). This sums it up. There is not a thing belonging to the world that does not classify under one of these three.

"THE LUST OF THE FLESH"

"The lust of the flesh" simply means the uncontrolled indulgence in the satisfying of our physical appetites. Every appetite that is natural to man is right, and God has provided for its legitimate satisfaction. Hunger, thirst, the sex desire, all have been provided for in God's wisdom and love, and as long as we remain within the divinely appointed limitations to find satisfaction for the flesh no wrong is committed. But surrounded by temptations, it is easy for us to let these appetites to lead us into forbidden paths. While we are on the subject of fleshly appetites, I would like for some Baptist, Presbyterian, or just anybody who believes the doctrine of hereditary depravity (if anybody does) to tell me what appetite, desire, or impulse a man is born with that is wrong, in and of itself. James said, "Lust when it has conceived bringeth forth sin, and sin when it is finished bringeth forth death." You have heard people say, "You might just as well do a wrong as to want to do it." That is not so. "Lust when it hath *conceived* bringeth forth sin." Let us illustrate what we are talking about here. Suppose a drunkard is converted to the Lord. He turns his back upon sin, the world and the devil. And that's what repentance is—making up your mind to quit doing wrong, whether a Christian or a sinner. Lot of folks in the church need to repent! They visit their good-for-nothing kinfolks on Sunday, or let their kinfolks visit them, and keep them from coming to church, then perhaps ask the Lord to forgive them, when they know they will do it again when they feel like it, and come back next Sunday, sit on the front seat and sing, "Oh, How I Love Jesus!" Such is not repentance. Make up your mind that you won't do that thing any more. That's repentance. A man is a drunkard. He hears the gospel. He repents of his sins, makes up his mind that he'll never take another drink.

But you know conversion doesn't change a person physically. He gets just as hungry after he becomes a Christian as he did before. He is just as tall, or just as short, as he was before. His physical impulses, his desires, remain exactly the same If he wanted to drink liquor before he was converted, he'll want it afterward. The difference between the converted man and the unconverted man is that the unconverted man is under the control of his flesh. His flesh has the ascendancy and controls the inner man. The converted man is quite the opposite. The inner man controls the outer man. This drunkard is converted. He becomes a Christian. One day he is walking down the street, looks in the liquor store and the old desire seizes him. He wants a drink just as much as he ever did before. But then the thought comes back to him, "I am a Christian now. I said I wouldn't and I won't" He turns and walks away. I tell you, that man hasn't committed any sin. The desire was there but he overcame that desire, walked away, and won a victory over the devil; and it will be easier for him the next time. This old idea that "you just well say it as think it" is not so. James said, "Lust when it hath conceived, bringeth forth sin." The sin comes when the lust conceives. Suppose the man, when he is tempted, loses the fight. His flesh is stronger. He decides to take the drink. He starts in the door with his mind made up, and sees his wife coming down the street. He turns around and walks out, goes on and doesn't take the drink. As far as the sin is concerned, he might as well have taken it, because the lust conceived. He made up his mind; he gave over to the devil. Lust of the flesh is not necessarily wrong, but giving over to it and allowing our physical desires to lead us beyond restraints which God has laid down, breaking through the divine restrictions and prohibitions which inspiration has placed around the child of God, that's when the sin takes place.

"LUST OF THE EYE"

"The lust of the eye," the desire for earthly, material things. It isn't wrong to make money. I don't know of a passage of scripture in all the Bible that condemns a man's making money. I know several that condemn him for the misuse of it. And the manner in which some people get it is wrong. But making legitimate money is not wrong. I remember in Mark 10th chapter, Jesus said, "It is easier for a camel to go through the eye of a needle than for a rich man to enter the kingdom of heaven." I used to hear, when I was a boy, preachers try to soften that; and I don't know why either, for there were not any rich folks in our congregation, where I was brought up. I don't know why a preacher would want to soften that, by saying that there was a hole in the wall of Jerusalem where a camel had to get down on his knees and go under. That was called the needle's eye and that's what Jesus meant—that a rich man had to get down on his knees. That's an explanation but that isn't what Jesus meant. It doesn't say the needle's eye, but the "eye of a needle." But Brother Preacher, that would be impossible. That's the point. That's it exactly! It is impossible for the kind of rich man here described to enter the kingdom of heaven. The twenty-third verse explains it. "How hardly shall they that trust in riches!" The man that makes getting money his aim and his goal and then sits down and holds that money while suffering and dying humanity all around him cries out for help. That's the man that is wrong and not the man that makes money legitimately. Any man who makes money for the sake of making money, for the sake of saying, "I can write a check in six figures," or "I want to leave my children a lot of money," has the wrong attitude and the wrong idea. He loves his money and Jesus said, "You cannot serve (love) God and mammon." Paul said in I Tim. 6:10, "The love of money is the root of all evil." And he said,

"They that would be rich fall into temptation and a snare." Not just the fellow that is rich, but "they that would be rich." Notice the expression: *"THEY THAT WOULD BE RICH."* That spells greed and vanity.

Some men want to make a lot of money that they might help build church houses and preach the gospel. I know a fellow who is an elder in the church and he makes a lot of money. He gives it very liberally. He said to me recently: "I believe that the Lord is going to let me live a long time and use me in his kingdom. I have thought about cashing in all of my assets, and I could live comfortably the rest of my life; but I'd destroy my earning power, and I have quite an earning power like it is. I don't want money; that doesn't concern me; and I don't care whether I leave my children very much or not. If I can educate them and give them an even start in life, that's all I want. But I want to spend my money to preach the gospel and to save men and women who are lost." God give us more rich men like that. I don't know of a passage of scripture in the Bible that condemns a man for making money, but the Bible is full of passages that condemn a man for not spending that money.

I want to notice a passage over in the fifth chapter of James: "Woe unto you rich men. Weep and howl for your miseries that shall come upon you. Your gold and silver is cankered." Cankered! How do things get cankered? "And your garments are moth-eaten." How do garments get moth eaten? Mine never do, for I have mine on, and moths don't get in them when you have them on. Garments get motheaten in the closet and money get cankered when it is not being used. Inspiration didn't put those words in just to fill up space. "Your gold and silver is cankered." Having it doesn't hurt anything; it's cankered. It is the rust that's hanging on it that is going to send your soul to hell. "Your garments are moth-eaten." You don't wear your Christianity. You hang it up in the closet and live for the devil. "And the rust of them shall be witness against you, and shall eat your flesh as it were fire."

Some things I can't figure out; I just can't. I once knew an old man who had a lot of money; and you know, that old fellow wouldn't eat enough. He didn't eat very much and I honestly believe that it was that he might save the money. And he'd tell a lie for a nickel anytime. If he could gain a nickel by telling a lie, he would do it. Of course, he didn't call it a lie. He was like the little boy that had the lemonade. He was selling his lemonade for five cents a glass; the other boy down the street was getting three cents for his. Someone asked him how he could get two cents a glass more for his lemonade, and he said, "You see, there didn't any cat fall in mine while I was making it." And that's all he said. Pretty soon the other little boy came around and asked him what he meant telling folks that a cat fell in his lemonade, and he said, "I didn't tell anybody a cat fell in your lemonade. I just said one didn't fall in mine." But he lied just the same, didn't he? The old man had more money than he needed, or ever would need, and yet, he'd lie for a nickel. And nearly any rich man will do that, just nearly any of them. They may not lie for a nickel but they will lie for a lot. They serve mammon and that is why there are such a few rich men in the kingdom of God. And that's why some who are don't do anything for the Lord. They trust in their riches. It is a hard thing for a man to have money without trusting in his money.

"THE PRIDE OF LIFE"

"The pride of life;" that means desire for fame and power —the thing that has sent so many people on the wrong road. Some time ago I had occasion to be in New York. Many of you remember when I was here last July (in a meeting at South Summit) I had some trouble with my throat, and had to go, or did go, up to Philadelphia for treatment. I had always wanted to see Broadway at night. Well, I did. As I stood there and looked up and down the great white way, the theatrical center of the world, where somebody said, "there are a million lights and a broken heart for every light," I thought of all the young people who had offered their souls upon the altar of ambition. Sacrifice themselves, their virtue, and their very souls for a career. And there are a lot of little girls in this country tonight, and maybe some in Fort Worth, who would give everything they have on this earth, virtue and all, if they could get a contract in Hollywood or become the toast of Broadway—"see my name in lights." Other men are crazy for power. Mussolini, Tojo, Napoleon, Alexander, all are examples. "What shall it profit a man if he gain the whole world and lose his own soul?" What if a man gain all the pleasure, satisfy every impulse and every physical desire of his flesh; suppose that a man has all the money that he wants—nobody ever did I guess—but suppose a man did. Suppose that he could satisfy every vain impulse and every particle of vanity that he has; suppose that he was the ruler over the universe, that all earthly governments were under his rule and dominion; suppose that he was so notorious and so popular that everybody knew and used his name in every nation on the earth; if he died without Christ and lost his soul, Jesus said he'd be a failure. Put all that on one side of the scale and put one human soul on the other, and Jesus says that this one human soul weighs more than all that, everything the world has to offer. Then no wonder Jesus said, "What is a man profited if he shall gain the whole world and lose his own soul?" I don't know how many of you have ever come face to face with the thought that perhaps this is the time I must die; this is it. This is my call to go out into the great and boundless beyond. A lot of people never think about the hereafter until they are faced with that reality. Let me tell you something, my friends. It is just as real as if it had already happened to you; it is just as real as if it were going to happen tonight. If I had it in my power (and wanted to do it) to tell you that this is the last hour that you are going to spend on this earth, that at 9:00 o'clock your life would be snuffed out, if you believed me, there isn't a person in this audience that wouldn't come down that aisle in tears and give his heart to the Lord Jesus Christ and his life to his service—if he had the opportunity. But you keep putting it off. Why? Because you have some more of the world that you want to enjoy.

TRADING A SOUL FOR THE WORLD

I was preaching in a little East Texas town, and I preached on "Hell" one night. A lady who had been coming to the meeting said, "If you don't quit preaching like that, I won't come to hear you, because at night I can't go to sleep." I said, "Well, why don't you do something about it? You know how to fix that." And she said, "Yes, I know, but, preacher, I just love the world too much." She was honest about it. And till this good day she is still in the world. She still belongs to the devil, and I guess always will, because she isn't willing to give up the world. But Jesus said, "What shall it profit a man; what is the profit?" In the first place, no one ever gained the world, but in the second place, what if he could? He'd be a fool to trade his soul for the world.

TRADING A SOUL FOR A HUSBAND

Some young ladies have traded their souls for a husband. They fall in love with some boy who doesn't care a thing on earth about the church. And when folks get in love, you know, that entitles them to trample everything that God ever said under their feet—Christianity, father, mother, morals and everything else. "I'm in love and I'll marry him, no matter what. Oh, I'll convert him. I am going to do different to what the rest of them did." It is her business if she wants to trade her soul for a husband, but it is a bad trade. It is a bad deal.

But let us notice another thing about the vainglory of life. A great many people have too much pride with regard to their religious connections. Some people remain in denominations because the church of Christ is unpopular and small. Some people who are convinced of the truth have too much pride to give up their big church, give up their big party denominational connections and come into the church of the Lord Jesus Christ, even when they know it is right. I had a friend who gained quite some reputation as a student in the school he attended. He won a scholarship in Europe and studied in Switzerland. Some of the denominational preachers in that town approached him and tried to get him to leave the church. They said, "You are too big a man to be going down there to that little place. Why don't you come up with us?" But they happened to hit a fellow, in that case, whose pride couldn't be appealed to in that way. A good many people will not give up the important and popular side in order to walk with Christ. "What would a man be profited if he should gain the whole world and lose his own soul?"

ONE QUALIFIED ON THE "WORLD"

I think Solomon was, perhaps, as well qualified to speak on the instability of the world, both by inspiration and experience, as most anybody about whom I have ever read. And if you will turn to Ecclesiastes and read it, you cannot but be impressed with the deep melancholy note Solomon sounded there. He begins it by saying: "Vanity of vanities, all is vanity." But let's take a look at Solomon's life. Solomon was given wisdom, you know, and a lot of folk think that is the summum bonum of all that could be desired. As I was driving a young preacher to his appointment, he told me his plans for the future. He was going to school till he had a Ph. D. I thought about the old gentleman who said, "My boy has his B. A. and his M. A. both, but his P. A. still supports him!" A young preacher asked one of our old pioneer preachers (I won't tell you his name) what he thought about his going to school. He already had his Master's degree and was getting his Ph. D. He replied, "It just depends on what you intend to do, son. If you intend to preach the gospel, you already know too much." It's fine to have an education if you have sense enough to use it, but it's just like riches. When you make it the aim and the end and the goal of life, of course, it becomes a hindrance. Oratory and eloquence. worldly wisdom and college degrees are not to be confused with the gospel of Christ. Solomon had wisdom. He was the wisest man who ever lived upon the earth, but that wisdom did not bring him satisfaction.

Not only did he have wisdom, but he came as near, I suppose, as anyone ever did, to satisfying every physical desire that he had. He gave himself over to the satisfaction of his desires until he became a dissipated wretch, just like everybody else that does that will do.

Not only did he satisfy all of his physical desires and impulses to the fullest, but Solomon was a very wealthy man. The coffers of Israel were overflowing during Solomon's reign, and enjoyed the wealthiest wealth of the world. Not only

THE WORLD FOR CHRIST

did he enjoy the satisfaction of his physical desires and the wealth, but he was famous. Why, the Queen of Sheba came to see him and when she left, she said, "The half hasn't been told." "Solomon, I have heard about you, but I hadn't really heard all the story." And when Solomon reached the end of the journey, had time to reflect upon his folly, and the curtain was ready to drop upon his little earthly drama, he said, "Vanity of vanities, all is vanity." And in the recapitulation of the last sermon, in the last verses of Ecclesiastes, he said, "Fear God and keep his commandments, for this is the whole duty of man." In the first chapter of Ecclesiastes he talks about the instability of life. He compares it to a tread-mill. Why, he said, "Generations come and go, but the world goes on. The sun rises in the morning, then it goes down and returns to the place from which it rises. All the rivers run into the sea, and yet the sea is not full; from the place from whence they come, thither they return again." Life is a tread-mill, and when I live my little span, bid good-bye to earthly friends and relationships and go the way of all the earth, I'll be like other men, forgotten except for the good or evil that I have done. Solomon, in spite of his wisdom, learned too late the purpose of life. He had been blinded by the glitter of the world.

MOSES AND THE WORLD

But there was another fellow, a man by the name of Moses. The Bible says, "By faith Moses, when he had come into years, refused to be called the son of Pharaoh's daughter, choosing rather to suffer afflictions with the people of God than to enjoy the pleasures of sin for a season." (Heb. 11).

Yes, there is pleasure in sin, but the pleasure that goes with sin is only temporary, lasts only as long as the act which provides the pleasure is being performed. Moses "esteemed the reproaches of Christ greater riches than Egypt, for he had respect unto the recompense of the reward." He left the land of Egypt in spite of the fact that he was heir to the throne and to all the wealth that Egypt had. It was his; he was reared as the son of Pharaoh's daughter. But he knew enough about God and this world to know that all this earth can afford is but a bubble, and as Solomon said "vanity." And so, when the crucial test came, Moses turned his back upon that Egyptian throne, upon the power that he could have wielded as the king of Egypt, and upon all the wealth, the joy and the pleasure that Egypt and the world had to give him, and cast his lot with a group of emancipated slaves. He wandered back and forth in the great and terrible wilderness until God called him from his labor and put him to rest. Moses could have gone down in history as a great Egyptian king, but he preferred to be a servant of his God. That was Moses.

PAUL AND THE WORLD

Take last of all, the apostle Paul. He was reared in the city of Tarsus and educated in the city of Jerusalem at the feet of Gamaliel. In Philippians the fourth chapter, he said, "If any man think he hath whereof to glory in the flesh, I more. Circumcised the eighth day, of the stock of Israel, of the tribe of Benjamin, a Hebrew of the Hebrews, as touching the law a Pharisee, concerning zeal persecuting the church, touching the righteousness which is of the law blameless. But those things which are gain to me, I counted loss for Christ. Yea, doubtless, and I do count all things but loss for the excellency of the knowledge of Christ Jesus, my Lord, for whom I have suffered the loss of all things, and do count them but refuse that I may win Christ." Paul was brought up at the feet of Gamaliel, a doctor of the law. He had a prominent position among his people. He had letters of authority in his pocket to bind and bring back to the city of Jerusalem those whom he found worshipping the name of Christ, because he thought with all sincerity that he ought to stamp out and abolish that hateful and despised sect of Christians. But from the time that the light shone on him on the Damascus road, and he fell down and said, "Lord, what wilt thou have me do?" From that time, I say, "until his old grey head rolled off the chop block in glorious martyrdom," not one single time did he waver or express any doubts about the ultimate finish of it all. I suppose Paul is my ideal of all men of the Bible; to me he stands out because of his unwavering loyalty to the things he believed to be right. He gave up his home; he gave up his family; he gave up his kinfolk; he turned his back upon his religion, venerated for its antiquity, and given to Moses amid the terrible scenes of Sinai, and cast his lot with the despised Christians. Enemies of the truth persecuted him from place to place until, finally, under the rule of old Nero, he was put to death and his spirit went back to God who had given it. That was Paul for you! He gave up the world but he gained Christ. He said, "The things that were gain to me, I counted loss for Christ, and do count them but refuse that I may win Christ." Coming to the personal part of the subject,

WHY I LEFT THE WORLD FOR CHRIST

I shall be as brief as I can. My primary reason for leaving the world, of course, was that I might be saved. I knew enough about the Bible, even then, to know that there could be no compromise between the two; that if I would win Christ, I must give up the world.

In the second place, I discovered that there is no peace, I discovered that there is no peace of mind in the service of Satan. A few minutes ago I referred to some men as examples of this very thing. Alexander the Great thought that happiness consisted in power. He conquered the world and then cried because there were no more worlds to conquer, according to the poet. He died young and disillusioned, "having conquered the world but unable to conquer his own lusts." Such a life is never happy. It doesn't have the ingredients for happiness. If Solomon with wisdom, wealth, power and everything that the world has to offer, could find no lasting happiness in these things, surely I could not hope to fare so well.

In the last place, I left the world because, at best, my days upon this earth are few. If the world could provide all that it takes to make one happy, our "three score and ten" would soon run out. What then?

PLEA TO LEAVE THE WORLD

My friends, let me suggest to you, until you come to the place in your thinking and in your attitude where you are willing to say with Paul, "I count the things of the world but refuse; I count all the wealth of the world but a thing to be used in the service of my God: I count all the pride and fame that I might gain as a man of the world a thing to be despised, if I may win Christ and die a triumphant and victorious death when this earthly life is done." I say, until you can come to the place in life where you can earnestly and conscientiously say, "Lord, use me; I am through with the world," you may just as well stay in the world because the Lord can't use you. There are a lot of folk in the church, and I suspect in Fort Worth, whose names are on the church roll, who have never actually given up the world. I plead with you tonight that you turn from the world, and from the pleasure that the world offers you. The world can offer no lasting peace. The world can offer no satisfaction that is permanent in its nature. The world can offer you none of the blessings that are in Christ, none of the comforts that you have as a Christian when you come to die. Let me tell you something, friends; if everything else in the world I ever did fails, if I go down in the memory of my friends as a failure and as a complete disappointment to all who knew me, as far as this world is concerned; if I can look up in the hour of death with an eye of faith and say with Paul, "I have fought a good fight, I have finished my course, I have kept the faith," I won't care a great deal about what the world affords and how much of it I have missed. Until we can come to that place where we can give up everything that the world has to offer and cling to Christ, no matter what the sacrifices may be, we are not fit to serve him as his children. I beg you tonight to turn from the world, to turn to Christ who is able to save you to the uttermost, to come believing in the Son of God, to answer the call to the highest duty and the greatest obligation that any man or woman ever accepted; come in the name of him who loved you and died for you, come believing and come turning from your sins, come confessing the faith that you have in your heart, and be baptized for the remission of those sins, and God will wash them away, blot them out and remember them no more and "give you an inheritance among all them that are sanctified," if you are faithful unto the end of the journey.

JOSEPH C. MALONE

Joseph Colby Malone was born on February 14, 1907 in Dallas, Texas, where he was reared and educated. After leaving school he tried the occupations of bank clerk, railway clerk and advertising artist which prepared him for his later task of being a cartoonist for one of the large Dallas papers. His sports cartoons became the most popular feature in the newspaper. His editorial cartoons were also well received. John Nance Garner, as Vice-President of the United States, requested several of his original drawings for his personal collection. Later, Joe Malone began to draw for a newspaper syndicate. One drawing made during this time, a biographical cartoon of Congressman Sam Rayburn as the Speaker of the House, was cast in bronze and presented to the late President Roosevelt.

Prior to his baptism into Christ Brother Malone began a study of the Bible which grew intense, and has continued unabated. He was soon used by the Pearl and Bryan congregation as the teacher in the young people's class, and as a substitute in the pulpit. Invitations from other congregations began to be received.

On March 9, 1940, Brother Malone became the regular minister of the Peak and East Side congregation in Dallas where he has continued to the present. Eleven hundred people have been added under his ministry.

He now restricts his art work and cartooning to the work of the church. He illustrated the book entitled, "Minute with the Master in Script and Sketch," and drew the now famous cartoon depicting the man, woman and child standing on the New Testament, which drawing has literally circled the globe, and of which some twenty-five million impressions have been made. He drew the headings for many of the religious journals among the churches of Christ. He is noted also for his interesting Chalk-talks which are given for the benefit of children in orphan homes, deaf schools, as well as church groups and others.

He is the father of two boys, Avon and David. (Avon is already a promising cartoonist for the Dallas Times Herald, the paper his father formerly served).

Why I Left The Catholic Church

By Joe Malone

Brethren and respected friends, I count it a profound privilege to have the opportunity to speak to you on the subject which has been assigned to me, "Why I Left the Catholic Church."

In the very beginning, let me stress that when people leave error which has been imbued into their consciousness so very keenly, it is not altogether easy. Further, there was a time, as you might well conclude, when I was adversely sensitive to any attack upon Catholicism. Bearing that in mind and realizing that there are probably those in the audience who stand where I stood, though I intend to speak plainly, I shall strive to show my interest in you and my consideration for you, whoever you might be, by speech that is free from rancor and that which is caustic. I trust that the spirit manifested will not only be discernible but agreeable to you, and that you will respond by lending an attentive ear .

CATHOLICS DISREGARD THE WORD OF GOD

I left the Roman Catholic Church because of its disregard for the Word of God. Should any be inclined to take issue with that statement relative to the attitude of the Catholic Church, let me remind you that the Catholic Church maintains that "the Bible is a dead letter and unable to interpret itself." Yet in the Bible, whether Catholic or not, we read, "The word of God is quick and powerful (living and active), and sharper than any two-edged sword, piercing even to the dividing a-sunder of soul and spirit, and of the joints and marrow, and is a discerner of the thoughts and intents of the heart" (Heb. 4:12). That is Heaven's pronouncement in regard to the matter. Further the Catholic Church asserts, "We do not in any wise presuppose that the books of the New Testament are inspired, but, rather, they are only genuine, authentic documents written by honest men." John, one of the writers of the New

Testament, wrote, "And I heard a voice from heaven saying, Write, Blessed are the dead who die in the Lord from henceforth: yea, saith the Spirit, that they may rest from their labors; for their works follow them" (Rev. 14:13). That is either an inspired statement or John was dishonest, and, in either case, the Catholic Church would be in error. Paul, another one of the writers of the New Testament wrote, "If any man thinketh himself to be a prophet, or spiritual, let him take knowledge of the things which I write unto you, that they are the commandment of the Lord" (I Cor. 14:37). The attitude of the Catholic Church is the attitude of Diotrephes, "who loveth to have preeminence among them, receiveth us not. Therefore, if I come, I will bring to remembrance his works which he doeth, prating against us with wicked words" (III John 9, 10). My friends the Bible becomes a "dead letter" to those whose doctrine it condemns; but, in the words of Paul, here is the attitude toward the Bible of those who respect heaven's way. "Every scripture inspired of God is also profitable for teaching, for reproof, for correction, for instruction which is in righteousness: that the man of God may be complete, furnished completely unto every good work" (II Tim. 3:16, 17).

CATHOLICS CLAIM THAT NEW TESTAMENT IS UNINSPIRED

Not only does the Catholic Church contend that the Bible is a "dead letter" and the New Testament is uninspired, but it maintains that the apostles appointed a "divine, infallible apostolate" to direct us. That, my friends, is essentially the way the Catholic Church endeavors to make room in the realm of religion for papal edicts and the decrees of the Romanish councils. But consider this: "For if the word spoken through angels proved stedfast, and every transgression and disobedience received a just recompense of reward; how shall we escape, if we neglect so great a salvation? which having at the first been spoken unto us through the Lord, was confirmed unto us by them that heard" (Heb. 2:2-3). Those who heard the word were the ones to confirm it, and that is in keeping with the following statement of Peter, "Of the men therefore that have companied with us all the time that the Lord Jesus went in and went out among us, beginning from the baptism of John, unto the day that he was received up from us, of these must one become a witness with us of his resurrection." This was said in regard to one "to take the place in this ministry and apostleship from which Judas fell away" (Acts 1:21, 22 and 25). Can this so-called "divine, infallible apostolate" qualify? And after the word has been spoken and confirmed, what purpose could such an office serve?

GOD'S DIRECTIONS FIXED AND NOT FLEXIBLE

I submit to you that the means of direction from earth to heaven is thereby fixed, complete and final. Listen to the apostle Paul, "I marvel that ye are so quickly removing from him that called you in the grace of Christ unto a different gospel; which is not another gospel: only there are some that trouble you and would pervert the gospel of Christ. But though we, or an angel from heaven, should preach unto you any gospel other than that which we preached unto you, let him be anathema. As we have said before, so say I now again, If any man preacheth unto you any gospel other than that which ye received, let him be anathema, For if I am now seeking the favor of men, I should not be a servant of Christ. For I make known to you, brethren, as touching the gospel which was preached by me, that it is not after man. For neither did I receive it from man, nor was I taught it, but it came to me through the revelation of Jesus Christ" (Gal. 1:6-12). Thus we are caused to better understand why the same apostle declared, "Now these things, brethren, I have transferred to myself and Apollos for your sakes; that in us ye might learn not to go beyond the things which are written....." In keeping with that statement is this declaration of John's with its awful consequence, "Whosoever goeth onward and abideth not in the teaching of Christ, hath not God" (II John 9). In closing the Book of God, John said in the last chapter, "I testify unto every man that heareth the words of the prophecy of this book, If any man shall add unto them, God shall add unto him the plagues which are written in this book: and if any man shall take away from the words of the book of this prophecy,

God shall take away his part from the tree of life, and out of the holy city, which are written in this book" (Rev. 22:18, 19). That statement, as already shown, is consonant with the tenor of the whole New Testament. Hence, this very vital conclusion is sustained: the Word has been spoken and confirmed; it is fixed, complete and final; and there is, therefore, absolutely no place or purpose in God's design for a so-called "divine, infallible apostolate." Please remember this conclusion. It is essential to a proper understanding of what we shall say henceforth. The weight of that conclusion, as it is readily arrived at in the Scriptures, might well account for why the Catholic Church contends that the Bible is a "dead letter."

Now, my friends, perhaps it can be better understood why the Council of Trent in its twenty-fifth session, decreed that a council under the pope should draw up and publish an index of books which were to be prohibited in the church. Among these is the Bible, which is said to have been the first prohibited in the Council of Toloso. In the fourth of the ten rules concerning prohibited books as set forth in the Council of Trent, license to read the Bible is put under control of bishops and inquisitors. He that presumes to "read without such license cannot receive absolution of sins."

WORD OF GOD INJURIOUS TO ROMAN CATHOLIC CHURCH

Recently, I had a conversation with a young lady who had been a government engineer and a Catholic. She is now employed in a vital capacity with the American Bible Society, a non-profit organization which has as its purpose the distribution of Bibles and Testaments. Last year, that institution in the pursuit of its noble course distributed throughout the world some twelve million Bibles and twenty-nine million New Testaments, and, remember, without cost to the recipients. Several months ago that young lady went to confession. While there, the priest asked her where she was working. She told him that she was working for the American Bible Society. He said, "You'll have to stop that." She inquired why—adding that she thought it was a wonderful thing to spread God's Word. His answer was that such furthers Protestantism. If

THE CATHOLIC CHURCH 185

the distribution of Bibles and Testaments free from anything other than the Word of God itself furthers Protestantism, what can you say for Catholicism? Could there be any stronger indictment of the Catholic Church as a man-made religious organization than that? Incidentally, you might be interested to know that I baptized that young lady into Christ.

REARED AS A CATHOLIC

My father was a Catholic, and was largely educated by the monks. My mother, who survives him, was not, and is not, a Catholic. However, she permitted him to rear us children as Catholics. We attended a parochial school in the beginning of our formal education. We went to confession, took communion, attended mass and studied the Catechism. But my mother encouraged our study of the Bible, and I recall quite well that often she gave us Bibles as presents and the text would be the King James version. For where I am today, I owe much to her through the grace of God.

DOCTRINE OF DEPRAVITY OF INFANTS CAUSES DISCONTENT

If memory serves me rightly, the first thing that caused me to suspect the fallacy of the Catholic Church, and, consequently, the beginning of the "why" I left that apostate body is this reading which I found in the Bible: "..... Jesus said, Suffer little children, and forbid them not, to come unto me: for of such is the kingdom of heaven" (Matt. 19:14). Though but a youth who was otherwise little informed in the Scriptures, I could not reconcile Catholic doctrine of little children being born depraved with the statement of Jesus to the effect that the kingdom of heaven is of such as little children. I've grown some since then, and now, dear friends, let me expound the matter a little further.

In the Bible we read, "And as they went on their way, they came unto a certain water: and the eunuch said, See, here is water; what doth hinder me to be baptized? And Philip said, If thou believest with all thine heart, thou mayest. And he answered and said, I believe that Jesus Christ is the Son of God" (Acts 8:36, 37). When the eunuch asked to be baptized,

Philip, by the inspiration of God, laid down a provision to be met: "*IF* thou believest with all thine heart, thou mayest." Whereupon the eunuch confessed his faith in Christ and was baptized. Now this question: can a baby do that? In Hebrews 11:6 we read, "But without faith it is impossible to please him: for he that cometh to God must believe that he is, and that he is a rewarder of them that diligently seek him." He that comes to God must believe that God is. Can a baby qualify? Now we can readily understand this verse: "Then they that gladly received his word were baptized" (Acts 2:41). Who were baptized? They that gladly received his word. Well, that eliminates babies, does it not? Jesus said, "He that believeth and is baptized shall be saved" (Mark 16:16). That word "and" is a co-ordinating conjunction. It connects words, phrases or clauses of equal importance. Therefore, belief is just as essential to your salvation as is baptism, and baptism is just as essential to your salvation as is belief. It is a case of two-plus-two-equals-four. It takes everything on the left-hand side of the equation sign to equal that which is on the right-hand side. Therefore, we are not saved by faith only; neither are we saved by baptism only. We are saved by faith plus baptism, and that eliminates babies. Some one may yet ask, "Well, what of babies? What if they die without being baptized?" My friends, you cannot be s-a-v-e-d until you are l-o-s-t; a baby is s-a-f-e. Remember, Jesus said, "..... Of such is the kingdom of heaven." When one reaches an age at which he or she can understand the gospel of Christ as it concerns the primary steps of obedience; faith, repentance, confession and baptism.

SPRINKLING FOR BAPTISM

Before we pass from the consideration of this subject, let me say that the Catholic Church ordered sprinkling or pouring of water upon one's head as baptism about 1311 A. D. Thirteen centuries after God's order was given to the world the practice of sprinkling for baptism was commanded by the Catholic Church and every religious body under heaven which practices such is merely apeing the Romanish church. Here is God's definition of baptism: "Buried with him in baptism, wherein also ye are risen with him....." (Col. 2:12).

THE CATHOLIC CHURCH

SEEKING FOR THE TRUTH

As my conviction mounted that the Catholic Church was in error, I began to grope for the truth elsewhere. I eliminated certain churches from consideration on the basis that their names seemed, even then to me, to be foreign to the Scriptures and to the church which I was persuaded that Christ had established. It was on such a basis that I eliminated the Baptist and the Methodist churches. Since then I have found there is overwhelming justification for maintaining there is something in a name. How can one read in the Bible that God changed Abram's name to Abraham, and Sarai's name to Sarah, and Jacob's name to Israel, and named Jesus and John before their births—and yet contend that the names by which the church is called in the New Testament have no significance! I've learned of other disparities in the religious bodies mentioned as time has passed, but I still maintain that the name being wrong is, in itself, sufficient error.

ATTENDS THE CHURCH OF CHRIST

One Sunday afternoon in September, 1928, as I was sketching at the Dallas zoo, three young ladies approached. One of them lived in my neighborhood, and we had attended the same high school. She introduced the others, who proved to be her sisters, to me. Toward the close of a none too lengthy conversation, one of the sisters invited me to Bible school and church. I inquired, "Where?" She named a church of Christ meeting in south Dallas. I attended the following Sunday. Truth compels me to say that I was not very much impressed with the Bible class and its study seemed to make no lasting impression, but I was very much impressed with the young lady—that may, or may not, account for the lack of impression otherwise. Anyway, several times thereafter I attended the worship there with her, but the preacher's sermons, to me, seemed to carry little force and less clarity and conviction. In due course the young lady suggested that we begin to read the Bible together. It was agreed, and we began the study of the New Testament.

Then in the spring of 1929, while in the home of a certain

young man, I listened to a radio sermon which he had seemingly flipped to just in order to employ my time while he took care of some household chore. The sermon was a plain exposition of the Scriptures with frequent reference thereto, and it was masterfully delivered. The young man remained away until the entire sermon had been preached and congregational singing in the form of an invitational hymn had been sung. Then I learned that I had been listening to the broadcast of the regular Sunday morning worship of the Pearl and Bryan Streets Church of Christ in Dallas with preaching being done by C. M. Pullias. That was a pioneering venture in religious broadcasting in Dallas or, perhaps, elsewhere for that matter. The fruits of it in magnitude only eternity itself will disclose. My own experience impresses on me its possibilities for others. I am an advocate not only of the pulpit, for which there is not and can never be a substitute, but also of the press and the radio and various new and usable means of visualization which are now being introduced for the promulgation of the gospel. The casual way in which I became a part of the audience of that radio sermon might suggest to many that it was strictly a matter of chance; I do not share that view. Jesus said, "Ask, and it shall be given you; seek, and ye shall find; knock, and it shall be opened unto you: for every one that asketh receiveth; and he that seeketh findeth; and to him that knocketh it shall be opened" (Matt. 7:7, 8). I was seeking the truth; I had no personal axe to grind religiously, and, by this time, I had little interest in attempting to exonerate the religious views of others. In short, I wanted to know what God would have me to do. I believe implicitly in the providence of God; and I, for one, am quite persuaded that the instance of which I now speak is an example of it, for which I give thanks to the Father of lights.

BAPTIZED INTO CHRIST

After hearing that sermon, I suggested to the young lady that we attend the services of the Church of Christ at Pearl and Bryan Streets in Dallas. She was agreeable. We attended. The truth I learned in our Bible study together was augmented and clarified frequently by what I learned from the

THE CATHOLIC CHURCH

pulpit there. That young lady, to whom I owe so much, was formerly Miss Glendelle Myers, but for the past eighteen years she has been Mrs. Joe Malone. Coming to a knowledge of the truth and recognizing my responsibility before God, I was baptized into Christ on April 22, 1934 by C. M. Pullias, to whom I owe a profound debt, at Pearl and Bryan, where a congregation meets which I shall ever hold in grateful remembrance.

CATHOLIC ERROR WHY "I" LEFT

One's conversion is, in its nature, a personal matter, and to it we have given some attention; but, my dear friends, when I am called upon to speak with regard to "Why I left the Catholic Church," the motives which prompted my conversion are brought into focus; and those motives, which constitute the "why" with me, far transcend mere personal experience and localized circumstance. Broad principles of truth are unalterably opposed by the Catholic Church. When I expose the error of the Catholic Church and show the danger therein, I am setting forth why I left the Romanish Church. Others are welcome to whatever seems plausible to them, but Catholic error is the "why" with me. Hence, let us examine that error in the light of Truth as it is reflected in the Bible; and, as we do, let it be borne in mind that thus I am continuing to establish why I left the Catholic Church.

CATHOLICS CLAIM THE CHURCH IS AUTHORITY

When I speak of examining the church in the light of the Word, the Catholic Church will immediately contend that the church is authority for the Word, and not the Word for the church. Jesus said, "He that rejecteth me, and receiveth not my words, hath one that judgeth him: the word that I have spoken, the same shall judge him in the last day" (John 12:48). Let those contend that the Catholic Church is authority who will, but, as for me, I am going to accept that authority by which I shall be judged in the last day: the Word of the Lord. Remember that He said, "All authority hath been given unto me in heaven and on earth." (Matt. 28:18). Jesus said of those whose religion is based on the tradition of men, "This people draweth nigh unto me with their mouth, and honoureth me with their lips; but their heart is far from me. But in vain they do worship me, teaching for doctrines the commandments of men." A bit later in the same connection He said, "Every plant which my heavenly Father hath not planted shall be rooted up" (Matt. 15:8, 9, 13).

DID THE CATHOLICS GIVE US THE BIBLE?

Again, the Catholic Church relative to the Bible is prone to say, "If you accept the Bible, you must accept us for the Bible has been preserved by us and has come to you through us." My friends, the Lord is responsible for the preservation of His Word as He said, "Heaven and earth shall pass away: but my words shall not pass away" (Mark 13:31). Should it even be granted that the Catholic Church were the agency through which the Word was preserved for a season, what would it signify? Further, should one be ready to concede that the Bible was handed to us, in a sense by the Catholic Church, does it follow that we must believe in the Catholic Church in order to accept the Bible? If I must repossess the newspaper from the mouth of my neighbor's dog, does it follow that I must believe in my neighbor's dog in order to accept what I read in the paper? Those who accept the Bible and the Bible alone, plainly show that they reject all else.

EXPOSED ERROR CALLED "INTERPRETATION"

Also, the Catholic Church is very prone to say (and she has a host of allies in this matter) that the force of any scriptural argument which is brought to bear upon her fallacy is "merely your interpretation." That reminds me of that classic poem about an owl critic. He proceeded to criticize an owl over the open door of a barber shop while the barber went on shaving. The critic pointed out that the fellow that stuffed that owl should have considered a live one. He said it was hunched over unnaturally, the expression in its face was all wrong, its claws were out of shape and so on and on. Finally, the owl with some to-do, left its perch and flew out the open door. Thus some will profess the Bible to believe and yet deny the very thing they see, and, we might add, others will read the Bible with their father's specs upon their heads and see the thing just like their father said. The Catholic Church would have the people think that they cannot understand the Scriptures and that they must rely upon the priest for the proper "interpretation." Thus millions of people are kept in the bondage of ignorance, and are coached to say, "That's just your interpretation" when some passage from the Bible is brought to consideration in opposition to Catholic error. Here is the point: let the Bible speak for itself, and when you see it in the Book believe it for what it says. Paul said of Timothy, "From a child thou has known the holy scriptures." If a child can understand it, can't you? Further, if you say that you cannot understand it, you are charging God with requiring of you more than you are able to perform, for we read, "Study to show thyself approved unto God, a workman that needeth not to be ashamed, rightly dividing the word of truth." (II Timothy 2:15). We urge you to follow the example of the Bereans: "These were more noble than those in Thessalonica, in that they received the word with all readiness of mind, and searched the scriptures daily, whether those things were so" (Acts 17:11).

Now it is greatly to be hoped that we are ready to consider Catholicism in the light of God's Word, and in doing so, we will understand why I left it.

THE ORIGIN OF CATHOLICISM: ONE-MAN RULE

Hardly had the second century begun, until certain people thought they saw the wisdom of setting one man over an entire congregation and designating that man as priest. All Christians are priests, for Peter plainly states that such compose a "royal priesthood" (I Peter 2:5, 9). But, as to the oversight of an entire congregation of people, let us see what the scriptures say. In I Timothy 5:17 we read, "Let the elders that rule well be counted worthy of double honor, especially they who labor in the word and doctrine." The elders then are to rule in the church. We might add they rule "not as lords over God's heritage, but as examples to the flock" (I Peter 5:3). What is the extent of their rule? In Acts 14:23, we learn that elders were ordained in every church. Thus we are caused to know that there is to be a plurality of elders in each individual congregation. Since the elders rule jointly in every local congregation, it is evident that no one man is to appropriate all such authority unto himself. Furthermore, you do not read in the New Testament of any man, or set of men, having more authority under heaven, in the church of the living God, than do the elders in the church. That means that, in the matter of organization, there can be nothing larger than the local congregation with the oversight under a plurality of elders.

THE ORIGIN OF BISHOP, ARCH-BISHOP, CARDINAL AND POPE

More time passes, and the same people thought it prudent to bring many local congregations in a given district under one head, and so the Bishop was introduced. The name "bishop" is synonymous with elder in the Scriptures, and, as for the office given to the one so designated by the Catholic Church, there is absolutely no grounds in the Bible. With the passing of additional time, it was thought to be a part of wisdom to bring all the districts in a state or province under one head, and so the archbishop was introduced. Both name and office are unscriptural and anti-scriptural. Then in the course of time it was thought wise to bring all the states or provinces in a continent under one head, and so the cardinal was introduced. Both name and office unscriptural and anti-scriptural. With the passing of further time—in fact, in 606 A. D.—old emperor Phocus, who was himself a murderer and an adulterer, appointed Boniface III, the first pope. Should anyone be inclined to call that in question, being mindful as I am that Romanism proposes a certain lineage from the time of Peter, I think this one argument is enough to settle the matter: for the first six centuries there was no ecumenical council called but what was called by an emperor—never by a pope! The decisions of those councils were considered authoritative and nowhere in them was there the slightest or barest allusion to a pope. Why not? If there had been such, quite obviously there would have been acknowledgment of the same.

WHY PETER COULD NOT BE A POPE

Now we have reached a vital juncture in our consideration. A pope has been appointed. The pope is supposed to be the successor of Peter; and yet, is it not strange, that Peter in neither of his epistles recognized the eminence of that office? Rather he referred to himself as a servant, as an apostle, as a fellow-elder. Further, is it not strange as recorded in Acts 8, when it was desired to have men sent from Jerusalem to Samaria that they might lay hands on certain ones, that Peter and John were sent? Have you ever heard of a pope being sent anywhere? Can you, beloved, in the greatest stretch of your imagination conceive of the present pope being sent on a mission by anyone? Does then Peter being sent to Samaria indicate the pre-eminence which is ordinarily attached to the office of pope? Something more: in the council held in Jerusalem as recorded in the fifteenth chapter of Acts, was it not James, if any one at all, who presided? Was it not James who handed down the finality of the decision? Did not Paul say, "For I suppose I was not a whit behind the very chiefest apostles." Does not Paul in the Galatian letter tell of withstanding Peter to his face, because he stood condemned? Peter associated with the Gentiles in Antioch before the coming of the Jewish brethren, but when they came, Peter withdrew himself from the Gentiles. Paul condemned Peter because he would have Gentiles live as did the Jews. Does that indicate the pre-eminence of Peter? You have heard it said that the Catholic Church never changes. Peter had a wife as shown in Matthew 8:14. The Catholic Church would have you think he was the first pope. Can his successor take a wife? Peter being right, the Catholic Church is wrong. He was certainly not in harmony with it.

TOO MANY POPES

Let us consider just for a moment this matter of papal lineage. Did you know that, after the papacy was introduced, there was a period of seventy years in which there was no pope at all? Did you know that for another period of fifty years there were two lines of popes? And did you know that at one time there were three popes? They were Benedict

XIII; Gregory XII, the French pope; and John XXIII, the Italian pope. Where does all this leave papal lineage and infallibility?

THE POPE: RULER OF THE WORLD

When the pope is declared to be the pope, on his head is placed a three tiered tiara, or triple crown, which means, according to Romanism, that he is the father of kings and princes, ruler of the world, and vicar of Jesus Christ. The Prompta Bibliotheca, an official Roman Catholic almanac published by the press of Propaganda Fide in Rome, in its article under the heading of "Papa," states: "The Pope is of so great dignity and so exalted that he is not a mere man, but, as it were, God, and the Vicar of Christ. The Pope is of such lofty dignity that, properly speaking, he has not been established in any rank of dignity, but rather has been placed upon the very summit of all ranks of dignities. He is likewise the Divine Monarch and Supreme Emperor, and King of Kings. The Pope is of so great authority that he can modify, explain or interpret even divine law." Pope Gregory said, "The Pope is the representative of God on earth; he should then govern the world. To him alone, pertain infallibility and universality; all men are submitted to his laws, and he can only be judged by God; he ought to wear imperial ornaments; people and kings should kiss his feet; Christians are irrevocably submitted to his orders; they should murder their princes, fathers and children, if he command it; no council can be declared universal without the orders of the Pope; no book can be received as canonical without his authority; finally, no good or evil exists but in what he has condemned or approved." Now, my friends, I ask: Is there, or has there ever been, in all professed Christendom, a parallel to the foregoing in arrogancy and presumption?

THE POPE IN PROPHECY

Let us see now if you do not quickly recognize a certain prophetic description which we shall read from the Word of God: "Let no man deceive you by any means: for that day shall not come, except there come a falling away first, and that man of sin be revealed, the son of perdition; who opposeth and exalteth himself above all that is called God, or that is worshipped; so that he as God sitteth in the temple of God, showing himself that he is God." (II Thess. 2:3, 4). Who is the man of sin, the son of perdition? He is the one who, as God, sits in the temple of God, showing himself that he is God. If you were required to describe such an imposter, could you possibly do it more completely than is done by that apostate church herself in the description of her head?

But let us read from the Bible further beginning with the next verse: "Remember ye not, that, when I was yet with you, I told you these things? And now ye know what withholdeth that he might be revealed in his time. For the mystery of iniquity doth already work: only he who now letteth will let, until he be taken out of the way. And then shall that wicked one be revealed, whom the Lord shall consume with the spirit of his mouth, and shall destroy with the brightness of his coming: even him, whose coming is after the working of Satan with all power and signs and lying wonders, and with all deceivableness of unrighteousness in them that perish; because they received not the love of the truth, that they might be saved. And for this cause God shall send them strong delusion, that they should believe a lie: that they all might be damned who believe not the truth, but had pleasure in unrighteousness" (II Thess. 2:5-12). You notice that Paul states there was something which restrained, at that time, the revelation of the man of sin, even though the "mystery of iniquity" was already at work, but you will also note that the restraining force would be taken out of the way.

Now let us turn to the thirteenth chapter of Revelation. There we read, "And I stood upon the sand of the sea, and saw a beast rise up out of the sea, having seven heads and ten horns, and upon his horns ten crowns, and upon his heads the name of blasphemy..... And I saw one of his heads as it were wounded to death; and his deadly wound was healed: and all the world wondered after the beast..... And he opened his mouth in blasphemy against God, to blaspheme his name, and his tabernacle, and them that dwell in heaven. And it was given unto him to make war with the saints, and to overcome them: and power was given him over all kindreds, and tongues, and nations. And all that dwell upon the earth shall worship him, whose names are not written in the book of life of the Lamb slain from the foundation of the world..... And I beheld another beast coming up out of the earth; and he had two horns like a lamb, and he spake as a dragon. And he exerciseth all the power of the first beast before him, and causeth the earth and them which dwell therein to worship the first beast, whose deadly wound was healed. And he doth great wonders, so that he maketh fire come down from heaven on the earth in the sight of men, and deceiveth them that dwell on the earth, by the means of those miracles which he had power to do in the sight of the beast; saying to them that dwell on the earth, that they should make an image to the beast, which had the wound by a sword, and did live. And he had power to give life unto the image of the beast, that the image of the beast should both speak, and cause that as many as would not worship the image of the beast should be killed. And he causeth all, both great and small, rich and poor, free and bond, to receive a mark in their right hand, or in their foreheads..." On the basis of these various verses from the chapter stated, and bearing in mind the apostle Paul's description of "the man of sin" in the second chapter of second Thessalonians, let us consider a striking parallel as it is reflected in recorded history.

OUT OF PAGANISM GREW THE PAPACY

The empire of pagan Rome, like unto a cruel beast, truly wore the name of blasphemy. It was called the Holy Roman Empire. Can an empire be holy which killed the saints and supported with all its strength a worship of force and idolatry? There is blasphemy! As long as pagan Rome was in the ascendancy, her crowned heads claimed divine powers. Sufficient proof of this is seen in the fact that every ecumenical council for the first six centuries was called by an emperor. The cruelty of pagan Rome shows that she derived her power from the dragon, the devil. When the barbarian hordes swept down from the north in 476 A. D., the empire seemingly was "wounded to death." Babylon fell to rise no more. The Kingdom of the Medes and the Persians fell to rise no more.

THE CATHOLIC CHURCH

Apparently that would be the lot of Rome. But not so! The "deadly wound was healed," and "all the world wondered after the beast." Paul declared that the "man of sin" would not be revealed until that which restrained was taken away. History plainly shows that, as long as pagan Rome was in the ascendancy, papal Rome was held in check. In the fourth century, Emperor Constantine recognized his version of "Christianity" as the true religion; and, by his gifts to the church and at the point of the sword, he gave impetus to that movement which resulted in the ascendency of papal Rome. As pagan Rome declined, papal Rome ascended. Out of the casket of pagan Rome, emerges papal Rome! Thus the second beast makes his presence felt for "he exerciseth all the power of the first beast before him." And let me say just here that all the pageantry and display, and pomp and ostentation of the Roman Catholic Church as is evidenced in her ornately decorated altars, the flowing robes and richly embellished garments of her priests, and the tapers and incense—all of this, constitutes but relics of pagan Rome and speaks convincingly, itself, of the origin of papal Rome. And yet the uninformed are taken in by such stuff, thinking that it is the mark of the true religion. How unlike the Christ who, in the midst of Roman pageantry, was born in a stable and placed in a manger, and who, some two years before his death, said, "The foxes have holes, and the birds of the air have nests; but the Son of man hath not where to lay his head." And how unlike Peter who said, "Silver and gold have I none" is that one who sits pompously in the midst of the vast wealth of the Vatican while without her walls the impoverished Italians beg for bread; and yet many of them continue to pay allegiance to that imposter who in no small degree is responsible for their said plight. Thus the "strong delusion" works of which Paul spoke. Why cannot people see that, on the very face of it, such pageantry cannot be a part of the religion of our Lord Jesus Christ? We say with the apostle Paul, "I fear, lest by any means, as the serpent beguiled Eve through his subtility, so your minds should be corrupted from the simplicity that is in Christ" (II Cor. 11:3).

THE INTOLERANCE OF CATHOLICISM

Further, this second beast is described thus: "he had two horns like a lamb, and he spake as a dragon." How fitly that describes the Roman Catholic Church! Her outward appearance presents the meekness of a lamb, but her papal bulls and edicts disclose the voice of the dragon. "He doeth great wonders.....and deceiveth them that dwell on the earth, by means of those miracles which he had power to do....." Or, as Paul states in describing the man of sin, "whose coming is after the working of Satan with all power and signs and lying wonders." The so-called "miracles" of the Catholic Church, such as those of the scapular, are sufficiently familiar to most of you to continue this striking parallel. ".....As many as would not worship the image of the beast should be killed. And he causeth all, both small and great, rich and poor, free and bond, to receive the mark in their right hand, or in their foreheads....." Romanism is intolerant when and where that church has the ascendancy. Consider the Inquisition; consider the slaughter of the Huguenots; and even today, my friends, consider the rank intolerance in Catholic dominated and benighted Spain as she struggles under Franco, the henchman of the pope. Also, think, if you will, of the intolerance in Portugal, and reflect upon the cruel suppression of the activity of other religious bodies in many South American countries—particularly such countries as Argentina under the papal servant, Peron—as the intolerance there has been brought to light time and time again by the protest of those religious bodies in the American press.

CATHOLICISM SEEKS POLITICAL SUPREMACY

What has happened and is happening in other countries would happen here if the Catholic Church were in the ascendancy—that is my firm conviction. By their fruits, ye shall know them! All of this stems from the idea that the pope should govern the world. Do not be deceived, the Catholic Church still entertains that hope. Hear her own spokesman, Cardinal Gibbons in "The Faith of Our Fathers," page 150: "For our part we have every confidence that ere long the

THE CATHOLIC CHURCH 199

clouds which now overshadow the civil throne of the Pope will be removed by the breath of a righteous God, and that his temporal power will be re-established on a more permanent basis." (This quotation is taken from the 83rd revised edition of the above book, published in 1917). Further Paul tells us of the "deceivableness of unrighteousness in them that perish; because they received not the love of the truth, that they might be saved." Jesus tells us that God's Word is truth (John 17:17). The Bible contains that Word, and yet those in the bondage of Romanism permit themselves to be persuaded that "the Bible is a dead letter and cannot interpret itself." "And for this cause God shall send them strong delusion, that they should believe a lie: that they all might be damned who believed not the truth, but had pleasure in unrighteousness" (II Thess. 2:10-12).

CATHOLICISM OPPOSES SEPARATION OF CHURCH AND STATE

What has been said plainly shows that the Catholic Church bitterly opposes the separation of Church and State. When Jesus said, "Render therefore unto Ceasar the things which are Caesar's; and unto God the things that are God's," (Matt. 22:21), He forever separated the church on the one hand from the state on the other. That period of spiritual degeneration so aptly called the "Dark Ages" was the awful result of the merger of church and state.

Concerning this matter of the separation of church and state, one point which has been brought under very subtle attack is our public school set-up. As you perhaps know, some time ago the United States Supreme Court granted permission by a vote of five to four for parochial school children to be carried on public school busses. Later, a certain Paul Connell, a lawyer in a certain school district in Pennsylvania, endeavored to force the local public school board to carry his daughter to a parochial school in a public school bus. The public school board refused. The matter was taken to the county court which sustained the decision of the school board. It was taken in due course to the state supreme court which upheld the former decision. Ultimately it reached the United

States Supreme Court which, by its action, gave support to the decision originally arrived at by the school board itself. But do you not see the pattern? First permission is received, and then compulsion is striven for. Catholics will argue that they pay taxes and, therefore, they are entitled to the use of the public school busses. They are entitled to the use of the public school busses on the same basis that every other taxpayer is: that is, that their children might be carried to some public school. Everyone welcomes their use of the public school busses on that basis. But when any school—and I mean any school—teaches a peculiar religious dogma, it forfeits the right to state support, and it thereby forfeits the right to the use of public school busses. Indeed so!

THE BIBLE IN THE PUBLIC SCHOOL

There are those, some of whom ought to know better, who are urging that the study of the Bible be introduced into the public schools. The public school is a state institution, being supported by public funds. To argue that the Bible be taught therein is to wave aside the principle laid down by our Lord Jesus Christ concerning the separation of Church and state. To contend that the Bible should be taught in public schools is also to wave aside the First Amendment to the Federal Constitution. Further, let it be borne in mind that all people who pay taxes support the state schools and if all tax-paying religionists did not have a voice in the particular course proposed for study, could not the slighted taxpayers say with Patrick Henry, "Taxation without representation is tyranny!" And if, on the other hand, all religionists did have a voice in the course of study, tell me what kind of course would it be? Far better that there be no course than to have such a travesty. But the United States Supreme Court has ruled in this very matter, and I have here the decision as reported in the United Press dispatch dated Tuesday, March 9, 1948: "Washington March 8th—The Supreme Court ruled Monday that religious teaching in public schools, even on a voluntary basis, is unconstitutional." The 8-to-1 decision was made in a case challenging the voluntary religious instruction system used in the Champaign, Ill., public schools. The majority opinion, written by Justice Hugo L. Black was based on the separation of church and state as provided in the First Amendment to the Federal Constitution. Justice Stanley F. Reed was the lone dissenter. Black held that the First Amendment "has erected a wall between church and state which must be kept high and impregnable." He added that the Champaign plan "falls squarely under the ban of the First Amendment."

It might not be amiss just here to read the language of some of our men of state concerning this very matter.

JAMES G. BLAINE OPPOSES UNION OF CHURCH AND STATE

James G. Blaine presented this article in the House of Representatives as a Constitutional Amendment: "No state shall make any law representing an establishment of religion, or prohibiting the free exercise thereof; and no money raised by school taxation in any state for the support of public schools, or derived from any public fund thereof, nor any public lands devoted thereto, shall ever be under control of any religious sect; nor shall any money so raised, or land so devoted, be divided among religious sects or denominations." It was stated by Senator Blair, as a matter of history, on the 15th day of February, 1888, that the defeat of this amendment was brought about by the Jesuits. Who are the Jesuits? A former Catholic priest has referred to them as "that society of storm troopers and mischief-makers of the Roman Catholic Church."

PRESIDENT JAMES A. GARFIELD'S STATEMENT

President James A. Garfield said, "Next in importance to freedom and justice, is popular education, without which neither freedom nor justice can be permanently maintained. It would be unjust to our people, and dangerous to our institutions, to apply any portion of the revenue of the nation, or of the state to the support of sectarian schools. The separation of the church and state, in everything relating to taxation, should be absolute."

GENERAL GRANT SEES CONFLICT

General U. S. Grant declared, "If we are to have another contest in the near future of our national existence, I predict that the dividing line will not be Mason and Dixon's, but it will be between patriotism and intelligence on one side, and superstition, ambition and ignorance on the other. In this centennial year, the work of strengthening the foundation of the structure laid by our forefathers one hundred years ago, should be begun. Let us all labor for the security of free thought, free speech, free press, and pure morals, unfettered religious sentiments, and equal rights and privileges for all men, irrespective of nationality, color or religion. Encourage free schools, and resolve that not one dollar appropriated to them shall be applied to the support of any sectarian school; resolve that any child in the land may get a common school education, unmixed with atheistic, pagan or sectarian teachings; keep the church and state forever separate."

ABRAHAM LINCOLN VS. THE CATHOLIC CHURCH

Abraham Lincoln stated, "As long as God gives me a heart to feel, a brain to think, or a hand to execute my will, I will devote it against that power which has attempted to use the machinery of the courts to destroy the rights and character of an American citizen. But there is a thing which is very certain; it is, that if the American people could learn what I know of the fierce hatred of the generality of the priests of Rome against our institutions, our schools, our most sacred rights, and our so dearly bought liberties, they would drive them away, tomorrow, from among us, or would shoot them as traitors..... The history of the last thousand years tells us that wherever the Church of Rome is not a dagger to pierce the bosom of a free nation, she is a stone to her neck, and a ball to her feet, to paralyze her and prevent her advance in the ways of civilization, science, intelligence, happiness, and liberty..... I do not pretend to be a prophet. But though not a prophet, I see a very dark cloud on our horizon. And that dark cloud is coming from Rome. It is filled with tears of blood. It will rise and increase, till its flanks will be torn by a flash of lightning, followed by a fearful peal of thunder. Then a cyclone such as the world has never seen, will pass over this country, spreading ruin and desolation from north to south. After it is over, there will be long days of peace and prosperity; for popery, with its Jesuits and merciless Inquisition, will have been forever swept away from our country. Neither I nor you, but our children, will see those things." The beloved Lincoln made the statement just given at the conclusion of the trial of Mr. Chiniquy, author of the book, "Fifty Years in the Church of Rome."

According to the book, "America or Rome, Christ or the Pope" by John L. Brandt, it was published in the various papers that Lincoln was born a Catholic, baptized by a priest, and therefore was to be considered a renegade and an apostate. Although this was false, Mr. Chiniquy said to Lincoln at the time, "That report is your sentence of death."

The book further records that Lincoln's murder was planned in the home of Mrs. Surratt, a Roman Catholic. Booth, the murderer, was a Roman Catholic. Mr. Lloyd, who had the carbine that Booth wanted for "protection," was a Roman Catholic. Dr. Mudd, who set Booth's fractured leg, was a Roman Catholic. Garrett, in whose barn Booth tried to hide, was a Roman Catholic. John H. Surratt, who was hiding under the banners of the Pope when he was detected, was a Roman Catholic. The death of Lincoln was announced by Roman Catholics, several hours before it occurred, at St. Joseph, Minn., forty miles from a railroad and eighty miles from the nearest telegraph station. This fact is established in history.

After being apprehended, Booth said, "I can never repent. God made me the instrument of his punishment."

Prominent government officials said, "We have not the least doubt but that the Jesuits were at the bottom of the great iniquity." Mr. Chiniquy, Colonel Edwin A. Sherman and General Harris, friends of Lincoln, investigated the matter, and unequivocally affirmed that Rome was the instigator of Lincoln's assassination.

THE BULWARK OF DEMOCRACY

My friends, I realize that I have dwelt at considerable length on this matter of the separation of Church and state—but I consider it most vital, and I am persuaded that the great principle involved is, in this great nation of ours, being subjected to constant and insidious attack. As for our public schools, I salute them as the bulwark of democracy. The Catholic Church charges that our public schools are Godless and inept. I answer, by their fruits ye shall know them. Contrast the United States, the land of freedom and great achievement, with her public school system and high literacy standard with those countries burdened with Catholic education: benighted Spain and Portugal, backward Ireland, prostrate Italy, debauched France, and the groping countries of South America. There you have sufficient answer! If we would maintain democracy as we know it, let us maintain our public school system as it is!

CATHOLIC HOLY WATER

Now, my friends, let us proceed with our consideration of Romanish doctrine, and thus continue to establish the disregard for God's Word as reflected therein, and thereby further set forth why I left the Catholic Church. The introduction of "Holy Water" could easily have been the first departure from simple New Testament teaching. Where, pray tell me, do you read in the gospel of Christ of Holy Water? Peter tells us that God has given to us all things that pertain to life and godliness (II Peter 1:3), but God has not given to us anything that pertains to Holy Water. Therefore Holy Water is no part of life or godliness. Furthermore, let it be constantly borne in mind that, as already established, the revelation of God as it concerns our duty to Him is fixed, final, and complete. As Jude would say, it has been "once delivered unto the saints." Hence, beloved, to teach or practice something not authorized therein is to fall under the indictment pronounced by John in these words: "Whosoever goeth onward and abideth not in the teaching of Christ, hath not God....." (II John 9). So a little Holy Water become a violation of a great principle.

THE LATIN MASS

And then there is the Latin Mass. Wherever you go upon the earth—in this country, Canada, England, France, Germany, the countries of South America or Africa or Asia—the mass is said in Latin, a dead language. Yet the apostle Paul declared, "For if I pray in an unknown tongue, my spirit prayeth, but my understanding is unfruitful. What is it then? I will pray with the spirit, and I will pray with the understanding also: I will sing with the spirit, and I will sing with the understanding also. Else when thou shalt bless with the spirit, how shall he that occupieth the room of the unlearned say Amen at thy giving of thanks, seeing he understandeth not what thou sayest? For thou verily givest thanks well, but the other is not edified. I thank my God, I speak with tongues more than ye all: yet in the church I had rather speak five words with my understanding, that by my voice I might teach others also, than ten thousand words in an unknown tongue." (I Cor. 14:14-19). Let the Roman Catholic Church contend that the world-wide Latin mass is a mark of her universality and a sign of her cohesion; the truth remains that it is a flat violation of the teaching of the apostle Paul which has just been given. Thus, again, the Catholic Church disregards the Word of God.

THE SACRAMENT OF PENANCE

Let us now take a look at the Sacrament of Penance. According to this point of Catholic doctrine, which is everywhere embraced, acknowledged and studied by Catholics, when men sin they incur the wrath of God, and when they repent and receive the Sacrament of Absolution, they are forgiven—but not altogether! The Council of Trent sets forth: "If any man shall say that the whole penalty is always remitted by God, together with the guilt, and that the only satisfaction of penitents is faith whereby they embrace that Christ has made satisfaction for them: let him be accursed." Thus the Catholic Church teaches that there are two punishments for sin, the eternal and the temporal. Now, by the Sacrament of Penance, the eternal punishment is remitted, but the temporal punishment remains due. Man must do something to appease the wrath of God regarding the temporal punishment. The priest determines what is sufficient to satisfy God in this matter. In Peter Dens' Theology, a long list of suggested works of satisfaction practiced in the Romanish Church are given: fasting, rising earlier, enduring cold, praying, reciting litanies, reading the penitential psalms, hearing masses, visiting churches, wearing sackcloth, making gift of food, clothes, money, and so on. Let us see the gross offence to God's Word in this. First, it makes God's forgiveness incomplete. But hear the Lord in the matter: "Come now, let us reason together, saith the Lord: though your sins be as scarlet, they shall be as white as snow; though they be red like crimson, they shall be as wool" (Isaiah 1:18).

Second, it makes Christ only a partial Savior—the ministry of the priest is altogether essential; he must determine what more is necessary in order to satisfy God. But we read of Christ: "Wherefore he is able to save them to the uttermost that come unto God by him, seeing he ever liveth to make intercession for them." (Hebrews 7:25). Get it, my friends! Christ is able to save to the uttermost them that come unto God by him!

Finally, as already stated, it makes the priest an absolutely necessary mediator, and in this we see the design of the Catholic Church to bind the people to herself through her system of priests and sacraments which they alone can administer. But hear the apostle Paul in this matter: "For there is one God, and one mediator between God and men, the man Christ Jesus" (I Tim. 2:5). There is one mediator; that mediator is Jesus Christ—and that eliminates the Catholic priest from God's order.

CATHOLIC DOCTRINE OF PURGATORY

Let us now have a look at the Catholic doctrine of purgatory. The first council that mentions the subject of purgatory is the Council of Florence in 1438 A. D. It decreed, "If any true penitents shall depart this life in the love of God, before they have made satisfaction by worthy fruits of penance for faults of commission and omission, their souls are purified after death, by the pains of purgatory." In the Douay Catechism, we read: "Whither go such as die in venial sin, or not having fully satisfied the punishment due to their mortal sin? The answer: To purgatory, till they have made full satisfaction for them, and then to heaven. What is purgatory? The answer: A place of punishment in the other life where souls suffer for a time, before they can go to heaven."

As to the nature of the punishment, Peter Dens states that it is two-fold: one of loss and one of sense. The punishment of loss is merely a delay of the beatific confession; and the punishment of sense in purgatory is caused by material fire. Bellarmine maintains that the punishments of purgatory are more severe, grievous and bitter than the greatest punishments of this world. Damien, along with others, teaches the inhabitants of purgatory pass rapidly and painfully in baths ranging from cool to tepid, from torrid to frigid, from freezing to boiling. Thurcal tells us that, among other things, the sufferers have to pass over a bridge studded with sharp nails with points upturned; the souls have to walk barefoot on this rough road, and many ease their feet by using their hands; others roll with the whole body on the perforating nails, until, at last, bloodily pierced, they complete their way over the painful course. Thus, in due course, they escape to heaven. Such are some of the visions of purgatory depicted by some of the Romanish theological writers. Such tales are as silly as pagan mythology. In fact, Plato, Homer and Virgil taught the same doctrine. Protestants of today have so exposed these absurd notions that Roman Catholics are sometimes hesitant to acknowledge such a portrayal of purgatory. Yet the time was when the pope, the cardinals and their co-workers upheld such rigidly, and to deny it was a mark of heresy. Their modern writers still maintain the punishment is extremely severe and is caused by material fire.

WHERE IS PURGATORY?

As to where purgatory is, Catholic authors cannot decide. Gregory the Great thought it to be in the earth's center, and he considered the eruptions of Vesuvius and Aetna as flames arising from it. Bellarmine thought purgatory between heaven and earth with the demons of the air. Damien with others concluded it might be in some flaming cavern or icy stream. The truth, my friends, is, of course, that there is no such place. It is but the figment of Catholicism, and is used to fatten her purse and bind the people to the ministry of her priests as we shall see in our consideration of indulgences, invented to release the sufferers from the imagined purgatory and transport them to paradise. Beloved, the Word of God very plainly teaches that our eternal destiny is sealed at the time of our physical death. Paul declares, "For we must all appear before the judgment seat of Christ; that every one may receive the things done in his body, according to that he hath done, whether it be good or bad" (II Cor. 5:10). We shall be judged by what we do in the body, and James sets forth that "the body without the spirit is dead" (James 2:26). Hence, when we die in the body our eternal judgment and destiny are sealed! This, of course, is absolutely fatal to the theory of purgatory, a supposed place of further cleansing.

A GREAT GULF FIXED

Listen to Jesus, whose native home is the other world, as He gives us the account of the rich man and Lazarus. "It came to pass, that the beggar (Lazarus) died, and was carried by the angels into Abraham's bosom: the rich man also died, and was buried; and in hades he lifted up his eyes, being in torments, and seeth Abraham afar off, and Lazarus in his bosom. And he cried and said, Father Abraham, have mercy on me, and send Lazarus, that he may dip the tip of his finger in water, and cool my tongue; for I am tormented in this flame. But Abraham said, Son, remember that thou in thy lifetime receivest thy good things, and likewise Lazarus evil things: but now he is comforted, and thou art tormented." Now take notice: "And beside all this, between us and you there is a great gulf fixed: so that they which would pass from hence to you cannot; neither can they pass to us, that would come from thence" (Luke 16:22-26). After death, there is a great gulf fixed between them which cannot be crossed, and—mark it!—that is before the final judgment, for later the rich man pleads that Lazarus might be sent to his father's house in order to testify to his five brethren. Remember, too, the account reads, "... The rich man also died, and was buried; and in hades he lift up his eyes..." That is the sequence. So, we see that after death there is a great gulf fixed that cannot be crossed. What purpose, then, can purgatory serve? It is not strange that Catholicism rejects the Bible; to accept the Bible would be to destroy Catholicism.

INDULGENCES THE KEY TO PURGATORY

As soon as the Catholic Church had invented purgatory, she devised means of affording a fictitious key, namely indulgences, to unlock the door of that fictitious prison called purgatory. The Catholic Church tells us that "an indulgence is a remission of the temporal punishment of our sins, which the Church grants us outside the sacrament of penance. Can indulgences be made use of to the souls in purgatory? Yes, all indulgences which the Pope has indicated for that purpose." Pope Leo X stated, "We have thought proper to signify to you that the Bishop of Rome is able to grant to the faithful in Christ, indulgence either in this life or in purgatory—out of the superabundant merits of Christ and his saints." The bishop may grant indulgences in his diocese, and the archbishop throughout the whole province, but the pope is the supreme dispenser of indulgences. An indulgence may be received by a man before he enters purgatory, and so be happy. Or, an individual might operate retroactively in regard to certain works of alms, prayers and the like performed by someone for another. For example, a Catholic, with sympathy for his relatives in purgatory, might obtain an indulgence in the form of commutation of their sentence in that fiery region, securing in such a case an indulgence of a certain number of days or years.

According to a Catholic book of devotion, this brief petition, "Sweet heart of Mary, save me!" gives three hundred days indulgence every time it is repeated. From the infallibly authorized Book of the Scapular, we take note that: To those who wear the scapular during life, Mary makes this promise: "I, their glorious mother, on the Saturday after death, will descend to purgatory and deliver those whom I shall find there, and take them up to the holy mountain of eternal life."

To visit a Carmelite church on Saturday procures eighty-seven years of indulgence, and the remission of two-sevenths of all sins; to wear a blue scapular gives full indulgence, cancels all sins, and gives a free ticket to paradise.

AMERICA SPENDS TEN MILLION IN INDULGENCES

Indulgences have been used to prompt crusaders to rise up against those who have opposed Catholicism; they have been used to purchase the remission of sins, and to deliver souls from purgatory. Mr. Chiniquy, in chapter twenty-five of his book "Fifty Years in Rome," states that more than ten million dollars are expended annually in North America to help souls out of purgatory. At the time of writing, he stated that masses were said in Canada at twenty-five cents each, and in many parts of United States at one dollar each, and that it was, therefore, a common practice for the bishops in the United States to have masses said in Canada for the departed souls, and thereby make seventy-five cents on each mass. For many years it was a common practice for the bishops of Canada to send to Paris to have masses said at five cents each by the poorer priests there, thus saving twenty cents on each mass they were paid to celebrate.

LUTHER ARISES AGAINST INDULGENCES

When Martin Luther was serving as a priest in Whittenberg, Germany, Johan Tetzel, a Dominican priest, came through that region selling indulgences and telling the people that if they would buy those indulgences and couple with them severe penance, they would have the remission of their sins. That seems to be the incident that prompted Luther to put his ninety-five objections to the Catholic Church on the door of the church building, and then defy the whole Catholic hierarchy, pope included, to debate the merit of his objections. I might add that the money thus obtained by Tetzel was going to complete the building of St. Peter's Cathedral in Rome. There was no scruple about this business of selling indulgences. Tetzel went so far as to proclaim that he had saved more souls from hell by his indulgences than the apostle Peter had converted to Christianity by his preaching. If that is not making merchandise of religion, pray tell me, what is it? Coming to a knowledge of the truth and being honest with myself, I could not stay in the Catholic Church. That is why I left.

THE DOCTRINE OF EXTREME UNCTION

The Catholic Church practices what she terms "extreme unction." She describes it thus: "Extreme unction is a sacrament in which by the anointing with holy oil and by the prayers of the priest, the sick receive the grace of God for the good of their souls, and often also their bodies... It (extreme unction) increases sanctifying grace; it remits venial sins, and those mortal sins which a sick person repents of; it strengthens the soul in its sufferings and temptations; it often relieves the pains of sick persons, and sometimes restores him to health... We should receive extreme unction when we are in danger of death from sickness." This is a shining example of Catholic arrogance and presumption. Not only is there no mention whatever of such a practice in God's Word, but for the first eleven hundred years of this Christian era, there is no record of its ever being practiced among the people of earth. In the Converted Catholic Magazine of several months ago, there was an article, if I mistake not, having to do with the grave misgivings on the one hand or the fears on the other of Catholic youth engaged in World War II, who on the eve of actual combat reflected on the impossibility of Catholic chaplains being everywhere present to administer extreme unction. Protestant youth understand that there is one mediator, Jesus Christ, and that He is truly omni-present, and, hence, they are not concerned about the feigned mediation of one who, like themselves, has feet of clay.

CATHOLICISM ONLY AUTHORITY FOR INSTRUMENTAL MUSIC

The Roman Catholic Church practices, and thus teaches, the use of mechanical instruments of music in the worship. I want to say tonight that everyone who makes up this attentive audience and who is a member of a religious body using mechanical instruments of music in its worship has no higher authority for the use of the same than the Romanish Church. The New Testament teaches us to make melody in our hearts (Eph. 5:19) with the fruit of our lips (Heb. 13:15). It further teaches us that this melody, our singing, is to be with the spirit and the understanding (I Cor. 14:15). Can an insensate, mechanical instrument of music qualify? You may read your New Testament very, very carefully and you will not find the remotest hint of authority for the use of them. What does that mean? It means that whoever practices it in the worship goes beyond the authority of Christ, and John states that he "hath not God" (II John 9). Of course, instrumental music is not wrong in itself; if that were true, it would be wrong anywhere at anytime. But remember this one thing, it is wrong to introduce it into what is professed to be Christian worship when God has not commanded us to do so. We cannot infringe on the silence of the scriptures. When Pope Vitalian II introduced instrumental music into the worship in 666 A. D., it created such a furor that it had to be removed for about a hundred years. The matter of objection thereto, and division as a result thereof, has always followed in its wake. Indeed so!

CONFESSING SINS TO PRIESTS

Let me speak briefly of auricular confession and the arrogant contention that the priest can forgive sin. There is a curtained recess or box which is called the confessional in every Catholic Church. The penitent Catholic on bended knee there meets the seated Catholic priest; and, as the priest questions, the penitent recites his various misdeeds since they last met. This is called "auricular" because it is made into the auris, or ear, of the priest. It is but one of not a few abominable practices introduced during the medieval period. In fact, learned Romanists do not deny that auricular confession became a practice of the Catholic Church at the council of Lateran, 1215 A. D. Pope Innocent III, of the merciless Inquisition, was its founder. Catholics, generally, do not know that. Here is one reason why they do not: the Council of Trent declared, "Whoever shall say that the mode of secretly confessing to a priest alone, which the Catholic Church has always observed from the beginning and still observes, is foreign to the institution and command of Christ, and is a human invention: let him be accursed..." My friends, here is God's way: first, for the alien sinner—when in Acts 2, the believing Jews cried out, "What shall we do?" Peter said, "Repent, and be baptized every one of you in the name of Jesus Christ for the remission of sins, and ye shall receive the gift of the Holy Ghost." No command here to confess to any priest, or any other man, for the purpose of obtaining absolution.

Now concerning God's way for those in the church: when Simon, after his baptism as recorded in Acts 8, had committed a grievous sin, Peter directed him as follows: "Repent therefore of this thy wickedness, and pray God, if perhaps the thought of thine heart may be forgiven thee" (Acts 8:21-23). Peter did not direct him to confess his sins to a priest in order to obtain absolution. James, in giving instructons to those in the church, said, "Confess your faults one to another, and pray one for the other, that ye may be healed" (James 5:16). My friends, that states, "Confess your faults one to another;" it does not say to a priest.

CORRUPTING INFLUENCES OF THE AURICULAR CONFESSION

Now concerning another aspect of such a practice, Mr. Chiniquy, an ex-priest of good authority, says: "I have heard the confession of more than two hundred priests, and to say the truth, as God knows it, I must declare that only twenty-one had not to weep over the secret sins committed through the irresistibly corrupting influences of auricular confession. I am now more than seventy-seven years old, and in a short time I shall be in my grave. I shall have to give an account of what I now say. Well, it is in the presence of my Great Judge, with my tomb before my eyes, that I declare to the world that very few—yes, very few—priests escape from falling into the pit of the most horrible moral depravity the world has ever known, through the confession of females."

DO CATHOLICS TEACH THAT PRIESTS CAN FORGIVE SINS?

Let us look, just for a moment, at this question, "Does the Catholic Church really teach that the priests can forgive sin?" In Deharbe's Catechism, page 150, we read, "Question: Does the priest really forgive sins, or does he only declare them forgiven? Answer: The priest really and truly forgives sins through the power given him by Christ." How is the little child, or ignorant adult, or the one educated in a Catholic school going to recognize how much the Scriptures are perverted in that statement? To forgive sins is God's prerogative, and He has never delegated it to any priest! "He as God sitteth in the temple of God, showing himself that he is God." Such blasphemy!

"CALL NO MAN FATHER"

While speaking of the usurpation of that which belongs to God, let us consider the fact that the priest is called "Father." Jesus said, "But be not ye called Rabbi: for one is your Master, even Christ; and all ye are brethren. And call no man your father upon the earth: for one is your Father, which is in heaven" (Matt. 23:8, 9). The usual Catholic quibble is, "You call your paternal parent 'father'." Yes, and Jesus speaks of the earthly parent in that manner, but here it plainly has a religious designation as the context shows.

LORD'S SUPPER BECOMES LITERAL BODY AND BLOOD OF JESUS

Now let us briefly consider the Catholic doctrine of transubstantiation. The Council of Trent declared, "Whosoever shall deny that in the Sacrament of the Most Holy Eucharist are contained, truly, really and substantially, the body and blood, together with the soul and divinity of our Lord Jesus Christ, and therefore, the entire Christ; but shall say that he is in it only as in a sign, or figure of virtue: let him be accursed." From one of the Catholic Mission Books comes this: "Question: How and when are the bread and wine changed into the Body and Blood of Jesus Christ? Answer: This change is wrought by virtue of the words of consecration pronounced by the Priest during the Holy Mass." Thus the Catholic Church teaches that the priest has the power to change the bread and wine into the very body, blood, soul and divinity of Christ; and then, permit us to add, the priest proceeds, along with his fellow-communicants, to eat the very Lord whom he professes to have thus brought into being. This absurd doctrine and practice was, no doubt what prompted Crotus, the Jew, to say, "Christians eat their God." The cannibal never eats the object of his superstition, but the Roman Catholic eats the object of his adoration. Mr. Chiniquy, the ex-priest, declares, "The world in its darkest age of paganism has never witnessed such a system of idolatry, so debasing, impious, ridiculous and diabolical in its consequences as the Church of Rome teaches in the dogma of transubstantiation..... It seems impossible that man can consent to worship a God whom the rats can eat..."

In instituting the Lord's supper, Jesus took bread and said of it, "This is my body." When our Lord made that statement, He was very much in the flesh of his body and the blood was coursing through his veins. Yet He used the present tense of the verb in declaring, "This *IS* my body." Now this question: if the bread thus became the very body of Christ, what became of the One whose hand held that bread? Remember, He has but one body. Jesus also said, "I am the door" and I am the true vine," yet none of us have any difficulty understanding that Christ is not a literal door or vine. Why then should anyone have difficulty in understanding that Christ, in the body, said of a piece of bread, "This is my body" that He did not literally become that piece of bread? Paul tells us, "That the Lord Jesus the same night in which he was betrayed took bread: and when he had given thanks, he brake it, and said, Take, eat: this is my body, which is broken for you: this do in remembrance of me" (I Cor. 11:23, 24). Notice, "This do in remembrance of me (Christ)." Now can the bread be, at the one and the same time, the memorial and the thing memorialized? Paul tells us that the Lord's Supper is a memorial of the death of Christ until He shall come (I Cor. 11:26).

Usually the Catholic will strive to justify his position by turning to the sixth chapter of John and reading, "Then Jesus said unto them, Verily, verily, I say unto you, except ye eat the flesh of the Son of man, and drink his blood, ye have no life in you ..... For my flesh is meat indeed, and my blood is drink indeed" (John 6:53, 55). Where is the Lord's Supper mentioned in that chapter? That was spoken before He instituted the Supper. To take a text from the context becomes a pretext. Continue to read the chapter and Jesus gives this meaning: "It is the spirit that quickeneth; the flesh profiteth nothing: the words that I speak unto you, they are spirit, and they are life" (verse 63). In Deharbe's Large Catechism, we read: "Have we to drink of the chalice, to receive the blood of Christ? No, for under the appearance of bread, we receive also the Blood of Christ, since we receive His living body." Let the very words of Jesus refute that Catholic teaching, "And he took the cup, and gave thanks, and gave it to them, saying, Drink ye all of it ..." (Matt. 26:27). And then we read in Mark 14:23, "And they all drank of it."

DOCTRINE OF CELIBACY

Let us view for a short while the Catholic doctrine of celibacy. The Council of Trent decreed: "Whoever shall say that the clergy constituted in sacred order, or regulars, who have solemnly professed chastity, may contract marriage and that the contract is valid: let him be accursed... Whoever shall say that the marriage state is to be preferred to the state of virginity, or celibacy, and that it is not better and more blessed to retain virginity, or celibacy, than to be joined in marrage: let him be accursed."

The Catholic Church imposes celibacy on the pope, the cardinals, the archbishops, the bishops, the priests and the nuns. Yet God said, "It is not good that the man should be alone; I will make him an help meet for him" (Gen. 2:18). We read in Hebrews 13:4, "Marriage is honorable in all..."

In the summer of 1946, a young lady, who was a Catholic and who was preparing to become a nun, attended the last service of a meeting in which I was preaching in Stratford, Oklahoma. Afterwards, she asked to talk with me. During our conversation, I pointed out that, if she became a nun as she planned, she was going to pervert the course that God would have her follow, and then I quoted this statement made by the apostle Paul, "I will therefore that the younger women marry, bear children, guide the house, give no occasion to the adversary to speak reproachfully" (I Tim. 5:14). I am happy to say that, after some two hours of our considering the Bible versus Catholicism, I had the very great pleasure of baptizing that young lady into Christ.

CONCUBINAGE IN CATHOLICISM

In the Moral Theology of Ligori, Volume 8, page 444, we read: "A bishop, however poor he may be, cannot appropriate to pecuniary fines, without license of the Apostolical See. But he ought to apply them to pious uses. Much less can he apply those fines to anything else but pious uses, which the Council of Trent has laid upon non-resident clergymen, or upon those clergymen who keep concubines." Think of it! If a clergyman of the Catholic Church marries, he is excommunicated, but if he keeps a concubine, he merely is subject to a fine. Indeed it is a strong delusion that can ensnare people in a religion that teaches such! It is no wonder that the St. Louis Republican of June 20th, 1887 printed a letter from Bishop Hogan of the Catholic Diocese of St. Joseph in which he gives a list of twenty-two priests received into his diocese the fifteen years prior to 1876 whom he was compelled to dismiss on account of immoralities. About the middle of the past century, Bishop Vandeveld, of Chicago, said of the conduct of priests in his diocese: "..... They are all either notorious drunkards, or given to public or secret concubinage."

Finally, concerning this matter of forbidding to marry, listen to this language from the Bible: "Now the Spirit speaketh expressly, that in the latter times, some shall depart from the faith, giving heed to seducing spirits, and doctrines of devils; speaking lies in hypocrisy; having their conscience seared as with a hot iron; forbidding to marry, and commanding to abstain from meats, which God hath created to be received with thanksgiving of them which believe and know the truth" (I Tim. 4:1-3). If ever God in His Word points the finger of inspiration at a religious body and brands it an apostacy, He does in this instance. Which body? That one which forbids to marry and commands to abstain from meats. But with Catholicism, the Bible is a dead letter. No wonder!

POPE BECOMES INFALLIBLE IN 1870

The Roman Catholic Church had considerable difficulty deciding that her pope is infallible, and the matter required much time. In fact, it was not until the Vatican Council in 1870 that the infallibility of the pope was adopted. Here is the result of that council's vote on the matter: 451 for, 88 against, 62 would accept if modified, and 70 did not vote at all! On the basis of that, a fallible cardinal becomes infallible, in the administration of his office, when appointed pope. Who can believe such? And remember, this was adopted more than eighteen hundred years after Christ had given to the world His fixed, final and complete revelation of what constitutes acceptable service to Almighty God.

IMAGES IN THE CATHOLIC CHURCH

The use of relics and images by the Roman Catholic Church is common knowledge. Suffice it to spend but a few moments on the matter. About 601, Gregory the Great condemned the use of images in the strongest terms. He very highly commended the Bishop of Marseilles for breaking the images to pieces. Yet at the Council of Trent, 1545 A. D. a decree was pronounced, and is authoritative today, to the effect that "images were to be retained and due honor and veneration to be given them as representing those whose likenesses those images bear." Thomas Aquinas said, "The same reverence is to be paid to the image of Christ, as to Christ himself."

Did you ever see a Catholic statue supposed to be a likeness of the adult Christ in which his hair was not shown as long—dropping, perhaps, to the shoulders? The apostle Paul declares that even nature teaches that it is a shame for a man to have long hair (I Cor. 11:14). Do you think that Jesus would violate that declaration which He moved Paul to record? Did you ever see a statue of Jesus in which He was not portrayed as being beautiful in body? Yet Isaiah said of Him, "when we shall see him, there is no beauty that we should desire him" (Isaiah 53:2). I have said the foregoing in order to point up this statement: no one knows how Jesus looked in the flesh, and I submit to you that here is sufficient grounds for withholding such from man, "Thou shalt not make unto thee any graven image, or any likeness of anything that is in heaven above, or that is in the earth beneath, or that is in the water under the earth: Thou shalt not bow down thyself to them, nor serve them: for I the Lord thy God am a jealous God....." (Ex. 20:4, 5). It is no strange thing that the Catholic Church has entirely eliminated the wording of this second commandment of the Decalogue from its versions of the Catholic Baltimore Catechism, taught in all its parochial schools. The Bible becomes a dead letter to that religion which it condemns.

Life Magazine, reporting the ceremonies in Ottawa, Canada, in June 1947 at the Marian Congress, pointed out that a great procession of devout people knelt and kissed the foot of the giant statue of Mary "until the paint wore off its toes." Pictures in L'Europeo, an Italian newspaper, of April 5, 1947 shows that devout Catholics in Naples continue to crawl at full length on their stomachs before the images of their Madonnas and lick the ground with their tongues on their way to the statues. Some years ago, the New York Department of Health was compelled to put a stop to this practice among the Italian people in the Bronx, because it resulted in so many cases of tetanus. Such idolatry!

THE WORSHIP OF MARY—THE GODDESS OF HEAVEN

Catholics pray to Mary, to their saints and here is a prayer, found in the Breviary for the 14th of September, addressed to the cross as if it were living: "O cross, more splendid than the stars, illustrious throughout the World, much beloved by men, more holy than all things, who alone was worthy to bear the treasure of the world, bearing sweet wood, sweet nails, a sweet burden, save this present multitude assembled this day in thy praise."

As for prayers to Mary, in a book published by the Excelsior Publishing House, New York, 1891 and which book is entitled "Glories of Mary" and which was approved by the Archbishop of New York, on page 84 we read, "Sinners receive pardon only through the intercession of Mary." In the rosary, Catholics call on our Father some fourteen times and upon Mary some fifty-three times. The Bible teaches that "whatsoever ye do in word or deed, do all in the name of the Lord Jesus, giving thanks to God and the Father by him" (Col. 3:17).

Nowhere in God's Word are we taught to pray unto anyone other than God, and nowhere in His Word are we taught to pray through anyone other than Christ, who said, "I am the way, the truth, and the life: no man cometh unto the Father, but by me" (John 14:6).

MOTHER OF GOD

Catholics exalt Mary thus: "Thou art called the Mediatrix of all grace, the Refuge of afflicted hearts, the Advocate of desperate causes, the unfailing succor of all in need. It is through Thy maternal Heart that all benefits come to us. Filled with confidence in Thy Immaculate Heart which we venerate and love, we come to Thee with our pressing needs and many supplications..."

The Catholic Church addresses Mary as the "Mother of God" even though the first four words in the Bible declare that it is not so. On occasion, Catholics pray "five Our Fathers and five Hail Marys;" and, at such a time, they pray the same prayers through five times in undelayed succession. But listen to Jesus, "When ye pray, use not vain repetitions, as the heathen do: for they think that they shall be heard for their much speaking" (Matt. 6:7).

According to a recent issue of the Time Magazine, next year, on the occasion, I believe, of the present pope's fiftieth anniversary of entry into the priesthood, the Catholic Church is going to proclaim the ascension of Mary as a tenet of Catholicism! And Catholics will accept it! Thus Catholicism, like paganism, has her high priestess! Now listen to the Bible: "And it came to pass, as he (Jesus) spake these things, a certain woman of the company lifted up her voice, and said unto him, Blessed is the womb that bare thee, and the paps which thou hast sucked. But he (Jesus) said, Yea rather, blessed are they that hear the word of God and keep it" (Luke 11: 27, 28).

HOW THE CATHOLIC CHURCH GAINS ADHERENTS

The Catholic Church gains her adherents through three principal channels: (1) immigration—those who come to our shores are largely Catholic; (2) the offspring of Catholics—usually educated in parochial schools; (3) the offspring born to a Catholic and non-Catholic union—the Catholic Church requires that children born to such a union be reared as Catholics. How can a man or woman find such attraction in one of the opposite sex as to be willing to consign their unborn children to such an apostasy?

Thus, my friends, I have set forth why I left the Catholic Church. The Catholic Church disregards the Word of God and is not the church of the New Testament. I believe that I have established that in the light of truth. I thank God that I am a member of the church of Christ, which takes its stand upon the Bible.

Beloved, Jezebel, with her idolatry, is at work in the land. We see bowed forms before her in the press and on the screen. This is no time for week-kneed Protestantism; this is a time for courageous, concerted action in behalf of truth. Cast out that evil influence, as was Jezebel of old! How? Exalt and spread the Bible's influence. No one can embrace Catholicism without rejecting the Bible. The sword of the Spirit is the word of God.

L. W. HAYHURST

(*A Biographical Sketch*)

L. W. Hayhurst was born near Claremore, Oklahoma, in the 1890's. When he was thirteen years of age he obeyed the gospel and began to more closely study the Bible. This caused him to go through Gunter College, to study awhile at Texas Tech, and to take some correspondence courses from the University of Texas.

While at Gunter College he met Miss Mamie Webster who became his wife. Five children were born to this union: the oldest daughter married a preacher of the gospel, Merle King, and the oldest son has been preaching since he was seventeen. The other children are still at home.

He has represented the brethren in public discussion eighteen times. These discussions covered most of the issues between the church of Christ and our religious neighbors. More than once he has conceded the truthfulness of an opponent's argument, and does not feel that he has lost in doing so. He has a keen logical mind and a special ability to deal with the detailed and tedious in argumentation. Five times he defended the anti-class brethren in their position.

At present he has devoted himself to the proposition that all the anti-class brethren can be brought to see the error of their way by teaching, patience, and counsel. He considers the work of conducting consulations and counsels with brethren one of the best means for bringing disrupted churches into "the same mind and the same judgment."

At present he is laboring as minister of the church of Christ in Raymondville, Texas.

Why I Left The Anti-Class Position

BY L. W. HAYHURST

The freedom and opportunities that we enjoy here in America are probably the greatest in all the world. May we protect and use them to the glory of the Lord, and when we pass, hand them down to oncoming generations.

We who appear on the program have changed and are asked to give our reasons for so doing. This is in harmony with Peter's teaching to be ready to give every man an answer (I Peter 3:15), and this we hope to do with the meekness and fear that he enjoins, and we trust that our answers may be beneficial to all who hear us.

I opposed Bible classes for twenty-five years and then changed. I did this because I was convinced that I had been wrong, and not through bitterness toward any one with whom I had once agreed. If any of my hearers still oppose Bible classes, all I ask is that they listen with the same honesty, sincerity, and candor with which I speak.

I quit opposing the classes because I saw that I had been mis-applying I Cor. 14:34, 35, binding it on schools as well as on "church;" because my theory of interpreting law excluded room for expedients, which are necessary in carrying out all commands; because I had been perverting passages like Deut. 31:11-13, making them forbid class teaching; and because I could not make one stonewall argument for the anti-class position.

NOT DISHONORABLE TO CHANGE

Many people are convinced that they are wrong, but will not change because they are adverse to doing so; they think it is dishonorable. Not long ago two neighbor women who had heard the gospel were talking about it when one asked the other, "If you knew you were wrong would you change?" Her expression indicated that she thought it a dishonorable thing to change even though she knew that she was wrong. And there was the Baptist preacher who got cornered on baptism by a farmer and admitted that he was wrong, but said, "That's right, but I couldn't change; my converts and connections all believe this way." To all this I would reply that Paul saw his mistake and turned a new leaf; Apollos saw his error and changed; and the Bible commands repentance which is a change. The only question with me is not whether a thing requires a change, but "Is it right?" If a thing is right, it should be accepted; if wrong it should be rejected regardless of immediate consequences. For I have the faith to believe that right turns out right, and that wrong turns out wrong, and that there are no exceptions to the rule.

WE MISAPPLIED SCRIPTURES

My first reason for changing is the fact that I saw that the anti-class brethren were applying I Cor. 14:34, 35, binding it on groups that are not the whole church "come together into one place." I did not come to disbelieve the passage, not to discount it, nor to set it aside. I did not even change my interpretation of it; it still means to me what it always has. I just quit misapplying it, quit trying to force it on schools. Our difference here comes not over the law, nor its interpretations, but over its application. Does the command apply to schools? If so, it applies to singing schools as well as Bible classes. From this conclusion no one has been able to show me any escape. And strangely enough, we differ over its application only in one point. Those who have Bible classes and those who reject them, when they have what they call "church," apply the passage alike: both groups keep their women silent. But in their other meetings—courts, weddings, schools—they do not require silence, although such meetings be formal.

The fight comes when we try to teach the Bible in groups. We think that the application is to be made when "The whole church be come together into one place" (I Cor. 14:23), and functions as such, whereas, they think it applies wherever we teach a Bible class. If any one of their number does not believe this, just let him start a Bible class on any basis that he wants to, individually or otherwise, and see what happens to him.

THE ANTI-CLASS POSITION

CONFUSION ON THE RULE OF SILENCE

We have been asking them, "If the rule of silence applies to a class to teach Matt. 28:20, why does it not apply to a group assembled to teach Col. 3:16? And, if the church can assemble one of these groups and it not be the 'Church,' why can it not assemble the other and it not be the 'Church'?"

Up to this time I have received two answers. One brother tells me that there is some science taught in the singing class. Well, do we not learn something about reading, the meaning of words, and the way to interpret language in Bible classes? And do not these fall in the class of science? Besides if a group is a church, and we teach some science in it, does that fact change the character of that group? And, if a group be not the church, and we teach Bible to it, does that change its character? Does it cause it to be a church? Take one good look at a class being taught to sing, and one at a group being taught lessons in proper conduct, and try and convince yourself that one is a church, and that the other is not.

The other brother tells us that these are not on a par. Well, is school on a par with school? Are arrangements on a par with arrangements? It is a known fact that the churches arrange for both the Bible school and the one to teach singing. Everybody knows that they are both schools, and that they both are sometimes divided into classes. Is one organized? So is the other, and on the same plan, and by the same people. If these are not on a par in essential respects, let some one show it; the assertion is not enough. It is obvious that if the sisters are to be bound by silence in one of these schools, they are not to be allowed to ask and answer questions in the other one, and for the same reason. From this I see no escape.

THE TWO FORMS OF THE CHURCH

If we could observe and keep in mind one fact it might help to clarify this matter. It is this: the church exists in two forms, its assembled form, and its non-assembled form. It is seen in its assembled form in I Cor. 14, and in its non-assembled form in such meetings as Acts 5:1-10; 12:12-13, etc. In Acts 5:42 it assembled as such in the temple, but we see it in its non-assembled form teaching all over Jerusalem.

A school may meet in "assembly" and function in that capacity. Afterwards it may meet for classes, but these classes are not in that assembly. In the same way the church may come together in one place and function as a church, then it may disassemble as such and have a singing school, a wedding, a church court, or a Bible class. All this the anti-class brethren readily see and admit, except the Bible class. To them I would ask this question, "If you can have a class to teach singing while the church as such is recessed, why can't you have one to teach Bible while it is recessed?" When pressed with this, they will leave the field of silence and bring in some other objection; but be not deceived; they have not abandoned their idea. And they will be back to this refuge just as soon as they are routed somewhere else and this one seems handy. Let me urge that we stay with the silence question until we decide whether or not it applies to all meetings of Christians. The anti-class brethren will say that it does not. Then to what meetings does it apply?

WHAT ASSEMBLY?

One brother contends that it applies to "all assemblies of saints." But he does not believe this, for he allows many assemblies of Christians that he does not apply the rule to. For instance, he does not apply it to the singing school. And it must be remembered that the singing school is a formal meeting, and one that is called and arranged by the church, and in the church house.

In a letter to me a brother said, "Church is an assembly for teaching or worship." I reminded him that if that were the case, then the aged women could never arrange to carry out Titus 2, for if they did, it would be teaching or worship, that they would have to keep silence. Then I got to looking around to see how many of the anti-class churches had made, or allowed, any arrangements for their sisters to obey this passage (Titus 2:3-5). To this good day I have not found one, although I have been asking for it in letters to brethren all over the country. The trouble lies in the fact that they so apply I Cor. 14:34 as to cancel the effects of Titus 2:3-5. How unfortunate!

TITUS 2:3-5 IGNORED

During one of their Bible readings at Abilene, Texas, they discussed women's work in the church. (In such meetings the sisters are allowed to attend but not to talk, except when singing is taught, then they may ask and answer questions). I asked them, "How many of you are here from a congregation that has assumed its obligation to God to carry out Titus 2?" I asked for hands. No hands went up. I then repeated the question a second time and a third time. Still no hands went up. Then I said, "We are the loyal brethren, aren't we?" They had people there from several different states, but not from any congregation that made any arrangements to carry out this command.

Not only does this doctrine set aside Titus 2, but many of their members try to so explain the passage as to limit it to family relationships. They will say, "I teach my daughters." One letter informs me that a certain sister teaches her daughters and nieces. Let any honest hearted person read the passage and say if it is a family duty. But some of their teachers will allow the aged women to teach the younger ones, "incidentally," which is to say accidentally. However, any time that the aged women get to meeting the younger ones and instructing them, some anti-class preacher will come along and kill it. I challenge for an exception.

BY THEIR FRUITS YE SHALL KNOW THEM

Jesus gave us a rule by which to measure a person or his doctrine: their fruits. What are the fruits of the anti-class doctrine? From this they seek to hide by saying that this does not prove the opposition right. This we freely grant, but the opposition is not under consideration. This is but a "slideover" to get away from being measured by their fruits. What fruits? What arrangements do they make to feed the widows and orphans? Hunt for yourself; I do not find them. How many missionaries have they sent during this time when doors are open to us to preach to all the world? They have sent not one. What have they done? They have applied I Cor. 14:34 so as to prohibit a prophetess from prophesying to any group, if they had one in their midst. Let it be remembered that Joel said that they would prophesy (Joel 2:28), and that Luke and Paul confirms the fact that they did do so (Acts 21:8-9; I Cor. 11:5). As compared to Titus 2, I Cor. 14:34 is a major doctrine, and it rises so high in their minds that certain duties drop out of consciousness. When interpreted in its true perspective, this means that the negative side rises much higher in their minds than the positive, consequently their churches are small, inactive, and usually found haggling over some technicality. Let him who is interested look around; demonstrations are not easily denied.

But we are not through with the silence question. One brother says that to exclude the classes, we must apply I Cor. 14:34, 35, and I Tim. 2:11-12. This being true, to show them that their application of these passages is wrong is to convince them. If this could be done many of them would be a power for good among those who are carrying on the work. It is being done to a greater extent than has been in the past. Many of them are changing; many more will do so; the truth will prevail.

WHEN IS THE CHURCH ASSEMBLED?

Brother Bonneau says, "When a local congregation calls a group together, that group constitutes a church assembly, be it large or small." (*Teaching the Word,* page 21.) He goes on to say that this is the way the classes are convened, and so he clamps on the rule for silence. He is wrong, for he allows the same local congregation to convene the same people for the purpose of teaching them Col. 3:16, and what is necessary to carry it out, and does not bind silence on it. This is one of the first things that I saw, and having seen it, I would like to put the idea where everybody will see it.

But suppose that the Bible class is a church assembly? It is so only in the sense that it is composed in part, or in whole, of church members and is arranged by the church, and this is true of the singing school, the church social, the group that eats dinner at church, the church court, etc. And if we bind silence on this group because it is a "church assembly," we will have to bind it on all these others, because they are as much church assemblies as it is. The thing to decide is

THE ANTI-CLASS POSITION

whether or not it is "THE ASSEMBLY" of I Cor. 14. If the Bible class is, then the other meetings which are composed of Christians and are arranged by the church are "Churches" too. If they are not that assembly, neither is the Bible class.

Brother Bonneau and I attended church court in Houston one time, about the first of November, 1944. We stayed two weeks and got many differences settled. These meetings had all the requirements that he and others claim as essentials for "The Assembly"—(1) arranged by the church, (2) called together by it, (3) called to order, (4) begun with prayer, (5) dismissed. Yet the women in them freely asked and answered questions, "No man forbidding." Not only so, but I, being the go-between, was frequently called on for some point of law which I stated and which was accepted. Others did likewise, so we had teaching.

Was that "The church?" Was it "The Assembly?" It certainly was not, although it had all the essentials of what they call "Church." Now if they can see this, why can they not see that we can get a group together and have a Bible class and that not be "Church?" That court was convened not by just one church but by two or three, and it had people in it from six or seven. You may call it a sort of church assembly, but it is not the one Paul bound silence in, and neither is the Bible class. It follows then, that if the Bible class is to be condemned, it must be by some other passage than this one.

WHAT IS CHURCH?

The word *ekklesia* is found in the New Testament 115 times. Three of these times it is rendered "assembly," the other 112 times it is translated by the word "church." The original word is used in five senses:

1. In Acts 19:32, 39, 40 is designated a mob that worshipped Diana.
2. Luke uses it to refer to the Jewish nation (Acts 7:38).
3. Jesus names his institution an ekklesia (Matt. 16:18).
4. In Romans 16:16 and I Cor. 1:2 it means a local congregation.
5. Paul uses it in I Cor. 11:18, and 14:19, 28, 34, 35 (and possibly others) in a peculiar sense. Here he uses it

to refer to a special assembly of a local congregation. In my study I have been unable to find it so used elsewhere in the Bible. Paul says, "If therefore the whole church be come together into one place.....", and then he goes on to give instructions to regulate such a meeting.

Now in which of these "churches" is it that the women are bound to silence? Not the mob of Acts 19, because they were a group of unbelieving idolators; not the Jewish nation, for it existed before Jesus built his church and was distinct from it after its establishment; not the institution, for women are in it all the time; and not the local congregation, for they are members of it all the time too. It must, then, refer to the whole assembly of the church as such. From this conclusion there seems to be no escape.

Somebody will ask if that meeting did not have miracles in it. The answer is, "Yes." Then, do we have such gifts today? We answer, "No." The conclusion will then be reached that since we do not have a meeting like that, the regulations of that meeting do not apply to us now. To this the anti-class defender will reply that every meeting that is recorded in the New Testament had at least one miracle worker in it, and that if we cancel the commands where there were miracles, we would threby cancel the entire law to us; that we would have to do away with baptism for the remission of sins (Acts 2:38), because there are no meetings like that either. Be that as it may, the Corinthians had "Church," and we have "Church." Here I think is the parallelism. Not only so, but the Corinthian women kept silence during that time, and so do ours. In all such meetings the men lead the singing, as you see here tonight. They read the lessons, lead the prayers, do the preaching, and the teaching, wait on tables and dismiss—the women keep silence.

The same practice prevails among the churches that are opposed to teaching in classes. Both groups interpret and apply I Cor. 14 exactly alike as it relates to this meeting. The difference comes when they try to stretch the injunction for silence to include the Bible classes which are not the "whole church come together into one place;" they are in different

THE ANTI-CLASS POSITION 231

places. Who could say that each class is a church? If that were true, when we operate ten classes we would have ten churches, and that will not do.

ANTI-CLASS BRETHREN HAVE TROUBLE IN DEFINING "CHURCH"

In my correspondence with the anti-class brethren I have been calling on them to tell us just what they mean by the word "church." Some said that they could not define the word; others said, "Anybody knows that." Those who tried to do it would first so define it as to include the Bible classes. When they were shown that this would include the singing school, they would re-define so as to exclude it, and when they did they also excluded the Bible classes from their definition. Seeing this they would back off and quit the discussion.

Suppose we try defining the word "church." Let us try the word "court;" just what do we mean by it?—a judge, plaintiff, defendant, witnesses, and those who plead the case? This would appear to be court if they are all in one place. But you may see all these together in the court room discussing a case, and it not be court, because court had not been convened. So it is with the word "church" too. What we want is room to have Bible classes when the church is not in session. If all the disciples may come together as a social group, and not be "church;" if they may assemble as a court and not be "The Assembly;" if they can come together as a wedding and not be "The Assembly;" if they can meet as a school, and not be "Church," pray tell me why can't they come together to have a Bible school and not be "Church?"

SECOND REASON: THE BLUNDER ON EXPEDIENTS

My second reason for leaving the anti-class position was our blunder on expedients. We reasoned that since the law is perfect, and since it does not mention the details of a Bible class, that, therefore, it is wrong. When seen in its true light this argument is against all expedients, all arrangements not stated in the law. We did not so use it; we just pointed it at the thing that we wanted to exclude by it. Such arbitrary handling of the sacred word was unconscious on our part, but it was, and is, real. We did not apply the argument to the singing school; we let it by, but the Bible class was sure to get full benefit of that argument.

We used Isaiah 8:20; James 1:25; I Thess. 5:21, etc., to exclude the arrangements of the Bible class. They were not stated in detail, therefore were to be excluded. Had we made a uniform application of it, we would have seen the mistake, for it would have excluded church buildings, deeds, singing schools, etc. Our blunder lay in the fact that we failed to distinguish between principle and expedient, principle and device, principle and arrangement. And, overlooking the fact that the class system is taught in principle, and failing to see modern arrangements in ancient times, we concluded that Bible classes are wrong. How we managed to fail to include the arrangements of radio preaching (it is rather modern), protracted meetings (they come to us as a tradition), and a thousand other expedients that we employ is more than I can see. It seems to me as certain as life itself, that if there is room for all these things under the perfect law, that there is room for a Bible class under it.

IS THIS A "DIGRESSIVE" ARGUMENT?

Their invariable reply to this is to stigmatize it "digressive" argument. This can have but one motive, and that is to arouse prejudice. Being unable to meet the issue, they presume the point, stigmatize the argument, and slide off on a detour. But this is not to be easily disposed of. It is a principle that enters into all applications of law, and one that they themselves use to defend their arrangements.

A few years ago an anti-class man and a one-cup brother were debating. The brother contending for a plurality of cups affirmed Paul's principle of expediency (I Cor. 10:23). Not being able to read of individual cups any more than any other expedient, he found room for his arrangements under the command to drink. Was this "digressive" argument? It is the same one that we use to defend the Bible class. If we are digressives, so are they, and so are the one-cup brethren for they put cloths and a plate on the table, and arrange for someone to carry the emblems from one to another, none of which is stated in the perfect law.

THE ANTI-CLASS POSITION

DERIVING AUTHORITY FOR EXPEDIENTS

From general commands we derive authority for the details that carry out such commands. From Col. 3:16 we derive authority for a song book, a song leader, fourpart music, although we never read of soprano, alto, tenor and bass; and from this passage we get authority for a school to teach all that pertains to our singing. All this we see clearly enough, and act upon in most things. But it is not in harmony with our arguments built on the perfect law of liberty which we used to exclude teaching the Bible in classes, and which some have used to exclude individual cups.

Paul's authorization, "Let every man have his own wife" (I Cor. 7:2) says nothing about courting a girl to get her to become a wife, nor a ceremony by a preacher or anyone else, yet the most "died-in-the wool" radical will derive authority from this general authorization for such details. What they need to do is to look at the commands "Go" and "Teach" in the same way. In the time of Jesus there were several ways of going, and several ways of teaching; and he used the different ways of traveling and the different methods of teaching.

CANNOT OBEY COMMANDS WITHOUT EXPEDIENTS

It must be remembered that an expedient carries out a command. You cannot obey one without some expedient; I challenge you to try it. Of course the thing (principle) must be enjoined, but the detail that carries it out must be chosen. Noah could never have built an ark without many expedients —an axe, nails or something with which to fasten the planks together, or the logs or in whatever form he used the wood. For all such things we derive authority for the detail that carries out the command. On no other basis can we apply law. Such detail is lawful but not law.

Someone will want to know, "If we may choose expedients, why not play an instrument in wroship?" The answer is easy: "play" is not commanded, and so cannot authorize an instrument, which could be an expedient under the command, if we had it. But "teach" is a command both to men and to women, and therefore must authorize arrangements that carry it out.

AREA OF REASON AND JUDGMENT

Paul affirms in Rom. 12:1 that our service is a reasonable service. Likewise the commands to "walk circumspectly" (Eph. 5:15) and to "walk in wisdom toward them that are without" (Col. 4:5) indicate the use of reason and judgment. The apostles appealed to reason in Acts 6:2, and Paul urges the Corinthians to be of the same mind and the same judgment (I Cor. 1:10). Let those who will refuse to study, to reason, and to endeavor to walk in wisdom under God's law. To refuse to do these things is to fail to obey him. Any law that had all of its details written out would be larger than this building—too large for a man to read or to remember in his short life time. The "law of the Lord is perfect" in the sense of giving all the principles needed to make men perfect, but neither that law nor any other law points out all the details involved in it. This not only makes room for reason, it demands the exercise of it. This is so obvious and so universally practiced in all other matters that it cannot well be denied with respect to teaching services. For a man to use his judgment in carrying out fifty commands, and then deny it a legitimate place in one, is to set himself in an odd light, and yet this is exactly what the one-cup man and the anti-class man do. Get on the Bible class question and hear them decry human wisdom, just as if God had not commanded the teaching, and as if the very methods had not been used by Christ and his apostles.

THIRD REASON: PERVERTING THE SCRIPTURES

My third reason for changing is the fact that we had been perverting such passages as Deut. 31:11-13. We argued that their teachers were to teach "all Israel" in one group, and concluded that it was wrong to teach in classes. It would be difficult to get one who argues this to state his connection between the fact and the conclusion. It is really no argument, but we thought it was, and we were wrong. To meet this argument (if it is an argument), is to meet the ones that they make on all such passages— Josh. 8:34-35, Neh. 8:1-3. And this we now do.

    1. The idea that teaching a large assembly excludes teaching a small one is a false idea. All schools have what

THE ANTI-CLASS POSITION 235

they call "assembly," and many times go directly from it to their classes. All churches that employ the class method of teaching also have large assemblies in which they preach. Thus the argument is built on a false premise.

2. Moses at the very time that he gave the command to teach all Israel was not teaching "all Israel," but a class of priests and elders whom he was telling to teach the nation. When I saw this, it silenced my mouth forever on this argument, for it appeared plainly to be a perversion. Honesty demanded a change.

3. The synagogue was organized and perpetuated by the Jews under the law to teach "all Israel." In it they did not gather the whole nation in one "undivided assembly," but conducted a school and public worship. The school had two classes of boys, those from about seven to thirteen years were instructed under one teacher, and those from fourteen to twenty in another room under a different teacher. If a class reached as many as forty, they were divided, and another teacher was given to a part of them. In such a school Paul was brought up, and after becoming a Christian he tells us that it was after "the perfect manner of the law" (Acts 22:3). Paul forever settles this question. Let us quit perverting the passage.

We built another misapprehension around Deut. 32:2: "My doctrine shall drop as the rain." This we said forbade class teaching, for the teaching was to fall like the rain undivided. Then we got to asking, "If a man teaches his family group, does the doctrine drop as the rain?" They answered, "Yes." Then we wanted to know if we can teach one small group and the doctrine drop as the rain, why not many small groups and it still drop as the rain? Besides, does the rain always come as a universal downpour, or does it shower in different places, and sometimes simultaneously? Such observations led me inevitably out of this error.

We even interpreted Luke 4:16-19 as teaching that Bible classes are wrong. We saw Jesus in public worship, and being ignorant of the fact that they had in the synagogues teaching done in classes, concluded that all teaching was done in one large assembly. The fact that Jesus asked and answered questions in the temple, one of their centers for teaching, failed somehow to indicate to us that they had schools and that they taught the Bible in them, and that by school methods.

This could go on indefinitely showing how we either misconstrued or misapplied the Bible, but time forbids.

FOURTH REASON: NO STONEWALL ARGUMENT

The fourth thing that drove me from my former position is the fact that I could not build one stonewall argument in its favor, nor one that would stand up. This is why the anti-class debaters hedge around on technicalities and dodge from one position to another, so that to argue with them is to run all over creation. When I began to doubt my position and called on their leading minds for help, many of them stated facts and admitted the difficulties. Others depended so much on dodges, enuendos, and personal questions that they convinced me that their strength lay in such tactics. Who can have faith in a position which demands such things?

EXACTLY WHAT DO THEY OPPOSE?

Since changing, I have been asking them what it is that they find wrong with class teaching. (1) Is it arrangements? (2) Is it who makes them? (3) Is it the method used in the classes? (4) Is it the fact that another class is in progress at the same time that makes a class wrong? (5) Is it separating the groups that is wrong? (6) Is it who does the teaching? (7) Is it the day on which it is done?

These questions have not been answered; no one has even undertaken the task. At one time it seems to be the method that they oppose, then it seems to be women teachers, but they allow both the method and women teachers. And all the while they do not make one argument that will stand the test of a close examination. Watch it and see.

On the first page of *Teaching the Word*, the author attacks the "method" of teaching in class twice. On the next page he condemns it again. Just what is he condemning? A "method of teaching." But it is not a method that he is opposing, although that is exactly what he argues from Deut. 31 and Neh. 8, etc. At the bottom of page 2 he says that there is no difference over methods of teaching in homes, but that it is not right for the church to use that method.

Again, they argue against women teachers long and loud, but are they really opposed to women teachers? Not long ago a sister who opposes classes got several of us preachers together just after preaching and tried to teach us that it is wrong for a woman to teach. Had we invited her back into one of the class rooms to teach us that lesson, she would have rebelled. But what would have been the difference? (At the end of this speech, not one but three women tried to do the same thing. One of them told me that she taught her daughter every night, and that was her answer to Titus 2. We wonder if they think that this is all that is embraced in that command).

AN INTERESTING STUDY OF BIBLE METHODS

Not long ago Brother Lamoine Lemley, of Kress, Texas, read the first four books of the New Testament to see just what methods were used. He made three columns under the heading of PREACH, TEACH, and CONVERSATION. He found where Jesus preached 27 times, where it is said that he taught 70 times, and where he engaged in conversation 86 times. (See last page). Let it be remembered that the conversation method, the dialogue method, is the one generally used in class teaching, and the one argued against by the anti-class preachers. We do not claim that the list is complete; if Jesus used a way 86 times, I would not be afraid for the church to arrange to use it.

Although we are branded as "Moderns" for teaching the Bible in classes, it remains a fact that none of the basic methods of teaching are modern. The Egyptians heralded out news to the people in the times of Joseph (Gen. 41:43). In the days of Esther and Daniel the Babylonians used criers to announce their messages (Esther 6:11, Dan. 3:4). When Jesus began his preaching, John the Baptist had preceded him in this. Nor did Jesus invent the dialogue method, for Socrates had made it famous 400 years before Christ. What Jesus did was not to invent, but to adapt and use the methods he found in vogue at his coming.

Much of the teaching and training given to the apostles by Jesus was by taking them aside from the multitude, and frequently this teaching was given by the question and answer method (Matt. 16:13-18, 20:17, Mark 9:9-14). This is in principle the procedure used in Bible classes today. Anyone who knows that they had school in their synagogues and that they both taught and lectured will see in Matt. 4:23 a distinction in preaching and teaching, for it is said that Jesus did both. If I say that some brother teaches and preaches at a certain college, those who know what college is will understand me.

NOT THE METHOD BUT SOMETHING ELSE

But if it be not the method that they oppose but the use of it by the church, it would then appear that all we have to do to make the Sunday morning Bible school right is to take the arrangements of it out of the hands of the elders and put them in the hands of some women! Brother Bonneau says that, "If a sister teaches a group, where the church has not convened it, nor called a plurality of classes in session, she is within her rights." According to this it is lawful for me to get me a class, for you to get one, for everybody but the church. But the responsibility for teaching the gospel to the world is on the church (Eph. 3:10, 4:16, I Tim. 3:15). Strange, is it not?

The anti-class defenders, failing to make their arguments stand up, shift from one to another. They do it so artfully that they are seldom detected at it. It reminds me of our bringing a man into court charging him as an outlaw. The judge would require a specific charge, so we accuse that he has no driver's license. No sooner does he produce it than we charge him of driving on the wrong side of the street. He immediately brings up witnesses who testify that he drove exactly where we did, but before the judge can render a decision or dismiss the case, we accuse the man of stealing a tire. What would the court say? This fairly illustrates the way the anti-class man argues against the class teaching and the women teachers. It is first the silence question. By the time we get that answered he condemns us for not having all the disciples together in one great assembly and have all the teaching done by men. Then he requires that the expedient be stated in the law, then an example that walks on all fours, then comes the "all Israel" argument, or the doctrine dropping as the rain argument, etc., until time runs out. They never stand on an argument long enough for it to be tested out. If they did they would lose it. I lost mine, and I changed.

LET US TEACH UNDER LAW

The idea in the mind of Jesus was "They shall be all taught of God" (John 6:45). Nor did he exclude any known method of teaching. He lectured to the people; he conversed with them, asking and answering questions, and he left an example as an object lesson. Shall we follow his example and use the same methods that he did? Then let us quit arguing against one of them.

When Paul was among the Jews he became as a Jew; a Roman when among the Romans; when among those without law, as without law. But he tells us that he was all the while under the law to Christ (I Cor. 9:20-21). He shaved his head when among the Jews, and conformed to the customs of the other people when with them, just so long as such custom did not run counter to the law of Christ. In this is illustrated liberty under law. These things were lawful to him, and when they were expedient, he took advantage of them. All this our brethren can see until it comes to teaching the Bible. Then they will say that if the church divides over a thing that it is not an expedient. To which we reply that when they divide, it is generally over an expedient. They should not divide over these things, but they frequently do. The trouble is they make laws where God has not, and try to bind them on others. When they quit this we will get along. I saw it, and I quit it, and from here on I expect to teach the Bible as opportunity affords, on the mountain, by the sea side, in the synagogue, in the pulpit,—"Being not without law to God, but under the law to Christ."

EXAMPLES OF TEACHING METHODS

PREACH	TEACH	CONVERSATION
Matthew	*Matthew*	*Matthew*
4:17	4:23, 5:1	8:18-21, 9:1-8, 12-13
4:23	7:28, 9:35	9:14, 10:7, 11:2, 12:1
9:35	11:1, 13:54	12:9, 12:25; 38
10:17	21:23, 26:55	13:10, 36-52, 15:1
11:1	28:20	15:12, 16:1, 5
11:7		16:13, 17:24, 1
13:1	*Mark*	18:1, 21, 19:2, 16
22:1	1:21, 2:13	19:23, 20:1, 17, 19
	3:23, 4:1, 33	22:17, 23, 34, 41
	5:35, 6:2, 6	24:3
Mark	6:30, 34	
1:14	7:14, 8:31	
1:38	9:14, 31	*Mark*
2:2	9:38, 10:1	2:1, 18, 24, 3:4, 4:10
3:14	10:32, 11:17-18	7:8, 8:27, 9:10, 28
6:12	12:35, 43	9:33, 10:2, 10, 17
12:1	14:49	10:28, 12:14, 18
13:10		12:28, 14:5
	Luke	
	4:15, 31, 5:3	
	5:17, 9:28, 43	
Luke	10:1, 23	*Luke*
4:17, 18	10:39, 11:1	2:47, 5:30, 6:2, 9
4:43	11:17, 29	7:18, 39, 8:9, 9:18
6:17	12:1, 22	9:57, 10:25, 45, 12:13
7:24	13:10, 22	13:14, 23, 14:3, 17:20
8:1	14:25, 15:3	18:18, 19:5-10, 20:2, 27
9:1	16:1, 14	21:7
16:16	17:1, 22	
20:1	19:47, 20:21, 45	
20:9	21:3, 37, 22:24	
	23:5, 24:27	*John*
	John	2:18, 4:7, 5:17, 6:25
John	7:28, 8:20, 30	6:43, 66, 7:14-16, 8:34
7:37	12:20, 14 Ch.	9:2, 10:22, 12:5, 13:15
10—	15, 16, 18:20	14 Ch.

www.ingramcontent.com/pod-product-compliance
Lightning Source LLC
Chambersburg PA
CBHW030314080526
44584CB00012B/572